TRANSACTIONAL ANALYSIS
FOR TRAINERS

Related books by the same author

The 1ˢᵗ edition of this book was published by McGraw-Hill 1992, and then by Sherwood Publishing in 1996.

That edition was also published in French as *Analyse Transactionnelle et Formation* Desclée de Brouwer 1994

Working it Out at Work - Understanding Attitudes and Building Relationships 1ˢᵗ Sherwood 1993, 2ⁿᵈ edition 2009

Ist edition translated into Slovenian, Romanian, Persian and Dutch

Donkey Bridges for Developmental TA : Making transactional analysis memorable and accessible Sherwood 1995

Transformational Mentoring: Creating Developmental Alliances for Changing Organizational Cultures McGraw-Hill 1995, Sherwood 1999

Dealing with Difficult People - The Workbook and Tape Set Sherwood 1998

Transactional Analysis Introductory Course – Workbook & Tape Set Sherwood 2001

Neuro-Linguistic Programming Practitioner Course – Workbook and Tape Set Sherwood 2001

Transactional Analysis for Coaches and Mentors Sherwood 2009

Transactional Analysis for Consultants Sherwood 2009

TRANSACTIONAL ANALYSIS FOR TRAINERS

Julie Hay

SHERWOOD PUBLISHING
• • • developing people

HERTFORD UK

Published by

Sherwood Publishing
Wildhill, Broadoak End, Hertford SG14 2JA, UK

www.sherwoodpublishing.com
email: sherwood@adinternational.com

This edition first published 2009

A catalogue record of this book is available from the British Library.
ISBN 978-1-907037-00-9

Design: Diane Richardson, info @drdm.eu
Printed by Athenaeum Press, www.athenaeumpress.co.uk

CONTENTS

LIST OF FIGURES

ACKNOWLEDGEMENTS

The acknowledgements I wrote in the first edition of this book still apply and are reproduced in full below. This was the first book I ever wrote and those mentioned then were significant contributors to my identity as an author.

Since then, there have of course been others. More authors who have stimulated me, even though I do not reproduce their work directly: especially Graeme Summers & Keith Tudor on co-creativity and Helena Hargaden & Charlotte Sills on recognising the significance of the relationship. Plus I have trained in Neuro-Linguistic Programming (NLP) with Richard Bandler and others – and this has alerted me to the deeper structures and the hidden hypnotic effects of the language we use.

There have also been many more participants on my programmes, including groups in India, Romania, Russia, Ukraine, the Netherlands, Australia and elsewhere. I have been privileged to be able to add a truly multi-cultural flavour to my transactional analysis (TA) work.

I have enjoyed working with a group of 'regulars' over the past three or four years, whilst I've updated and refined my TA knowledge – so thanks go to Diane Richardson, Mary Tobin, Min-Min Teh, Rebecca Galley, Lyn King, Richard Hall, Andrew Jackson, Ros Soulsby. Diane has also been responsible for book design and for nagging me to get this update written!

Finally, another group who were not there when I wrote the first edition – those who have signed TA contracts with me as their sponsor and allowed me to accompany them on their own professional journeys. Those included here are: those who are now Teaching and Supervising Transactional Analysis's (TSTA's) like me: Trudi Newton (who was there from the beginning – see below), Anita Mountain, Colin Brett, Suriyaprakash; those who are now Provisional TSTA's and continue to stimulate my thinking as we discuss theories and engage in supervision: Lynda Tongue, Sandra Wilson, Annie Murray, Chris Davidson, Bill Heasman, Debbie Robinson in the UK; Mohan Raj and Sebastian in India; Pia Bylund in Sweden; Bojan Pucelj in Slovenia; Anne Tucker in New Zealand and Croatia, and not forgetting Bogdan Serbanescu in Romania, who has attained his international accreditation as Certified Transactional Analyst (CTA) (Organisational) during the time I have been finalising this book.

ACKNOWLEDGEMENTS IN THE FIRST EDITION:

There are three groups of people that I want to acknowledge: the TA writers who came before me and provided my knowledge; the participants and trainees who have worked with me to turn concepts into practical applications; and the individuals who played a part in my introduction to TA.

My acknowledgements begin with my gratitude to the founder of transactional analysis, Eric Berne. I like to think that he would have welcomed this book as proof that his ideas are being spread in accordance with his own preference for teaching the material to the clients so they can apply it for themselves.

Next, I thank the authors who have given me permission to reproduce their diagrams, or my adaptations of them: Graham Barnes, Fanita English, Richard Erskine, Taibi Kahler, Stephen Karpman, Pamela Levin, Nelly Micholt and Marilyn Zalcman.

There are others too whose material I have described in my own words: Harry and Laura Boyd, Jack Dusay, Bob and Mary Goulding, John James, Ken Mellor, Jacqui Schiff, Aaron Schiff, Eric Schiff and Claude Steiner. I could not have written what I have without all of these authors' original contributions.

And then there are those many others, including particularly Michael Brown, Muriel James, Dorothy Jongeward, Thomas Harris and Stan Woollams, whose books I have read and absorbed. There are doubtless concepts and activities in this book that are heavily influenced by these other writers even though I no longer recall the specific sources of my ideas.

The second group I thank are those who helped me develop my own applications of TA theories. These include hundreds of participants on training courses over the years. Special among them are my "regulars", Patricia Croker, Trudi Newton, Stephen Slater, Heather Veevers, Elizabeth Hendry and Nick Williams, who have helped me take the theories apart and put them back together again with a greater understanding.

Shelley Dennison, James Drummond, Chris Grimsley, Glynis Judge, Maggie Mills, Josephine Pell, Jackie Poole and Ken Timms read draft chapters and gave me feedback.

The third group I thank are those who played a significant part in my initial introduction to TA. Michael Reddy ran the '101' course I went on; Mike Bruce, Peter Farey and Derek Hinson gave me organisational support for my training; and Archie Mills was my TA sponsor.

And most of all, I am grateful to Mark Greening for telling me about TA in the first place.

Finally, my thanks to two individuals who contributed in a different way. Terry Clark produced diagrams for me on his computer, and Sylvia Taylor developed the muscles in her right arm whilst printing the drafts during the unplanned absence of a paper-feed mechanism.

ABOUT THIS BOOK

I began the first edition of this book about transactional analysis (TA) by explaining my reasons for writing it. Most of these still apply:

- it was to impress my mother – it did and so will this new edition
- it was a challenge to see if I could do it – I did and it encouraged me to continue writing, as you will see from the list inside the front cover
- I wanted a satisfactory answer for the many people who asked me to recommend a book on transactional analysis in organisations – and now they ask for one that contains the newer ideas I now teach
- having gained a lot from previous TA writers, I wanted to be a part of the tradition of sharing the opportunities with others – and I still do.

Then there was also my (no longer) secret agenda, which also still applies:

- to convince you that transactional analysis is so valuable in your personal and professional life that you want to know more, so that you will join and enrich the worldwide community of TA people.

In 'The Different Drum', M Scott Peck (1987) subtitled his book 'The creation of true community – the first step to world peace'. TA already has a true community, which acts in advance of changes in the world. For example, overt TA activity increased in Eastern Europe many months before the Berlin Wall came down.

As organisations have recognised the need to develop cultures that value the whole person, and accept the human need for contact and community, so TA has assumed a higher priority in the toolkit of the organisational trainer. My hope is that this book will empower you as you play your part in influencing and advancing the progression towards a more caring society.

My specific objective, therefore, has been to provide you, the reader, with enough information and guidance for you to use transactional analysis theories and techniques competently in your work as a trainer so as to help people develop their potential and grow as human beings. To help you do so, I have kept in mind that what I write should support four stages:

- greater self-awareness
- increased understanding of your own issues
- identification of options for change
- practical strategies for self development

and that these must apply to you before you attempt to use the TA ideas with participants on your training events. I encourage you, therefore, to apply the material to yourself before using it on others. I also urge you to get super-vision of your own professional application of TA. I have added an extra chapter to this edition to explain why this is so important, and why I use a hyphen. I believe that when you realise how super-vision works, you will feel, as I did, that it is a fantastic way to increase competence – and something that no professional would want to function without.

Let me just add that the book is not written as a definitive account of transactional analysis theory. It is intended as a practical guide, in which I will show you how I have adapted theories developed in clinical settings, and applied them to organisational needs. I have given details of original sources of theories so you can refer to them if you wish; at the same time I have provided enough detail for you to use the ideas in the book without the need for further study.

HOW TO USE THIS BOOK

Should you be one of those strange people who read by starting at the beginning and reading through to the end, this book has a convenient structure. If you are not, you can still read chapters in any order. As I introduce particular concepts for the first time, I describe them in detail. When the same framework is used later in a different way, I give a brief summary relating it to the new topic. You can therefore work directly from each chapter. There are cross-references if you need them, or want a deeper understanding of a particular piece of theory.

Chapters 1 to 3 and 12 are aimed at you as a trainer. I begin by telling you (fairly briefly) about TA, so that you will understand how it has evolved and to alert you to some of the advantages and pitfalls of teaching it to others. Next I focus on methods for contracting so that your participants will learn more, and learn more that is truly relevant to them. In the third chapter I explain how attitudes, of both trainers and participants, will affect the amount learned. I introduce you to the suggestion that we often sabotage ourselves unknowingly; trainer awareness of this phenomenon will considerably increase the options available in the training process. In Chapter 12, I explain and explore the nature of super-vision and why this is such a significant developmental process for those of us in the helping profession.

From Chapter 4 through to Chapter 9 I have provided a range of TA concepts to suit a variety of typical training needs related to people skills. I have started with a focus on the individual, covering our personal styles, the ways we prefer to communicate, our characteristic working styles, and the ways we do our thinking and decision making. In Chapter 7 the attention moves to interactions; ideas on how to build good relationships are followed by some clues about what goes wrong between people. Chapter 8 extends this theme into consideration of teams and group processes. Chapter 9 is a relatively short chapter that pulls together several of the previous concepts into an overall model of leadership styles that is based on using TA to better understand the needs and preferences of those being led. Although putting people into boxes is risky, this chapter does provide a fun way of classifying people provided we do so tentatively.

Chapters 10 and 11 introduce some subjects that are commonly tackled as organisation-wide initiatives. There can be few trainers who do not need good ideas for helping participants deal with change; similarly, most organisations now aim to encourage creativity and innovation from their people.

I have left the chapter on super-vision until the end so that by then you will have a good understanding of many TA frameworks, have hopefully related them to yourself, and are ready to find out how you can continue to develop yourself personally and professionally.

CHAPTER FORMAT

Each chapter begins with a brief overview to alert you to the structure and content. With the exception of Chapters 1-3 and 12 which are aimed at helping you increase your understanding and control of the process of training, I have retained a roughly similar format throughout. I begin by explaining an appropriate theoretical model and demonstrate how it can be applied to the organisational world. I have generally done this in a language and style that matches the way you might present it to participants.

I go on to give examples of how you might use the concepts to analyse what is going on in your classrooms, so as to gain a better understanding of what occurs between participants and with you. Separately, I also show how you can use each model to analyse your own behaviour and increase your competence and professionalism.

After theory comes practical – in the book but not necessarily in the classroom. I suggest activities that will help participants to understand the concepts and how to apply them. The activities are presented in an order which matches the chapter content; depending on time available you could use them progressively or select only those which relate to your choice of key topics.

At the end of each chapter I have included notes and references. This gives you the sources of original concepts and also explains some of the differences you might spot if you read other TA publications. At the back of the book are some appendices, with details of where you can get more information and involvement with TA.

I hope that this book will have as much impact on you as my early exposure to TA had on me – and I look forward to welcoming you into the worldwide TA community.

DONKEY BRIDGES

Donkey bridges is a term borrowed from German trainers and explained by John Townsend in 'Making Messages Memorable' <u>Training and Developmental Journal</u> January 1994. They are the gimmicky ways that trainers use alliteration and similar techniques to provide memory aids for the learners.

Those who study with me soon learn that I am an avid donkey bridge fan, and they often help by providing ideas and words. You will, therefore, find several donkey bridges within the book. Misery is optional – if you hate gimmicks like this, feel free to change the words!

And if English is not your language, my apologies that the donkey bridges will probably be lost in translation.

NON-TA CONCEPTS

After publication of the first edition of this book, I became concerned to find that people were claiming non-TA concepts as if they were TA. I realised that I had inadvertently caused some of this by including them within my book.

I have therefore been careful in this updated edition to label all non-TA concepts as such. I have done this within the text when first mentioning a concept, as well as within the end-of-chapter Notes where I state the sources of what I have written about.

Please take careful note and avoid teaching non-TA material as if it is TA. TA has enough great material of its own so let's not inflate it by claiming ideas that come from elsewhere.

CHAPTER 1:   APPLYING TA IN ORGANISATIONS

This is very much an introductory chapter, in which I aim to whet your appetite, give you some of the background to transactional analysis and show in general terms how it may be applied in organisations.

I begin with my thoughts on why TA philosophy is such a useful framework to apply in organisations, with an introductory section that gives some idea of the range of topics to which it can be related.

Then I explain the TA philosophy, something which I believe distinguishes it from many other approaches. I also describe the range of TA concepts that now exist, because I have found that many people have had contact only with a fairly restricted selection of the earliest ideas.

I go on to write about some of the unfortunate myths that have arisen concerning TA and the ways in which the concepts and techniques have been gradually and unintentionally misrepresented. Associated with this are my thoughts on uses and abuses of TA. By giving you a clear account of these aspects, I hope that you will be better equipped to form a true judgment of the usefulness and appropriateness of TA within organisations.

The final section of this chapter is a rather ambitious attempt to show you how the different TA models fit together. Included here for those of you who like your learning to be structured in advance, I have done my best to explain some of the links.

I have necessarily used TA labels for the constructs; if you do not recognise them you may well find it easier to return to this section after reading the rest of this book.

WHY USE TA

I use TA because I find that individuals and teams achieve more when I teach it to them, and I achieve more when I apply it to myself. I also appreciate the simplicity of the theoretical constructs, the diversity of the models, and the way there are different elements to suit different needs whilst maintaining a coherent overall approach.

Although you may not be familiar with the TA terminology, I list below just a few ideas for how TA concepts can be matched to specific training topics:

TRAINING TOPICS	TA CONCEPTS
relationships	working styles/drivers
attitudes	windows on the world/life positions
change	cycles of development, competence curve
stress	racket system, BARs to success and PRO, working styles/drivers
creativity	ego states
problem solving	discounting, steps to success
assertiveness	racket system, BARs to success and PRO
teamwork	psychological games, group imagoes
motivation	strokes
customer care	ego states, strokes
counselling skills	transference
coaching/mentoring	transference
leadership	personality adaptations, AP[3]

I also use TA in combination with a variety of other non-TA approaches including action learning, behaviour analysis, synectics, enneagram, neuro-linguistic programming and psychometric questionnaires such as MBTI, KAI and FIRO-B.

My first contact with transactional analysis was back in the seventies, when it still had a novelty value but seemed to be going out of fashion rapidly within the training scene. Unlike many of my colleagues, I did not discard the approach when other ideas came along. Instead, I became intrigued by the way the transactional analysis concepts complemented other training methods, and particularly by the ease with which participants on training programmes were able to think their way through problems after being given only a simplistic introduction to basic transactional analysis models.

When I first began to include TA within programmes, I was impressed by the way I was at last able to deal with course members who approached me during breaks to confess that they had relationship problems outside work that corresponded to the difficulties identified in their performance at work. The TA models gave me a framework that they could apply to these personal situations.

More importantly, it provided me with the means to check my own professionalism at dealing with these requests for help as I discovered that there existed a process for thorough professional training in transactional analysis for use in organisational settings, organised by an international association. This training included supervision (which I now write as super-vision to avoid confusion with the function of first line managers). Super-vision is a process of self-reflection with a 'guide'. I found that it made an amazing difference to my self-awareness and hence my professional competence (see Chapter 12 for more about this).

There are of course alternatives to TA for people skills training. The range of options is wide, from macro level frameworks such as when people are likened to Greek gods, through to the micro level of specific analyses of what they say and how they say it. Somewhere in between are approaches such as body language and representational systems.

These alternatives vary in terms of how objective/subjective they are. Some depend on the perceptions of individual participants, of the trainer, and occasionally of any visiting managers who may come along as observers. Some include the subjective views of colleagues, as when pre-course questionnaires are distributed and the results collated by the trainer. At the more objective end of the scale, there are techniques such as Behaviour Analysis where trainers can check out their own classifications against those of their colleagues.

Another way in which such models vary is around who is doing the analysis. I classify them into three formats, each with advantages and disadvantages:

1. the participant analyses themself – the participant can include information that is hidden from others – but the participant may lack self-awareness
2. the participant completes a questionnaire from which the result is computed – the participant benefits from the framework for analysis that has been carefully developed by experts – but how a person believes they behave may not match up with how in fact they do behave
3. someone else analyses the participant – the participant gets feedback on how they are seen by others – but the person doing the assessing may be projecting their own characteristics onto the assessee.

I believe that the TA models generally combine the advantages mentioned above with a reasonable degree of objectivity. They are macro enough for ease of comprehension and micro enough to identify specific actions that could be taken to increase a person's interpersonal skills. They allow us to balance the input from others against the individual's capacity for recognising their own strengths and weaknesses. And they place the responsibility firmly in the hands of the individual and do not enforce on them the preferences and opinions of others, even if those others are 'experts'.

WELCOME TO TA
What is Transactional Analysis?

Transactional Analysis is a wide-ranging set of theories and techniques that can be used by individuals and groups to enable and help themselves and others to grow and develop to their full potential. The underlying philosophy is one of self and mutual respect and caring.

Formulated originally in a therapeutic context, it is equally valid for application in organisations and by individuals who want to take the initiative in their own development. Certified Transactional Analysts operate in four specialist fields: Psychotherapy; Organisational (training, organisational development, consultancy, management); Educational (children and adults, personal development); and Counselling (often one-to-one, problem solving, coaching).

TA is now taught and used worldwide, in settings as diverse as therapy groups, manufacturing and service industries, churches and religious orders, local and national governments, schools and universities, prisons and police forces, hospitals, and by individuals working alone to improve their personal adjustment to the world.

The TA Philosophy

The underlying philosophy of TA was encapsulated in the title of an early book by Thomas Harris: *I'm OK, You're OK*. This statement reflects a belief system that each of us is of value, each of us has the right to seek to meet our needs, and that we can behave towards others in ways that maximise our chances of getting on with each other. In other words, we can aim for win-win options.

This belief system is an important aspect of TA. It is not true TA if someone merely grasps the theory without the associated values. Similar to Rogers' concept of unconditional positive regard in the counselling situation, TA practitioners need to be committed to the encouragement and development of human potential, and to the principle of personal responsibility. National and international TA associations publish Codes of Ethics which call for all involved to establish ways of working that reflect such values.

Eric Berne, the originator of transactional analysis, specified the goal of therapy as being *autonomy*, which has three components:

- *awareness*, which means being in the here and now. This includes recognising your own sensations and feelings in response to current reality – and being able to set aside emotional responses that 'belong' in the past;
- *alternatives*, which means feeling free to choose from options for your own behaviour – and knowing that there will always be more than one way to behave;
- *attachment*, which is an open, trusting interaction with another person during which you can show and share your true feelings – and that they will accept you as you are, 'warts and all'.

These are just as relevant in organisational settings. Awareness is encouraged in organisations which respect the feelings and opinions of employees and take them into account when decisions are made. Alternatives are generated when employees are trusted to show initiative and make decisions relating to their own work. Attachment is the result in organisations when managers are willing to share their own hopes and concerns with employees, so that open two-way communication is established.

Developments in TA

The style of continual development modelled first by Berne has continued over the years. He developed the early theory and the philosophy during the period 1949 to 1958. He gave us detailed descriptions of well-known concepts such as ego states, games and strokes, and the basic ideas for many other aspects that were subsequently developed with and by others.

Over the years, many of the major theoretical advances have been recognised through a series of annual awards, given in memory of Eric Berne. A full list of the Eric Berne Memorial Scientific Awards is given as Appendix 2 – you may like to see which ones you recognise as many of the TA concepts get taught within organisational training courses without the source being credited. All have relevance in organisational settings even though they may have been developed originally for therapy. The following are some that I will refer to in detail within this book:

1971	Steiner	Script
1972	Karpman	Drama Triangle
1977	Kahler	Drivers
1980	Mellor & Schiff	Discounting
1984	Levin	Cycles of Power

The current range of topics encompasses enough variety of constructs that nowadays, when I run training programmes for those who seek TA qualifications, I can include workshops in the following groupings:

- professionalism: contracting for clear agreements with clients/participants, etc; the importance of self-reflection, super-vision and continuing professional development; and the application of ethical codes of practice;
- individual development: stages of childhood development and how these repeat later and can therefore be re-worked where necessary; how and why we created our life scripts when we are only children; what we can do to 'dismantle' unhelpful scripting and achieve increased autonomy;
- ego state analysis: usually labelled within TA books as structural and functional, I adjust the theory somewhat to produce models of internal ego states and how they have been formed, and behavioural ego states or how they show up to others;
- interactions, or transactional analysis proper, which is about the ways we interact with other people and therefore includes topics such as complementary, crossed and ulterior transactions, strokes (units of recognition), and the ways we structure our time;
- what can go wrong, or game and racket analysis: game analysis looks at the repetitive ways in which our interactions lead to negative payoffs - in other words, analysis of transactions but with a particular focus on how we fail to communicate and how we unknowingly sabotage our efforts to create trusting relationships; racket analysis, which might also be called intrapsychic or intrapersonal analysis as it concerns our internal processes of thinking, feeling, perceptions and interpretations; and the concept of stamp collecting;
- groups and teams: group imagoes, which are unwitting mental representations of groups and may unduly influence our behaviours; stages within groups as we get to know each other and (hopefully) work or play together;
- leadership: ways to combine several TA concepts, such as ego states and preferred channels of communication, strokes and motivation patterns, and working styles into a framework for leadership styles;

- organisational analysis: various models for analysing organisations and how they function; a metaphor as a framework for reviewing the various elements of organisational cultures;
- various 'work skills' such as creativity and innovation; stress management, assertiveness, change management, problem solving

Schools of TA

It was accepted for many years that there were three main 'schools' of TA but over recent years these have been extended and there is not yet general consensus about the additions. The original three schools were referred to as classical, redecision and cathexis. More recent approaches include integrative, systemic, constructivist, cocreative and relational.

The Classical school follows most closely the original style of Berne, which was to teach the TA theories to the patients and to work with them on the basis that understanding would enable them to select new options for changed behaviour. This is the approach that is closest in overall approach to that required for most organisational applications.

The Redecision school, led by Bob and Mary Goulding, focuses on the need to rework some of the decisions we made as children. We may no longer be conscious of these yet they influence our current behaviour. We need, therefore, to regress temporarily to the age at which we made the decision so that we can remake it in the light of our greater experience of the world. There are many ideas from the redecision school that have relevance in organisational work but the technique of regression is more appropriately used within a therapeutic relationship.

The Cathexis school arose from work done by Jacqui Schiff, and subsequently by members of her family and colleagues. Schiff adopted adult schizophrenics and enabled them to repeat their childhood in a different set of circumstances. This total regression involved them in being treated as babies and then 'growing up' again under the care of the therapists acting as parents. Again, this school generated many useful ideas for use in organisational work although the technique itself is not appropriate.

I do not propose to describe the newer approaches to TA in much detail here but include references in the Notes at the end of this chapter so you can follow up if you wish. For me, the key additional contributions to organisational TA from the later schools have been:

- constructivist – reminds us that perceptions of the world are 'constructed' within our minds, that we use 'narratives' to describe our perceptions, that different people will construct different realities
- cocreative – explains that communication brings into being another perspective that is mutually constructed
- relationship – describes how the relationship is the professional tool, so that an understanding of processes such as transference (see Chapter 12 Professional Super-Vision) becomes essential.

A few years ago I began referring to developmental transactional analysis (DTA). I chose this term to label the non-psychotherapy applications of TA, where we aim to help people develop themselves rather than seeking to cure them. I had by then devised many adjustments to TA theories so that the focus was on healthy functioning and not on pathology.

This focus on development was for me a theme shared by the organisational and educational fields, as well as by the counselling field when practised in line with the defined competencies (when it might more accurately be called the coaching field) rather than as a form of therapeutic counselling. Also shared by those fields is the approach of teaching the TA theory to the clients (as in the classical school), plus generally the need to contract, or define agreements, for our professional services, taking into account more than just one client, e.g. the HR director who brings us in as well as the course participants, the line manager who asks us to work as an internal consultant with their subordinate(s), the teacher who must juggle with the expectations of the pupil, parents, head teacher and maybe more.

The content of this book, whilst owing much to the full range of TA schools, is an example of DTA in action.

A Brief History of the TA Community

I have already mentioned that Eric Berne developed the basic concepts from 1949 to 1958. In 1958 he started the San Francisco Social Psychiatry Seminars (SFSPS), which was chartered as a non-profit educational corporation by the State of California in 1960. Seminar meetings are still running nowadays in San Francisco even though Berne himself died in 1970. The seminars have always been an important aspect in the sharing and development of TA theory. The SFSPS itself became the International Transactional Analysis Association (ITAA) in 1964.

Sometime after that, the European Association for Transactional Analysis (EATA) was established. Unlike the direct membership arrangements of ITAA, EATA comprises delegates from national TA associations across Europe.

More recently, the Western Pacific Association of Transactional Analysis (WPATA) has been set up in Australia. ITAA, EATA and WPATA are each responsible for professional training and accreditation in their areas of the world although ITAA operates this through a separate legal entity known as the Training & Certification Council (T&CC). The three organisations work to maintain similar processes and operate a policy of mutual recognition of each other's qualifications. There are also many national TA associations within South America, with an over-arching Asociación Latinoamericana de Anàlisis Transaccional, www.alatnet.org (ALAT).

In 1959 Berne was running what have since been known as 101's and 202's. Borrowed from the US education system, the terms refer to introductory courses (101) and advanced courses (202). Again, the notion has survived Berne. The 101 is an internationally-accredited introductory course in TA, with a set syllabus that applies wherever it is run. 202 is used to refer to advanced training run by people who have passed examinations and reached an appropriate level of endorsements as teachers of TA.

The first TA conference was run in 1963 and these have become regular international conferences. EATA and WPATA also run annual conferences and every three years all three organisations work together to run a World TA Conference. Most national TA associations run their own annual conferences.

Publication of a quarterly Transactional Analysis Bulletin began in 1962; this became the Transactional Analysis Journal in 1971. This continues to be the major international publication in TA, although there are now several equally important national journals.

In 2009 I am becoming the Editor of a new e-journal being launched by EATA; this will be all about research into TA and its applications.

The TA community operates a unique way of smoothing out the inequalities in the world's financial system. Known as the TAlent, it is a TA unit of currency. This converts payments due from members at different rates for different countries. In this way, we reflect the different income levels that apply in, say, Canada and India. Members in more prosperous areas of the world are charged more, so that others can pay less. The TAlent is a practical expression of TA principles of mutual respect and caring.

DISPELLING THE MYTHS

I continue to meet managers and trainers who are surprised to find a real-life Transactional Analyst, especially one who has specialised in organisational applications. Many have assumed that the approach is defunct as the publication of 'popular' books ceased years ago. Some even claim not to use TA, only for me to find that it has become part of the everyday language of their organisation. Do your employees and trainers talk about strokes, games, I'm OK, You're OK, without realising the source of these concepts?

Unfortunately, over the years the true nature of TA has become disguised. Be warned – if you tell people that you plan to use TA in the training you offer, you may hear remarks such as: "It was around years ago but no-one uses it now!" - "It doesn't work!" - "It's therapy, not training!" - "It's too simplistic!"

These are typical of the comments that emerge when you mention transactional analysis in some organisations. In a sense, I have written this book to challenge these statements. Let me own up right away to being biased in favour of transactional analysis. I have spent many years teaching and applying transactional analysis in organisations and with individuals, and am more used to hearing comments about how useful it is. I hope that this book will lay to rest some of the myths and allow you to share my enthusiasm for this potent approach to developing and empowering people.

There will of course always be some people who reject outright anything to do with 'psychological brainwashing'. However, these will be few when TA is taught effectively, within the TA philosophy that allows people to decide for themselves what, if anything, they want to change. In these circumstances, the feedback will typically begin with expressions of awareness and insight, followed by enthusiastic questions along the lines of "So is that why I... (take an instant dislike, or liking, to someone; dread talking to them, or prefer to spend time with them; get that feeling of here I go again; and similar examples).

Next will come the ability to relate the TA concepts to incidents in their day-to-day work and social lives, closely followed by the realisation that they can now identify options for change. Finally, the comments on course evaluations will include positive responses concerning the amount learned and the relevance of it.

Superficiality

Many of the common misconceptions have arisen from the over-reliance on just the few TA concepts that were publicised in best-sellers during the 'sixties'. The developments mentioned above have been overlooked, perhaps because they have often appeared only in scientific journals and have not been published for the general market. Some of the early books were rather simplistic in themselves, as the authors sought, quite reasonably, to make the new theories accessible to the reader.

Over the years the theories have been extended, new concepts have been developed, and applications have continued to grow. Much has been done to convert ideas originally devised by psychotherapists into practical models for use in organisations. TA models have been integrated with other approaches to give greater understanding and enhanced impact.

The international spread of the TA community has brought together contributions from around the world, so that the body of knowledge now encompasses a range of cross-cultural ideas.

Any new approach risks being misused; the very straightforwardness of basic TA meant this risk was greater. The simplicity of the concepts meant that we could read a book and believe that we understood. At one level this was true, and teaching TA at this depth certainly did no harm to anyone. Indeed, many people were able to recognise valuable lessons within such an overview. However, when presented too simplistically, audiences quite reasonably came to the incorrect conclusion that the TA itself was superficial.

Distortion

Along with superficiality came distortion. TA is about how people function and fail to function effectively. Trainers are people. We are therefore subject to the very problems that TA theory addresses – but we cannot always recognise our own issues. Our blind spots mean we overlook some of the options contained within the concepts. We then teach these concepts in a way that incorporates our own lack of awareness.

A common example of this arose with ego states; writers and trainers tended to give undue emphasis to the ego state attributes that they themselves possessed. As with all people skills training, our own value systems influence our choice of teaching material. Our potency as trainers is therefore constrained by the limits of our self-awareness.

This was why so many of the earlier works on TA implied, or even stated outright, that Adult ego state was the only 'good' ego state. As you will read in Chapter 4 on Interpersonal Styles, Adult is the ego state that appears as logical and problem solving. However, there is more to life than that. We need also to be caring, to have fun, to be creative, to be assertive. Someone who is highly rational may well overlook these other good human characteristics. Classical TA, as developed by Berne, appeals to people who are highly rational, as it is very much a thinking person's approach. Hence the omissions and incorrect emphasis on Adult ego state in the past.

Therapy

I have also heard tales about the inappropriate use of therapy techniques in organisational settings. Occasionally, trainers failed to recognise the boundaries. Asking 'macho' managers to sit on cushions is not the best way to convince them of the practicality of a new approach. Encouraging participants to share intensely personal information without ensuring it will not be used against them later is unprofessional.

I doubt that these incidents were the responsibility of TA-trained therapists. Instead, what happened was another version of the superficiality problem. Someone learned a little TA, experienced or read about some of the techniques, and failed to realise the true impact of some of the activities. They then recreated them without having the experience and expertise required to handle the results of such activities properly. Their participants quite rightly decided that this was not for them.

I have already mentioned the different schools of TA; for organisational work the Classical approach is the most appropriate. This involves teaching the theories to the participants, and helping them to choose how they wish to apply their new knowledge. In ego state terms, the trainer works with the Adults of the participants, who remain in the here-and-now and are not expected to re-experience previous scenes in their life. They may well remember the earlier situations, and thus be able to work out why they now respond as they do, but they do not regress.

We can all achieve a considerable amount of self development in this way. Participants who need to go further, or deeper, can then opt to continue their contact with TA in different settings if they wish.

The Singer is Not the Song

As you introduce TA into your work, you will need to be sensitive to the sort of concerns I have described. People may need help in distinguishing TA as a general approach and TA as it has been put over by specific individuals. An approach may only seem as effective as the person using it. The singer is not the song.

However, the relational and co-creative schools of TA are relevant here. You need to keep in mind that, whether you intend to or not, you will be engaging in a relationship with each participant, you will be co-creating reality with each of them – and when working with a group there will also be multiple relationships and multiple-creating. This is why it is so important that you engage in processes that will enhance your self-awareness.

It is not essential that you repeat my process and complete professional training in TA, although you will find it an enlightening and competence-building exercise if you do. However, I strongly urge you to work with the TA concepts and techniques on yourself before you use them with others. TA is a great approach for uncovering what we are unaware of, so that we can choose from a wider range of options. There is no shortcut because we do not know what we do not know. This is why super-vision, as described in Chapter 12 Professional Super-Vision, is so important

You will find certified TA practitioners who are willing to help you understand yourself and the TA theory better. There are also internationally-accredited TA supervisors. Appendix 3 gives details of TA associations; contact them to find out who is in your area.

USES AND ABUSES
Benefits of TA
The rest of this book will give you many ideas about applications of TA. Here I want to draw your attention to some of the general benefits from the use of TA as an approach for organisational work. As you read, check them against your value systems about training and learning. To the extent that they resonate, TA will make a valuable addition to your existing methods.

Learning TA in order to teach it to others has a major impact on trainer effectiveness. Working through the exercises will improve your skills in the same way that practice at technical tasks will build up your expertise. Teaching is basically an interpersonal skill, so concentrating on this for others will generate many insights if you are open-minded enough to look for them. In a sense you will also be operating at two levels; as you apply the techniques you are teaching to others, you will also be recognising their relevance to the way you are doing your teaching.

TA provides participants with an understanding that they can continue to use long after the trainer has left the scene. By equipping them with theories and models, and coaching them in their application, you enable course members to take with them a method of dealing with situations rather than a fixed checklist for a limited range of circumstances. They can analyse interactions, assess their own and others' reactions, and select from options whatever the occasion.

The TA approach relates to the whole person. As participants learn new ways of behaving, they are also helped to understand their attitudes and emotions. Often it is these under-the-surface aspects which really determine how successful we are. Knowing an assertive way of refusing a friend's request for a favour is not much help if you are unable to handle the flood of guilt you experience at the merest thought of saying no. If it were that simple to change, trainers would be superfluous.

Linked with the comment on understanding is the ongoing nature of TA based awareness. Once started on the route to self discovery, most people just keep going. The realisation that they can in fact analyse and understand their own behaviour and the responses of others gives them licence to continue the process of self development.

The changes they make as a result of additional awareness will continue to benefit them into the future. And just as your training skill improves as you teach TA, so will you recognise more effective modes of relating to others generally as you see how participants change.

The philosophy underpinning TA encourages people to take responsibility for themselves and their development. They become a partner with the trainer instead of a willing or unwilling victim. The basic belief of I'm OK, You're OK invites mutual respect and places a value on the experience and existing skills of the course member. They are not there simply to obey an 'expert' trainer; they are respected individuals who will work with the trainer to develop a greater range of options for themselves.

Abuses of TA

If you share the values implicit above, and work through the activities to gain self awareness before you try your TA out on other people, you are unlikely to do (or come to!) any harm. Regrettably, trainers have not always done this and have instead misused the TA concepts in various ways.

We all know the trainer who sets up the students, making them look foolish in order to make a training point. There are plenty of ways to help students gain awareness without belittling them. Activities in which normal human failings are exposed need to be handled with care and respect. Participants should end up feeling they have learned a valuable lesson and know what to do differently in the future. The aim is not to prove that the trainer is cleverer than the participants.

I recall a colleague who once gave deliberately vague instructions to a group in order to demonstrate how poor communication can affect outcomes, and how we often fail to clarify. Unfortunately, he was so intent on making his point that he criticised them strongly for failing to complete the task properly – and then discovered they had in fact determined their own parameters only after establishing that they were unable to check his requirements because he had deliberately left the site. They disliked him so much for his manipulation that little of his subsequent teaching was accepted.

Equally unprofessional is the trainer who creates an upsetting experience and tells the participants afterwards that it was for your own good. TA is based on mutual agreement, a concept explained in detail in Chapter 2, Contracting for Learning. In essence, this means that all parties have agreed, knowingly, to whatever is to happen to them. This does not mean that you have to spell out the detail of every activity; it refers to giving students a choice of whether to take part and an honest assessment of the likely impact.

Sessions in which participants experience strong emotions may indeed be good for them but they should be the ones who make the decision. Claiming, as I once heard, that "participants were reduced to tears because you need a cathartic experience before you can change" is unacceptable when participants have not even indicated that they want to change. Organisations who want employees to change do not have the right to use training as a way of imposing such views on unsuspecting course members.

Playing the TA expert is a trap that many of us fall into from time to time. Indeed, there is even a psychological game ('game' being TA jargon for unhealthy interaction) called 'Transactional Analysis'. The TA expert is the person who has learned some TA and is now ready to analyse everyone else and tell them their shortcomings. This is a one-up stance for the trainer, with the participant as victim. The participant resembles a butterfly that has been pinned to a board. They are held there, unable to escape, while the trainer exposes their psychological underbelly.

TA was devised as a tool to be used by individuals for self enlightenment; not a tool with which to change the shape of other people. Analysing someone else is acceptable only when done at their request, tentatively, tactfully, gently and respectfully. Even though we are unlikely to comment on anything that is not already apparent to others, feedback should not be given unless we are sure the recipient is in a good psychological position to absorb it.

It is often suggested that we help others as a way of dealing with our own problems. In itself, this is no bad thing. Counsellors often work in fields where they have experienced personal difficulties; it means they can empathise with the client and speak from a common understanding. However, competent counsellors ensure they have adequate super-vision so that their own issues do not interfere with the needs of the client. They learn from their clients but work on their own problems elsewhere until they have resolved them.

Trainers are often attracted to approaches like TA for the same reasons. This is reflected in the old joke: 'Those who can do. Those who can't, become trainers.' Provided we are aware of the potential conflict of interests, we can arrange appropriate support. We can never eliminate every issue of our own but we can check to see that they do not interfere with our effectiveness in the classroom. Having our own super-vision arrangements is a key element for ensuring we are as competent as possible, as I emphasise in chapter 12, Professional Super-Vision.

Permission, Protection and Potency

There are three essential elements in the helping relationship: permission to do things differently, protection while you learn to do so, and potency to overcome the habits and beliefs of the past. These can be considered from the perspective of the trainer and the participant.

The effective trainer will provide permission to be different by: the way they present information; an emphasis on the possibility for change; quoting examples of successful changes made by others including themselves; modelling an open-minded approach to change; and by not being critical.

They will provide protection by: careful selection of individual and group activities; structuring feedback sessions to provide constructive criticism only; intervening when necessary; maintaining boundaries between the training session and the workplace; promising confidentiality for information shared with them; not making promises they cannot guarantee (such as on behalf of others); providing advice and guidelines on how participants implement changed behaviours; and by not rescuing or doing it for them.

The trainer will demonstrate potency by: showing their own enthusiasm for what they are teaching; commending the achievements of participants; describing the advantages of making changes; quoting examples of previous successes; showing their belief in the capabilities of participants; helping participants devise ways to overcome obstacles to change; and by not being passive and low key.

The participants' part in this will include: giving themselves permission to change by actively considering alternatives; getting reinforcement from colleagues, managers family and friends; planning rewards for successful implementation; reviewing their successes regularly; not criticising themselves for lack of progress; not dwelling on the sins of the past.

They can organise protection for themselves by: carefully considering the implications of any change; organising a support network; agreeing change objectives with management; selecting appropriate circumstances in which to initiate the changes; not changing without first considering the consequences; not waiting for someone else to take the initiative.

Participants can develop potency in themselves by: allowing their natural enthusiasm to show; sharing with others who are also changing; recalling past successes; getting congratulations from people who care about them; not spending time with people who don't want them to change; not expecting others to change instead.

UNDERSTANDING THE LINKS

There are a number of concepts within the broad field of TA. It is not easy to see how they fit together. At the risk of confusing you with jargon, I finish this introductory chapter with an overview. I will use terms that you may not yet know, so I will accompany each with a brief explanation. As you work through the book, you will learn more about each. I suggest that you refer back to this section, and especially Figure 1.1, from time to time so you can see the links between the constructs.

Please keep in mind that there is little point in spending time and energy trying to compare different elements. I use the analogy of a diamond, with a person inside it. The different concepts are the facets of the diamond. What goes on inside the diamond does not change

Figure 1.1: Understanding the links

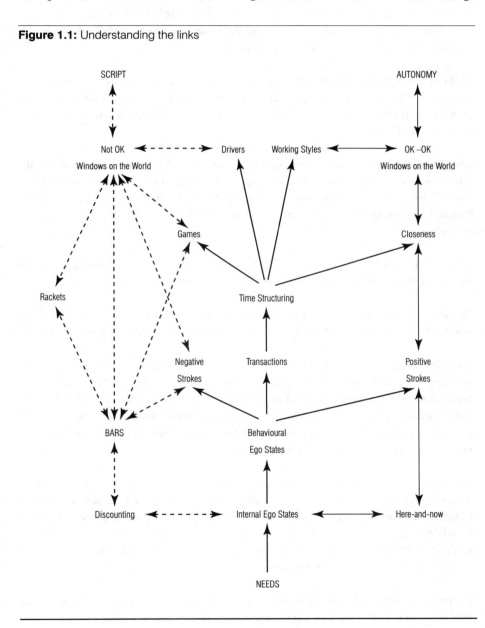

– only our perception of it alters. We can select which facet to observe through, to suit our purpose and to gain the best understanding. We may choose to view through more than one facet to build up a more rounded picture. Or we may decide that one perception has given us enough information to work on.

At the base of the diagram are our *needs*, such as for growth and development, for human contact, for structure and protection. At the top are the alternatives: *script*, which is our unconscious life plan, versus *autonomy*, which means we are in the here-and-now, we choose how we behave and we can form relationships.

Between the base and the alternative apexes, I show three 'routes'. The middle path is basically neutral, the left hand option is shown with dotted lines to indicate unconscious processes that are inferred but cannot be observed directly, and the right hand route is the positive way of behaving.

The dotted lines are shown with double arrows to indicate the way in which the unconscious processes create reinforcing loops. A couple of solid lines are also double-headed: being in the here-and-now allows us to update our *internal ego states* and choosing our *working styles* depends on and also reinforces our non-distorting *window on the world*.

Taking first the middle route, needs refers to our biological *needs* and *hungers*, for contact with other human beings and for some structure and predictability in our lives.

Our *internal ego states* are the 'organs' by which we store experiences and make sense of the world. Our *behavioural ego states* are the observable ways in which we operate in the world.

We then engage in *transactions*, or interactions with others. Our transactions can be analysed in terms of clusters, which are our ways of *time structuring*. These range from being *alone* through varying levels of intensity of interactions with others. They culminate in the positive option of *closeness* or the negative option of *psychological games*, which are repetitive patterns of failing to connect. These options feed into either the positive or negative sequences towards *autonomy* or *script*.

Above time structuring, I show another two options: *drivers* or *working styles*. These are two ends of the same phenomenon. We are said to be in driver when our behaviour drives us and in working style when we choose our behaviour. Drivers operate on a principle of *I'm-OK* if (I act in a certain way), or sometimes a You're OK if (you act in a certain way), and end up reinforcing our *not-OK* windows on the world. Working styles are seen as our strengths and reinforce our OK-OK perspective.

On the right hand side I show an alternative explanation for what can be observed. Provided our internal ego states are functioning well, we will experience ourselves as in the here-and-now rather than regressing to past situations. Being in the here-and-now will mean that we exchange mainly positive *strokes*, or units of recognition, with other people. Strokes are shown alongside transactions as they are alternative concepts for analysing interactions – any time we interact it is both a transaction and a stroke.

Positive strokes may occur through the various forms of time structuring but the key outcome is that they enable us to achieve genuine *closeness*. This in turn is a key ingredient of having an OK-OK, non-distorting window, or frame of reference, through which we view the world. And that window is an essential component for achieving *autonomy*, which is the aim of TA therapy and development.

On the left hand side I show how unconscious processes lead us away from the here-and-now and into script instead of autonomy.

A key element here is *discounting*, which means that we minimise, exaggerate or overlook some aspect of reality. We then fail to recognise opportunities to get our needs met in a healthy way and instead we repeat familiar patterns even though they have been unsuccessful in the past.

We filter the world through *BARs*, which stands for self-fulfilling loops of beliefs leading to actions leading to reinforcements of the beliefs. The BARs lead to several unhelpful ways in which we maintain our distorted, not-OK perspectives.

Rackets are short sequences where we mentally run through a familiar pattern of unhelpful thoughts and feelings and finish up feeling bad again. We can do this without any contact with others, although the existence of rackets can sometimes be surmised through observable manipulative behaviours. *Games* are similar, except that we interact with at least one other person and end up feeling even worse. Worse may include feelings of one-up, superiority, smug; not all of us opt to be put down.

The game behaviours are observable but the unconscious processes are not. Likewise, negative strokes are observable but we can only speculate about the internal beliefs that lead to them.

I am aware that I have finished this section with a description of what goes wrong, and an explanation that much of it is due to unconscious processes. This sounds somewhat depressing so let me remind you that:
- we also have the neutral 'middle' path and the positive route to autonomy
- unless we were in extremely unfortunate circumstances as a child, we have many experiences of things going well
- the aim of TA, and of this book, is to provide enough information for us to understand why we don't always choose the healthy option – and then to make the redecisions that will enable us to opt for autonomy for more of the time.

NOTES & SOURCES

Eric Berne – any book about TA must acknowledge the debt owed to Eric Berne, the founder of TA. He laid the foundations for the approach, developing the basic theories, the underlying philosophy and the characteristic style of application that is so respectful and empowering.

Berne's books are listed later. The one I recommend for an overview by Berne himself is *What do you say after you say Hello?* Corgi 1975. Issued after Berne had died, this book covers many of the concepts developed by him.

Berne also wrote an 'organisational' book, entitled *The Structure and Dynamics of Organisations and Groups* Grove Press Inc. 1966. However, this is a difficult book to follow and is largely restricted to hospital and psychotherapy group examples. The chapter on Management of Organisations occupies only 10 pages out of 236. I recommend this only for readers who intend to study TA in depth and suggest in that case that you read first an article by Elliot M. Fox entitled *Eric Berne's Theory of Organizations* in Transactional Analysis Journal Oct 1975 Vol 5 Iss. 4 pp 345-353 as this captures the key points of the book in an accessible way.

Similarly, *Games People Play* by Berne, Penguin 1967/1968 is geared to clinicians. Although a bestseller originally, three-quarters of the book consists of examples of psychological games, with much clinical detail. The first quarter of the book contains a useful overview of TA concepts but this information is now available elsewhere, such as in *TA Today* by Ian Stewart and Vann Joines, Lifespace Publishing 1987. This is an excellent introductory book for individuals who want to understand the main TA concepts.

If you do return to the original sources, be aware that Berne was writing in the 1960's so he may well sound sexist and even racist, as so many authors of that era do because of norms such as managers always being referred to as men. I am sure that, were he still alive, he would have wanted to update his books.

I'm OK, You're OK by Thomas Harris, Pan 1973 is also a good guide to general TA concepts, although it obviously lacks references to concepts developed since it was written.

Autonomy – Berne labelled the components awareness, spontaneity and intimacy.

Ego states – Berne wrote of structural and functional ego states, contaminations and exclusions. My version of internal and behavioural ego states is a variation developed as a result of my experiences with teaching the original models. See Chapter 4, Interpersonal Styles and Chapter 11, Creativity and Innovation, for more detailed descriptions.

Working Styles – I use this term for those behaviours that were previously called drivers but which appear as our strengths and are useful provided we do not link them to our sense of okayness. For more details see Chapter 5, Working Styles.

For more details on the original three schools of TA, see *Transactional Analysis after Eric Berne: Teachings and Practices of Three TA Schools* edited by Graham Barnes, Harper's College Press, 1977.

The *Redecision School* is described by its originators in *The Power is in the Patient* Robert L Goulding and Mary M Goulding, TA Press, 1978, and in *Changing Lives through Redecision Therapy* Mary M Goulding and Robert L Goulding, Grove Press Inc, 1979.

Cathexis School principles are given in *Cathexis Reader* by Jacqui Lee Schiff (in collaboration with others), Harper & Row, 1975. The practical side of this work is described movingly in *All My Children* by Jacqui Lee Schiff with Beth Day, Jove Publications Inc, 1979.

Integrative TA – see Richard G. Erskine & Rebecca L. Trautmann, *Methods of an Integrative Psychotherapy* in Transactional Analysis Journal, Oct 1996 Vol 26 No.4 pp 316-328.

Constructivist TA – see Bruce Loria *Integrative Family Therapy: A Constructivist Perspective* in The Stamford Papers: Selections from the 29th Annual ITAA Conference, Omnipress 1991

Cocreative TA – see Graeme Summers & Keith Tudor *Cocreative Transactional Analysis* in Transactional Analysis Journal Oct 2000 Vol 30 No.1 pp 23-40.

Relational TA – see Helena Hargaden & Charlotte Sills *Transactional Analysis: A Relational Perspective*, Brummer-Routledge 2002. I have extracted the relational concept from that book, although the book itself is targeted at psychotherapists.

Systemic TA – see Bernd Schmid in the list of Eric Berne Memorial Scientific Award Winner in 2007 (Appendix 2).

Permission, Protection, Potency are concepts for which Pat Crossman gained the Eric Berne Memorial Scientific Award in 1976. See Appendix 2 for publication details.

Training to apply TA – details of the requirements and procedures for obtaining international certification in the competent application of transactional analysis are given in Appendix 4 Professional Training in Transactional Analysis.

Unconditional positive regard– nonTA - for more information see *Client Centered Therapy* by Carl Rogers, Constable & Co, 1951 or any other book by the same author.

CHAPTER 2:   CONTRACTING FOR LEARNING

I am going to concentrate now on how some TA frameworks can be related specifically to the way we set up the situation to do our jobs as trainers. During 2009 I expect to complete the other books on TA that I am writing specifically for coaches and mentors and for consultants, plus the update of *Working it Out at Work* which is of course the book for your participants to read.

In this chapter I will include models that have been devised with a one-to-one helper/client focus in mind, as well as showing how these can be developed to take account of the additional complexity that occurs when we provide training to meet organisational as well as individual needs. I will also explain how some of the more general TA concepts can be applied to ways we help participants gain most from the teaching situation.

TA is a contractual approach; this means that there must be a clear agreement, or contract, between a practitioner and the one who is to be 'practised' upon. I will describe first the elements of a contract that might apply between two parties; this is a useful model for considering how we should conduct ourselves when providing training. I will then extend this into the situation that so often prevails in the organisational setting – when we have three or more parties involved as we make contact separately with managers, participants and others.

Having described the nature of three-way contracting, I give examples of what may happen if the psychological distance between the parties is not evenly balanced. There are some clear effects if the trainer becomes too close to either the organisation's management, or to the participants. It is even worse when the participants and the organisation appear to reject the trainer.

I will then go on to look at the additional complications that arise when we have more than three parties and when some of the links are implicit only – such as when the trainer does not meet the line managers of the participants but must still take into account that said line managers will have a major impact on how the ongoing performance of the participants will be evaluated.

Contracting leads us into the notion of participants contracting with themselves about the changes they want to make. A section on action planning is therefore included, in which I show how TA models can help to flush out those potential sabotage mechanisms to which human beings are apt to fall victim.

This chapter includes some activities, related to the text, that you can use with participants. I strongly recommend that you work through them yourself first; as well as knowing them better you will also gain in self-awareness.

Finally, I end with a very short section on sources and references for the TA concepts covered in this chapter.

CONTRACTING

Contracting is one of the major principles of TA. In normal use of the word, a contract is an agreement between the parties about what they expect to happen. Although the term is generally used to imply some form of legal document, it is recognised that verbal contracts can also exist.

TA uses the term in a similar way and places great emphasis on the advisability of having clearly defined verbal contracts before working with someone. Indeed, without a contract it is incorrect to claim that true TA is being practised. Berne proposed that there are three aspects that need consideration: administrative, professional and psychological. These might also be regarded as three different levels at which our contracts must operate. Some of these aspects will be set down in writing but much may depend on what is said, and the really significant elements of the contract will be the unspoken ones.

I have renamed administrative as procedural in order to create a donkey bridge of PPP.

Procedural

The procedural level of the contract should spell out the arrangements agreed concerning matters such as timings, venue, payment and task responsibilities. It includes items such as where the course is to be run, dates and session times, how many participants can attend, are there follow-up sessions, and payment to the trainer. This last point might of course be taken for granted if the trainer is an employee within the organisation, although compensation for overtime could need clarifying. Independent trainers may need to include cancellation arrangements as well as fees in their contract details.

Some typical oversights occur in this area, such as lack of clear allocation of responsibility for joining instructions, so that students receive a brief note from a manager instead of detailed advance notification from the trainer. Less expected was the occasion when I arrived to run a one day time management course to find that the room had been booked for a late afternoon session so please would I finish 45 minutes earlier - a significant - and ironic shortfall. Another example I recall was of a training manager notifying participants of dates and venue for a course on presentation skills, but omitting to advise them to bring the prepared talk or the supporting materials that I had specified. If you find that administrative matters are interfering with the effectiveness of your training, it is a good idea to draw up your own checklist.

Claude Steiner suggests also that we need 'consideration' to have a contract. This term is borrowed from the legal world, where there must be some consideration that passes between the parties to make it a valid contract. This is why we sometimes hear of agreements in which a peppercorn rent is paid; this token payment keeps the contract legal. In organisational work, the issue here is ensuring that a realistic fee is charged for the level of service provided. Cancellations must also be considered as training is a perishable product in the sense that days not used cannot be put back on the shelf to sell again later.

In this age of cost centres, the question of consideration becomes just as relevant for those of us employed within an organisation. Clarification of the financial arrangements has become essential for demonstrating the productivity of the training department. We are expected nowadays to calculate our overheads accurately and be able to cross-charge, even for non-attendance. Good administrative control is essential.

Professional

The professional level of the contract relates to the aim of the work to be done together. As professional trainers, we should have clearly defined objectives, stated in terms of what the students will be able to do after receiving the training. These objectives will be worded in a way that participants and their managers can understand, and ideally will be in measurable terms so that the outcomes can be checked. At the very least, there will be a description, albeit subjective, of what they can be expected to have gained from the course.

The professional part of the contract is also about how the trainer and the student will contribute to the learning. For the trainer, this refers to the special knowledge, skills and experience we bring to the training. This includes any technical expertise we may have as well as our abilities as professional teachers. For the participants, it relates to their willingness to undertake the range of learning activities proposed by the trainer, as well as the prior knowledge, skills and experiences that they too will bring to the training.

Related to this is the question of competence. We owe it to our students, our organisations, and ourselves, to provide only that training which we are competent to undertake. I can recall being expected by my employer to run interpersonal skills courses of a type which generate considerable discomfort in some participants.

The organisation concerned had neglected to check whether I was competent to handle the inevitable counselling sessions which used to be requested. Until I was able to organise counselling training for myself, the training was compromised in two ways; I sought to avoid giving challenging feedback in case participants were upset, and those who did solicit counselling got little benefit from my unskilled attempts to do my best.

Psychological

The psychological contact is potentially the more difficult element to handle satisfactorily. Psychological refers to the underlying dynamics between trainer and participant. Generally, this aspect of the contract is unspoken and may well be outside the conscious awareness of the parties. It will form the most significant strand of the overall contract; if the psychological level is not 'clean' then the objectives may not be achieved.

A healthy psychological contract will be based on mutual respect and trust. The trainer will respect the ability of the participant, will recognise the validity of their previous experience, and will trust them to make their own decisions about how they apply the training. The participant will respect the competence of the trainer and will trust the trainer to structure the training activities effectively. Trainer and participant will therefore be putting their psychological energies into a collaborative effort.

An unhealthy psychological contract will contain unresolved issues between the parties. There may be an imbalance, as when trainer or participant believes they are more capable than the other person. Equally, they may be convinced that they are less capable. Alternatively, either may suspect that both of them are incapable, of learning and teaching respectively.

Or the issue may be around trust, as when participants assume the trainer is out to set them up in some way, or trainers believe that participants cannot be trusted to work unless there is a trainer actually in the room at all times. In any of these instances, although they will not say so directly, their behaviour will contain indications of their attitude and this will sabotage the learning process.

An important element of the psychological contract will be mutual consent. At the macro level, does the student want to be on the course? There can be few trainers who have not been presented with a participant who has been 'sent'. Even worse is the situation where they have also been 'told' that they have a problem and that the trainer will sort them out.

At the micro level, trainers can inadvertently misuse the power of their role to coerce participants into training activities which they resent. Whenever students are not given a free choice about their participation, there will be psychological repercussions.

Trainers too need to have control over their own input to the training. Being expected to use a course design developed by another trainer is only reasonable insofar as we have the same values and preferences as the course designer. If we have serious reservations about the training methods we are required to use, our lack of conviction will dilute the effect of our training. A simple lack of training experience would figure under the issue of competence; I am thinking of more significant matters here. Mutual consent means that we have freely chosen our training style and are allowed to operate within our own ethical framework.

THE THREE CORNERED CONTRACT

The ideas above refer to contracts as if they are made between two parties. Fanita English pointed out that trainers in organisations are actually involved in contracts between three parties – and she coined the term 'three cornered contract' to describe the situation shown in Figure 2.1.

Her original suggestion referred to the situation where a trainer from outside is brought in by organisers to work with a group. The model works equally well if we apply it to an internal trainer. The first contract is set up between the trainer and the organiser; this may be external trainer with training manager, or internal trainer with line manager. Sometimes the organisers are a group of people, which tends to make the process yet more complex as each may understand the contract differently.

You may already be thinking about training situations with more than three parties involved – for example, the line manager, as well as the trainer, the organiser and the participants. For ease of understanding, however, I will continue to concentrate on the simple model of three and will explore the other possibilities later in this chapter. The three-way model is also the most useful in the classroom when you want to explain and agree the contract with your participants.

The trainer/organiser contract will have procedural, professional and psychological elements. With your own thorough checklist such as the one mentioned earlier, the procedural part can be straightforward.

We begin to enter more troubled waters when we work out the professional aspect. The organiser will probably have taken care of this by checking the credentials or prior experiences of the trainer, to ensure an appropriate track record for the topic in question. At the same time, the trainer needs to check what the organiser expects the training to cover. Often, the parties will agree on the training objectives and the course design.

Figure 2.1: The Three Cornered Contract

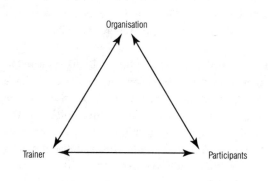

Herein lies a potential problem; at this stage there may well have been no involvement by the participants.

Subsequently, the trainer and the participants arrive in the classroom. Unless the joining instructions have been atypically informative, the participants and the trainer will have somewhat different ideas on what is going to take place. At worst, the participants may be there for the wrong reasons.

Over the years, my personal experience has included:

- being asked to run letter-writing courses where none of the participants ever wrote letters (they filled in numbers onto standard letters);
- having a non-supervisory participant arrive on a supervisory skills course. When I suggested that perhaps the skills would be useful if he were promoted, he pointed out that he was due to retire within months;
- being assured that participants had received no previous training in leadership, and then listening as they described their face-to-face discussions with Herzberg, Maslow and other famous names.

These 'quirks' occurred in spite of careful checking with the organisers. Sometimes the organiser was at fault; sometimes the nominating manager had put forward the wrong individual. In each case, the course still ran successfully but it required some careful readjustment to the programme. (For those of you who are wondering: in the first case we worked on personal letters; in the second he decided he might as well enjoy the few days break from work; and in the third the programme was quickly amended into an advanced course in which they shared previous knowledge.)

The psychological level of the contract may need even more careful attention, especially as it is so often outside our conscious awareness. We need to explore the underlying expectations of the organiser, and the organisation's management. Are we seen as surrogate persecutors who will make participants aware of their shortcomings? Are we expected to report back to management about individual participants? If managers will be attending the course, what will be their role? How successful can we be – does the organisation really want us to empower participants so that they come back to work full of challenges to the status quo?

In addition to the ideas described in the rest of this chapter, many other TA frameworks will provide useful models to help us understand this aspect of contracting. *Symbiosis*, as described in Chapter 6, Thinking Styles, will help you analyse your contracts; analysis of your own games, as suggested in Chapter 7, Working with Others, will enable you to sidestep potential pitfalls; knowing your characteristic approach, as explained in Chapter 5, Working Styles, will help you control pressures you might otherwise transfer to participants through your programme designs. And of course Chapter 12, Professional Super-Vision will prompt you to review your contracting and get the benefit of another's perspective.

Multi-party Contracting

There are often training situations in which more than three parties are involved. I have on occasion produced a series of interlocking triangles that looked rather like a deformed umbrella, to show the ways in which the same party may be involved in more than one contract. Adding the line manager into the equation can do this: we then have one triangle consisting of trainer, organisation and participant, associated with another that contains manager, organisation and trainer, associated with another that contains manager, organisation and participant as subordinate. Other options bring in clients (e.g. for social workers), the Health and Safety Executive or similar bodies, the customer or consumer associations, the parents (for schools and training schemes) and many more.

CONTRACTING IN THE CLASSROOM

English suggests that we use the three cornered contract in the classroom, by drawing a triangle on the board, (see Figure 2.1) talking about the contracts between the parties in each corner, and entering the details on the board as a summary.

What we take care of with this process is the psychological level of the contract. We bring the secret agendas and covert concerns into the open, where they can be discussed and dealt with. Participants hear from us the details of what the organisation has asked for, and what we are prepared to do.

I use this approach by describing first, in some detail, the agreement I have with the organisation. I explain that my discussions were with a representative of the organisation (training, personnel or line manager) but that essentially I have a contract with the organisation that employs them (or of which they are part, in the case of volunteer or religious organisations). To fulfil this contract, I have agreed to be in a certain location, on a certain date, to teach a certain subject – and here I am. In return, the organisation has agreed to pay me (or reward in some other way if for pro bono work).

The organisation has a similar contract with them. They have agreed to come to work in certain locations, on certain days, and to undertake certain tasks. As a part of this, they have implicitly agreed to attend training courses if the organisation requires it – so here they are. In return, the organisation pays them, and usually continues to pay them during their training as they are learning how to do their job even better.

That is the most straightforward part of our contracts with the organisation. I also point out that some of this will be in writing: I usually have at least a purchase order or letter of confirmation and they have a contract of employment. There may be other paperwork too: I may have produced training proposals and course outlines, while they may be expected to operate at work according to procedures manuals.

In addition, much of both contracts is likely to be verbal. I will have talked to my contacts about how I will do the training and what my training style is like. Participants will have talked with their managers about how they do their jobs and what level of discretion they have. In preparing for the course, I may also have talked with potential participants and with nominating managers to find out more about the work and the training needs. The participants may have discussed their individual needs with their managers. They may have talked to previous participants to find out what to expect of the course. We bring all of this verbal information with us as part of our understanding of our contracts with the organisation.

Now we need to establish a contract between us – between this trainer and these participants who are here today.

We can begin from the perspective of the trainer or the participants. From the trainer's corner, I describe those areas of the training/learning process that I take responsibility for. First, I point out that I cannot learn them anything; I can teach but only they can learn. Teaching therefore belongs at my corner, learning at theirs.

Next, structure goes into my corner and involvement in theirs. In order to teach well and enable them to learn, I take responsibility for the design and structure of the programme. As a professional trainer, I will select appropriate activities to help them learn. They have to make the decisions about whether to undertake the activities I propose. I will not (and cannot) force them to do so but if they opt out then any loss of learning opportunity is their responsibility. Conversely, the more effort they expend the more they are going to gain from the training.

Much of the training I do is centred on people skills. For this type of training, I add theories to my corner, experience to theirs. I expect participants to bring their experiences and problems to the course so we can work on real examples. I can provide them with models and frameworks for understanding human behaviour, and can give general examples. However, my aim is to equip them to apply the theories for themselves, so they can continue to increase their effectiveness after they have left the course. I invite them, therefore, to share their examples and to ask questions until they are satisfied they can use the concepts in the real world. This will apply also to technical training: the corners then might read theory for the trainer and practice for the participants. I show a typical completed three cornered contract in Figure 2.2.

When English first wrote of the three cornered contract, she referred to the organisation as the 'Great Powers'. This was because she found that the participants often arrived with fantasies about what the organisation had arranged; by introducing an element of fun she was able to defuse any bad feelings before they interfered with the training. She suggests we do this by listing the fantasies on the board, while identifying which are realistic expectations and which are not. This is usually enough to ensure that the more extreme fictions are laid to rest. English thus provides us with a neat process for clarifying, and if necessary retrieving those situations where there are significant differences in expectations.

Figure 2.2: A Typical Completed Three Cornered Contract

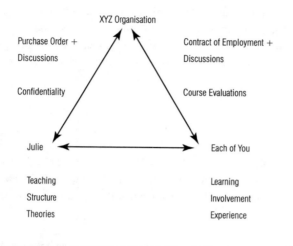

I find that her model makes a useful addition to any training session, even when I do not expect there to be any discrepancies. If there are no difficulties, the process is quick and sets the pattern for a partnership between trainer and participants. If there are unanticipated problems, describing English's model will bring them to the surface so they can be dealt with instead of emerging later when it will be more difficult to put them right.

Confidentiality

One other area I always mention is that of confidentiality and feedback to management. I can make my teaching more relevant if individuals let me know about the difficulties they encounter, whether these are at work or during the course. I think that people will be less likely to confide such details to the trainer if they believe the trainer makes a report to management after the course. My usual contract with an organisation therefore includes an agreement that I will keep confidential whatever I learn about the participants. (I will report it if someone fails to attend.) Confidentiality is therefore added to my corner of the triangle. On the other hand, I recognise that organisations need some way of checking the performance of a trainer. I therefore accept that the participants should complete a course evaluation. Feedback to management goes in their corner.

I do not normally ask for a blanket contract of confidentiality on courses I run. When this is done, particularly at the start of a course, participants are put under considerable pressure to agree to it. I do not believe this is a sound basis for a genuine contract. I prefer, therefore, to recommend rather than insist that they should refrain from talking about each other after they leave the course. I then point out that I have no way to guarantee that people will maintain silence, and no sanctions to apply if they do not. Because of this, I invite them all to consider carefully what they decide to share in the group and what they tell only to me. They are responsible for taking care of themselves in this way; I can only promise total confidentiality for things shared only with me.

PSYCHOLOGICAL DISTANCE

An important element in the psychological contract is what Nelly Micholt has called the psychological distance. This is the perceived distance in terms of relationship that exists between the parties. In a healthy training alliance, the sides of the contract triangle are all the same psychological length. Psychologically, the organisation, the trainer and the participants have matching degrees of closeness on each dimension.

Difficulties arise when any of the parties feels that the relationships are unevenly balanced. This can be represented by imagining that the triangle is drawn so that one side is shorter than the other two. Obviously, there are three variants of this, as shown in Figure 2.3 shown below.

Figure 2.3: Psychological Distances

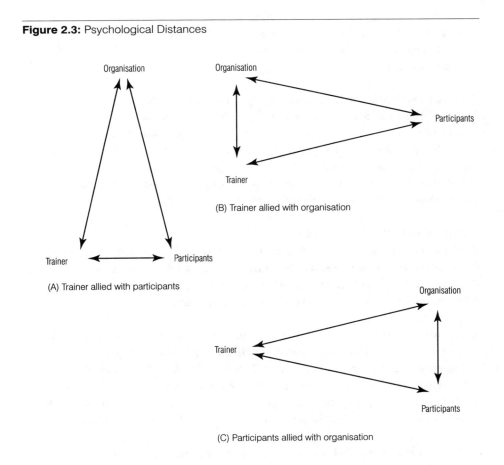

Trainer allied with Participants

There is a danger that the trainer identifies too closely with the participants. This may happen, for instance, with an in-company trainer who shares participants' disaffection with the organisation after a period of reorganisation. Sometimes independent trainers may see themselves as a crusading avenger, there to help participants throw off the unreasonable shackles of the organisation. Trainers who seek to meet their social needs through work may become too intimate with participants in an effort to make friends.

Too close a relationship between trainer and participants leads to an unnatural euphoria in the classroom. The needs of the organisation are likely to be forgotten as the group concentrates instead on having a good time, or on topics that interest them rather than that arranged by the organiser. Coalitions may be formed to lead an attack on the corporate environment, or trainers may find themselves coaching participants in subversive techniques. This may sound far-fetched but it really does happen.

Think about your own response when a participant complains about a manager – it is a difficult boundary to maintain so that they feel understood and empowered without your teaching them ways to manipulate. It can be even harder not to agree with them when you have had difficulties with the same manager yourself.

Becoming too close to participants in this way will seriously dilute your impact as a trainer. If you see the situation in the same way that they do, you are unlikely to change their frame of reference. Such a change is essential if people are to solve problems effectively. Failure to do this will have longer term implications for them and you. They will return to continued problems, exacerbated now perhaps by their manager's disappointment at their lack of development. You will come to be regarded as a poor trainer because your participants learn little but rebellion from you.

Trainer allied with Organisation

Participants will be wary of a trainer who seems to identify too closely with the organisation. They want to feel that their own needs will be taken into account even though the organisation is looking for something specific too. If you are clearly an envoy of management, your training will be received with scepticism.

In-company trainers may give this impression when they have been involved in the development of organisational initiatives that are now being applied via training. Independent trainers may appear like this merely because their contact within the organisation has till now been limited to a select few. We may also fall into this trap because of strong opinions about the way things should be done; if our values match the organisational culture we may be intolerant of those who do not share such views.

In the classroom we are likely to experience an excess of artificial politeness. Participants will mistrust us so will not tell us what they really think. They may avoid challenging us in order to conceal their doubts. We may be faced with an unresponsive group who put minimal effort into the activities and discussions we have planned. If we push too hard, we may stimulate a mutiny. Course evaluations will contain comments about the irrelevance of the training to the real world.

Participants allied with Organisation

This is an extremely uncomfortable situation for a trainer. It happens on a large scale when organisations call in a trainer even though those responsible do not believe the training is needed – such as when legislation requires they 'do something' about equal opportunities or safety. The trainer then finds that participants are intuitively aware of the lack of management commitment, making it extremely difficult to achieve any real progress.

The same thing happens on a smaller scale when individual managers are expected to release staff for training under corporate programmes which they do not truly support – such as customer care for support staff. Although the organisation, in the person of the training manager or top team, is committed to the training, the individual participant's principal psychological contract is with their own manager. If that manager's views are out of line with corporate policy, the participant will carry this stance into the classroom.

I can recall an example of this in a publishing company. The organisation had an extremely 'macho' image, being led by someone who was noted for his hire-and-fire style. However, his second-in-command, in concert with the human resources director, decided it was time to introduce a more up-to-date managerial style into the firm. A training initiative was duly designed and implemented, using several well-established consultancies. At progress meetings, the trainers soon began to complain of difficulties. Participants were aggressive and cynical. They could see no point in changing their own behaviour towards their subordinates when the managing director was clearly continuing to treat them as he always had. Regardless of the expertise of the trainers, the programme did not have a major impact within the company.

ACTION PLANNING

I regard action planning sessions as a trainer's secret weapon: get participants to spend some time at the end of the course thinking through how they will use the learning and your strike rate will increase considerably.

Most of us have attended courses, left full of good intentions, put the file away temporarily while we caught up with work, and then forgotten all about our plans until we come across the course folder many months later. In therapy groups, clients are often asked to state out loud their commitment to take or avoid specific actions. This is done because it has been demonstrated that making such a statement adds considerably to the likelihood that those actions will follow. The organisational equivalent is careful action planning – getting participants to draw up an explicit plan of what they intend to achieve as a result of attending the course.

I include action planning in this chapter because it is the process whereby participants make contracts with themselves. They may also contract with you, and/or their managers, but the significant dimension is the commitment they make to themselves. Therapists know also that the commitment is increased if clients share their plans with a group. Again, the organisational equivalent is to invite participants to review their objectives in plenary, or at least to share them in small groups.

Objective Setting

One of the ways that we sabotage ourselves is to have action plans that are vague. Then we never know whether we have achieved our aims or not. To overcome this, we need to meet the criteria for 'proper' objectives: that they are specific and measurable; that they are realistic and achievable; that they are worthwhile and challenging. We also need to pay careful attention to the way we frame our objectives, so that they are worded in formats that lead to successful change.

I convert the three criteria into a donkey bridge that also matches the three main internal ego states - and often joke with participants that M & M's make a change from SMARTIES:

- *Measurable* – as in will my Internal Parent (e.g. grandmother in my head) be able to check I have "done my homework"?
- *Manageable* – does my Internal Adult think my objective is something I can realistically achieve?
- *Motivational* – is it something my Internal Child ego state really wants to do?

I have included more ideas about the internal ego state aspects of objective setting later in this chapter.

To ensure our action plans contain objectives that are measurable, we need to answer such questions as:

- What exactly am I planning to do?
- How will I behave?
- In what situation(s)?
- With which people?
- When will I do this?
- How will I know I have achieved my objective?

"Get on better with Harry", is not specific enough. We need something like "Spend 5 minutes at least 3 times a week chatting casually with Harry about his hobbies". This tells us what, how, when, with whom. It is measurable – we can check during the week that we are on target so we don't have to chat to Harry three times on Friday afternoon.

Measuring progress is very important. It provides reinforcement when we can congratulate ourselves on doing what we planned. Without adequate measures, we miss the satisfaction of knowing we have achieved our objectives. We also need the measure so that we can decide when we have incorporated the change into our usual behaviour; then we can move on to the next challenge.

The manageable element has a different set of considerations; how realistic and achievable is what we plan to do? Do you currently find Harry very difficult to talk to? If so, is it realistic to plan to spend most of the week with him? 3 five minute chats is probably realistic. Set the target higher and you might well find it too hard to achieve.

Objectives need to be selected so that we have a good likelihood of attaining them. Picking the biggest problem to tackle first is not the best route to success. Instead, start with something that can be realistically accomplished – you can always up the stakes later if you find it's too easy.

Manageability also relates to power to act. We can only change our own behaviour, not anyone else's. Chatting to Harry is only acceptable as an objective if we are sure that Harry will agree to talk to us. If he is likely to walk away and ignore us, the objective is not achievable.

We need to balance achievability with how motivational our selected objectives are; how challenging and worthwhile are they? There is no point having an action plan about things which are not important or are simple to put into effect. If we could easily go and chat to Harry a few times a week, why not just do it now we realise it would improve our relationship. It hardly justifies being part of an action plan, which should be reserved for significant developments.

We get little feeling of satisfaction from making easy changes. We need to tackle something that we recognise as a real challenge, so that we will have an incentive to persevere. Otherwise, our reaction is likely to be "So what?" after we have implemented our plan.

Objectives also need to be motivational in the sense that they contribute to our overall effectiveness. It may be nice to get to know Harry but hardly worthwhile if he is leaving the organisation shortly (unless we want to continue the relationship, or see Harry as a useful test case on which to improve our ability to relate to others).

The way we frame our objectives is also significant. Compare the action planning process with eating an elephant – you can do it if you go for small pieces at a time. Changing our behaviour or attitudes can be equally indigestible if we tackle too much at once. Picking a few priority areas allows us to spread the elephant eating over a sensible timeframe.

"Whatever you do, do not think about rabbits!" When someone says that to you, what do you think about? It is virtually impossible not to think about rabbits, even if it is only fleetingly. To avoid someone thinking about rabbits, we need to tell them to think about something else, such as elephants perhaps.

The think-rabbit syndrome applies to action planning. If we concentrate on our weaknesses, we are likely to reinforce them. We should instead identify alternative objectives that would have the effect of cancelling out our weaknesses. For example, to stop interrupting other people, focus instead on listening to the end of their sentences. To improve a relationship, look for things you may have in common; don't approach them thinking 'I must not lose my temper' or you will very likely do just that.

TA Analyses of Action Plans

The idea of action planning is not new; neither are the criteria I have mentioned. However, there are some useful dimensions that TA enables us to add to the planning process. In particular, the concepts of ego states (see Chapter 4, Interpersonal Styles and Chapter 6, Thinking Styles), strokes (see Chapter 7, Working with Others) and drivers (see Chapter 5, Working Styles) are valuable frameworks for checking the way objectives have been selected and structured.

The concept of internal ego states allows us to consider in more detail the decision making process involved in our action planning. Thus, our Internal Parent holds opinions and is a store of previous experience, including recollections of how we and others have behaved in similar situations to those covered by our action plan. Our Internal Child contains our anticipated feelings about being in the circumstances specified in the action plan, often mixed up with emotional memories of previous incidents. Our Internal Adult thinks logically about our plans, considering options and implications and weighing up the probabilities of success. If we are to succeed in our stated objectives, all three internal ego states need to be in broad agreement.

Our Internal Parent will want to check that the plan is based on reliable precedents, even if we cannot identify an exactly similar set of circumstances. This ego state will also be in action when we consider our value systems and beliefs about the right ways to act. A logical course of action selected by Internal Adult will not be implemented successfully if it is out of line with our principles.

Our Internal Child will put energy and enthusiasm into plans that we feel comfortable and excited about. This ego state will unconsciously undermine decisions which ignore our feelings of scare or anxiety. This does not mean we cannot do anything we feel nervous about; it means that we need to use the resources of our other ego states to reassure the Internal Child that the concerns will be taken care of. Perhaps we will plan some relaxation before we enact a stressful change in behaviour, or set up a reward for ourselves as an inventive to make the extra effort.

Our Internal Adult looks for evidence that the objective is well-founded. In this ego state there is a danger that we see the logical solution and take insufficient account of our true opinions and feelings. If we are used to doing this, we may have lost touch with our own underlying motivations. We then act like a computer, without the necessary attention to all aspects of the decision. We may also underestimate the responses of other people, expecting them to appreciate the logic of our actions in the same way that we do.

Strokes are units of recognition – all the ways that other people show us we exist for them. This recognition is essential and we all have familiar patterns within which it occurs. When we change our behaviour in line with our action plans, our stroking patterns will also shift. If we make significant modifications to our behaviour, we may want more recognition, or strokes, to reinforce our sense of well-being as we put extra effort into the change.

We can add the concept of strokes to our action planning by considering:
- how do we get stroked now? what for?
- what strokes might no longer be available if we change?
- how can we make up the deficit?
- how can we get extra strokes/recognition for the changes?
- how will we reinforce our success?

It is important to remember that human beings settle for negative strokes if insufficient positive ones are available. We would rather be shouted at than ignored. The behaviours we now want to change may well have been providing a steady supply of negative strokes, as people expressed their dissatisfaction to us in a multitude of ways. Introducing a more skilful way of interacting may prevent the negative strokes being given before the replacement positive stroking pattern comes into effect. In that case, we will be wise to organise extra strokes temporarily from other sources, such as by spending more time with friends while we develop new ways of relating at work.

Drivers are characteristic ways of behaving that are usually strengths but can easily become weaknesses when we are under stress. Planning to change our behaviour is somewhat stressful for all of us, so the drivers tend to creep in to our action plans.

'Hurry Up' shows up when we want to tackle everything in a rush. We draw up an action plan with many items, all to be completed in a very short time. We then accomplish the changes only superficially, so that we fail to reap the full benefit of the changes. Or we select our priorities so quickly that we overlook significant areas that we should be working on.

'Be Perfect' is in effect when we aim to produce the perfect action plan, with just the right priorities and a great deal of detail on how we will implement the changes. This takes us so long that we never quite finish drawing up the plan anyway. Or we make each objective so complex that it would take hours to put any one of them into effect – so we never have a long enough period to get started.

'Please People' affects us by requiring that whatever we do has the approval of other people. We may ask the trainer to tell us what should be in our action plan. If the trainer wisely refuses, we may ask our colleagues on the course, or go back to check with our manager.

We want someone else to determine our priorities in case we get it wrong. Or we worry about upsetting other people if we make changes to our own behaviour.

'Try Hard' is about trying but not succeeding. We tackle lots of things enthusiastically but never quite finish them. Our action plan is therefore likely to be crammed with good ideas, which we will initiate and then get bored with. We will have several, so we can move between them whenever there is a danger that we might actually achieve one of them. We may even get bored with doing an action plan, and sidetrack ourselves by starting to experiment with alternative layouts for the plan – and maybe even alternative designs for the action planning session.

'Be Strong' driver means we keep a stiff upper lip. We stay calm and emotionless. We fail to see why we need an action plan anyway, as we are loathe to admit to having any weaknesses. Our speciality is coping in crises, without help from anyone else. We may grudgingly put down one or two loosely worded items to keep the trainer quiet but will do our best to avoid facing up to any shortcomings. We cannot imagine why we would want to change when we are in control of everything already.

Plans into Action
You can help participants produce much better action plans if you use one or more of the frameworks I have described here. By much better, I mean that they will be more likely to achieve whatever they have selected as their priorities. Checking ego states will ensure their choices are balanced, considering strokes will remind them to include encouragement and reinforcement into their plans, and looking out for drivers will identify the characteristic ways they might sabotage their own efforts. You can apply similar processes for yourself when you draw up your action plans for providing training.

Another important element to take into account is the choice of situations in which to implement the action plans. Learning new ways of behaving towards other people is like learning to ride a bicycle – we are acquiring skills we did not have before. We did not simply get on a bicycle for the first time and pedal off; we went through a process of practising separate actions and eventually being able to perform several functions at once.

First we learned to pedal strongly enough to keep our balance. We probably fell off a few times until we got this right. Hopefully, we had picked a quiet spot to learn this and not a busy road. Then, if we got it wrong we did not fall in front of a car. Learning new people skills also needs a quiet spot – in other words we need to select carefully the environment in which to make the change. We should defer using the new behaviour in front of people who could cause us harm, until we have practised enough to be confident we will not lose our metaphorical balance.

We may also find that our new approach lacks the impact we hoped for. Perhaps it seems false, even to us. It may certainly feel disjointed. On the bicycle, it took time before we could pedal, watch the traffic, give hand signals and stop efficiently without leaving the saddle. Similarly, with people skills we have to practise before we can readily pull together the sequence of judging the situation, determining our desired outcome, interacting in an appropriate style, matching body language, tone and content and responding to the other party.

This need to co-ordinate may make our behaviour seem stilted and artificial. Participants need to be reassured that this is a normal problem, that it signifies that they are well on the way to making a definite change in behaviour, and that practice will take care of the rough edges. They may also need to be forewarned about the negative stroking that often occurs when people return to work and their changed behaviours are greeted with "Oh, you've been on a course – now it's time to get back to normal!".

ACTIVITIES
Activity 2.1 Three Cornered Contract
Explain the concept of the three cornered contract by drawing it on the board and working through the content with the group.

Activity 2.2 Key Problems
This exercise provides detail required as part of the professional contract. It ensures that you can provide training in a way that relates it clearly to the real needs of the participants.

Brief syndicate groups of 4 or more to draw up a list of common problem areas (related to the programme topic) that they face at work.

For example:
- Identify and describe typical difficulties faced by supervisors in motivating staff.
- Give examples of customer contact situations that are difficult to handle.
- Identify the key problems in negotiating effectively with trade union representatives.

Ask them to be as specific as possible and to be prepared to describe real examples when the lists are reviewed in plenary.

In the review, check you understand what is meant by each item. Make it clear if any are outside the scope of the course (such as structural or resourcing issues rather than skills needs).

Keep the lists on display during the course so that you can jointly check that each item gets dealt with. Ask participants to tick off entries as they are completed. You might also want to invite participants to add items they think of as the course progresses.

Activity 2.3 Individual Contracts
This activity encourages individuals to think about how they can benefit most from the training. They draw up self-managed contracts with themselves so that they can take responsibility for their own learning.

Step 1 Tell participants they are going to make some notes for their own use during the course. They will have an opportunity to discuss these but they will have complete control over what they choose to share with others.

Step 2 Ask participants to write down their responses to the questions below:

Note: Do not explain the questions beforehand. Doing so may encourage participants to regurgitate your thinking instead of working it out for themselves.
1. What do you want to achieve as a result of being here?
2. How will you know when you have achieved it?
3. What are you prepared to do to achieve it?
4. How might you stop yourself achieving what you want?

Note: Be careful with the wording. In Question 1, "want" is stronger than "would like to". In Question 2, "when" implies success; "if" would denote some doubt on the trainer's part. In Question 4, be sure to say "might" and not "will" – otherwise they may well respond to your implicit invitation at the psychological level.

Step 3 When most participants have stopped writing, add the following question:

5. In what other ways might you sabotage yourself? Have you given all the answers you can to question 4?

Step 4 Explain briefly the rationale behind the questions.

Question. Having a clear objective will enable them to focus. They can then ask appropriate questions and generally make sure that the trainer provides them with relevant content.

Question 2. Thinking through how they will recognise success adds detail to their objective. It also operationalises it, turning it into a more specific description of what they want to be able to do.

Question 3. This makes them think about their role in the training/learning process. Are they willing to undertake activities proposed by the trainer or do they expect to acquire skills by some magical process of osmosis? Will they take notes to reinforce points or rely solely on handouts?

Question 4. We all have techniques, outside our awareness, for sabotaging ourselves. If we think about it, we can identify many of them. We can then take direct action to overcome them. For instance, many of us are reluctant to ask questions. Perhaps we are afraid of looking stupid. Yet our very failure to ask is what leaves us confused. Others of us jump to conclusions without listening to the full message from the trainer. We realise too late that we have misunderstood. Perhaps we are too embarrassed to practice new behaviour in front of a group, or scared of being video-taped. Our fear prevents us acquiring new skills.

Somehow, once we admit to ourselves that these obstacles are there, we find it much easier to deal with them. Even better, if we tell others about them they will help us to avoid slipping into bad habits. We will also find that our concerns feel so much less serious once we realise that everyone has some quirks like this.

Question 4 extras. Our subconscious will hold back one or two of our sabotage techniques if it can, in case we become too successful and get conceited. Checking again may flush out some more.

Step 5
Option A Invite participants to share their responses in pairs or threes. Deal with any questions, perhaps individually rather than in plenary.

Option B Invite participants to review their responses in plenary. Discuss how their individual objectives fit within the programme. If appropriate, agree what help they want from others should their sabotage techniques become apparent.

Option C Ask participants to keep the sheets and refer to them as the course progresses. Invite them to monitor their own progress and check for signs of self-sabotage. Remind them at intervals to read through the sheets, and perhaps update them.

Activity 2.4 Action Planning
Prepare a sheet headed 'Action Planning', containing reminders of the guidelines described in this chapter about objectives being measurable, manageable and motivational.

Allow plenty of time at the end of the course for participants to prepare individual action plans which will be their contracts for themselves. 30 minutes for a two day course is about right.

Brief participants to:
- Review their notes and handouts for the whole course.
- Select no more than x items as priorities to work on back at work (x = one item per day of training).
- State what they plan to achieve for each item, in terms that meet the guidelines for statements of objectives.
- Put any additional items onto a separate sheet for action later, after they have achieved the first list of items.
- Reassure them that the action plans are for their own use only and will not be collected in. They can be honest about any shortcomings.
- Keep the list of priority items separate from their course notes, in a place where they will see it regularly and be reminded of their plans.

Review their plans using any of the TA frameworks mentioned in this chapter, or indeed in later chapters. Ego states, strokes and drivers are all useful concepts to apply.

Optional extras:
Create syndicate groups to review learning throughout the course before they prepare individual action plans.

Pair them up when the plans are written and ask them to act as 'devil's advocate' for each other, checking that the objectives are written in ways that meet the guidelines.

Have participants share the content of their plans with each other, to reinforce their commitment and provide encouragement from the rest of the group.

To add some fun, have a supply of M & Ms sweets available, perhaps with one of the M & M figures that dispense them (often available in airport shops), so that participants receive either a small bag or a handful of sweets once their partner confirms that their action plan fits the Measurable, Manageable, Motivational guidelines.

If you need action plans that will be shown to participants' managers, suggest that they might like to prepare two versions if they want to plan for personal as well as professional objectives.

NOTES & SOURCES
Berne's ideas on contracts are contained in *Principles of Group Treatment* Eric Berne, Grove Press Inc., 1966.

Steiner's ideas on contracts are in *Scripts People Live* Claude M Steiner, Bantam Books, 1975.

For the original description of the three cornered contract, see *'The Three Cornered Contract'* by Fanita English in Transactional Analysis Journal 1975 Vol 5(4), pp 383-4.

The concept of psychological distance was introduced by Nelly Micholt; see *Psychological Distance and Group Intervention* in Transactional Analysis Journal 1992 Vol 22(4) pp 228-233.

CHAPTER 3: UNDERSTANDING ATTITUDES

This chapter is similar to Chapter 2, Contracting for Learning, in that the focus is on increasing your knowledge and awareness as a trainer so that you can work more effectively to bring about the development of your participants. I cover two themes: frames of reference and overall life plans and patterns.

Under Frames of Reference, I offer a framework of ways of understanding why and how individuals approach the task of learning (and everything else) so differently.

Windows on the world is the name I use for *life positions*, which are the components of a model that helps us see how participants, and trainers, vary in their attitudes about whether they expect learning to take place.

The *Disposition Diamond* is an extension of the basic life positions model and shows how there can be different combinations of attitude, emotion and behaviour. I describe examples of several characteristic patterns.

The third framework in the Frames of Reference section is the *Miniscript*. This model concerns the specific sequence of life positions that occurs for an individual when things are going badly. I explain how we can minimise the impact of these occasions by paying particular attention to behaviour at the start of the sequence.

The section on life plans is based upon the TA concept of *Scripts*. I provide a description of the major aspects of this concept, to show how it affects our everyday behaviour even though it is an unconscious life plan adopted by us when we were small children. Also explained is the way our frame of reference is actually designed to enable us to view the world in ways that reinforce our script.

Knowledge of the theory of scripts can help us identify why things go wrong in our lives. With this awareness, we can plan changes in our beliefs and behaviours so that we spend more time being spontaneous and script-free. Sometimes we may do this directly as a result of insights gained from considering our script patterns to date.

We may also need more specific ideas, which we can get from using the other, more specifically targeted TA concepts that I have explained in the rest of this book.

I have provided this chapter mainly to offer greater background and understanding to the trainer. However, as with the previous chapter, you might want to teach this material to your participants. It makes a good basis for workshops on personal and professional development, so I have included individual and group exercises related to each of the main topics. I have also included a simple questionnaire for those who prefer this type of structured approach.

FRAMES OF REFERENCE

As trainers, it is essential that we understand the ways in which our participants view the world. I am thinking here not just in terms of the constructs they have or the knowledge they have already acquired before they arrive in the classroom. What we also need is a way of analysing and predicting their response in terms of their frames of reference, or attitudes. These will be the features that determine how much they learn while they are with us – in fact, their attitudes will control whether they arrive expecting to learn anything at all!

The frameworks I have selected to explain here all relate to our overall attitudes, or the frame of reference that operates at the level of our most significant, core beliefs. In other chapters I have described some other concepts that are valid for understanding the thinking processes we go through and how these show up as attitudes. In particular, you might want to review Chapter 6, Thinking Styles, if you plan to teach this material to participants.

Before I go on to describe the different ways of understanding our frames of reference, I want to mention briefly why we come to have such beliefs. We all have certain hungers, or psychological needs. If these are not satisfied, we will fail to develop properly as autonomous, psychologically healthy individuals. Throughout life, therefore, we are motivated by the desire to meet these needs; we may well do this unconsciously because we do not recognise the underlying stimulus to our actions. The less we are aware of our true needs, the more we are likely to be frustrated in our attempts to fulfil them.

The main hungers are for stimulus, recognition and structure. I mention in Chapter 7, Working with Others, that babies do not develop if they fail to receive any stimulation, and that we all learn as we grow up that much of our stimulation will come via recognition, or strokes, from other human beings. Our need for structure hunger is what leads us to find ways of occupying our time so as to get recognition. I describe this in Chapter 8, Working in Groups, when I write of the different ways we structure our time and the impact of this on the strokes we get and give.

These hungers are responsible for several decisions we make, when we are small, about how best to perceive the world so that we can predict events. We need to predict in order to select ways of behaving that we believe will achieve the result we seek. Unfortunately, as children we do not always make too good a job of our predictions because we do not have the necessary knowledge and experience of the world.

Windows on the World

One of the main frameworks we develop as children are our life positions. As originally described by Berne, life positions are existential positions, or attitudes which we adopt towards the world. The concept was popularised by Harris when he chose a life position as the title of a book: 'I'm OK, You're OK'. We can show the possible combinations in a simple matrix, which I think of as a set of windows through which we look out onto our world, as shown in Figure 3.1.

Berne and Harris differed in their opinions of which of the four OK/not OK attitudes was held by a baby. They agreed, however, that we experience each and make a selection of one which will become our major view on the world. As grownups, we will recognise most of the time that the position of mutual respect, 'I'm OK, You're OK, offers maximum comfort and possibility for getting on with people. When we have a bad day, though, we are likely to slide into one of the other life positions and see the world through a distorted frame of reference.

It seems strange to conclude that we would settle for a distorted view when a more reasonable one is available. To understand, we need to recall what it is like to be a young child. One of our basic needs is for structure in our world. We want to be able to forecast the consequences of our actions – to know how things fit together. We are all miniature scientists endeavouring to invent our own theory to explain events. Being children, we also make our judgements in terms of the interaction between us and the world. We believe that we cause things to happen.

Within that context, we note that we are smaller than just about everyone else, including our siblings. Only babies are smaller than us and they don't do anything as far as we can see. We are not able to do many of the things others can, such as eat with utensils instead

Figure 3.1: Windows on the World

of fingers, fasten buttons and zips, carry things without dropping them. We do not understand that we will be able to do these things when we are older so we begin to believe that there must be something wrong with us. We come to the conclusion that we are at fault and others are capable – the I'm not OK, You're OK life position.

Having devised our theory, we test it out. We observe what happens: do we continue to be incapable while others succeed? Perhaps people tell us that we are clumsy or a nuisance. If there is enough of this type of evidence to support our hypothesis, we conclude that we were right. We then begin to filter information, rejecting any that contradicts our theory and thereby reinforcing our selected life position.

If appropriate evidence is not forthcoming, we experiment with an alternative scenario. Perhaps everyone is at fault. One traumatic event in an otherwise satisfactory childhood may make such an impact that we jump to this conclusion. Maybe our parents are going through a difficult time and are unable to care for use properly. We test out the I'm not OK, You're not OK life position. Again, if it seems to fit we become selective about the data we then take notice of.

The third option is the I'm OK, You're not OK combination. This arises when we decide that our problems are purely temporary. As soon as we are older, we will be able to do all the things the bigger people can do. In fact, we will do them better. Now we look for evidence of other peoples' failings in order to check that our theory is correct. We pay attention only to the times when we do something well, and blame others for any shortcomings on our part.

Each of us is likely to have explored all three of the unhelpful life positions during childhood. We will also have experienced occupying the I'm OK. You're OK slot. Along the way, we will have become accustomed to spending different proportions of our time in each. Remember that these life positions are our underlying attitudes to the world around us. Usually, there will be plenty of time in I'm OK, You're OK. This is likely to be followed by one of the three unhelpful positions, which we will tend to revert to at times of stress. We recognise the other two but spend less time there.

Our life positions, or windows on the world, act like distorting glass and determine how we perceive events. They are our existential position, a somewhat academic sounding label for what most of us colloquially call attitude. It is often claimed that the I'm OK, You're OK position is actually different in kind and substance from the other three and represents the TA goal of autonomy and mutual respect. However, this may also be a distortion and therefore just as potentially unhelpful as the other three views. Indeed, I often add a 5th 'open' window, as shown in Figure 3.2, because there is a case for recognising that I'm OK, You're OK is also a perception and not a generally-accepted fact. For instance, some religious groups would argue that the reality position is I am not OK (i.e. in the eyes of God). There can also be problems when people adopt a 'Pollyanna-ish' attitude that everyone is OK, only to learn to their cost that people may, however, not behave as if that is true. The window on

Figure 3.2: An Open Window to Reality

the right, therefore, is to allow for a perspective that all we really know is that I exist and you exist – and even that may be in doubt if you have seen the film 'The Matrix'.

Whether you opt for the original model or my extended version, the need is to be able to recognise that other people may be viewing through their unhelpful windows. This means we understand that they will sometimes behave illogically because their perceptions are being filtered by an out-of-date pattern. We need to separate a person's behaviour from their innate worth as a human being. All of us have bad days sometimes, when we do things we regret afterwards. By keeping in mind that a skewed perception is occurring, we can be more tolerant of apparent shortcomings. In true assertive fashion, we can object to the behaviour whilst continuing to respect the individual.

The windows framework can also be extended to incorporate attitudes to others – Martin Groder adds three others to the basic I and You: we – e.g. the team or family; they – e.g. the management, the neighbours; and it – e.g. something you've achieved or failed to achieve. These additions help to explain some the dynamics we observe when groups are involved; examples of such 'group think' include:

- participants 'ganging up' to make life difficult for a trainer – I, you , we okay, they (the trainer) not OK, and probably it (the course) is also not OK;
- trainers sharing their complaints about how useless the participants are – I, you, we okay, they are not OK;
- someone believing that everyone except them is OK, or not OK – I OK, you, we, they, it all not OK;
- trainer and participants colluding to talk about how not OK the management are (as also explained in Chapter 2 under psychological distance) I, you, we OK, they not OK and probably it (the company) not OK.

Finally, a small donkey bridge way of referring to the windows on the world if you prefer to stay with the original model. This is taken from an article by Wilson (1972). He suggested that we use the terms IOKYOK (i.e. pronounced as iokyok) for the I'm OK, You're OK and SHNOK (shnok) for the other three positions, on the principle that it stands for Somebody Here is Not OK. SHNOK even sounds like it is negative and is a lot quicker to say than having to list all three options.

Disposition Diamond

When we are viewing the world through one of the SHNOK windows, we may experience a similar variation in our emotions and behaviour. We may also find that the positions do not necessarily coincide – we may behave in a one-up manner to disguise the fact that we feel one-down, or we may believe we know better than others but still act outwardly as if we accept their control. The disposition diamond is a diagram that allows us to represent attitudes, behaviour and emotions as if they were three different levels, as shown in Figure 3.3.

At the top of the diamond is our attitude, or existential life position. This uses the concept described above, so that we may insert any of the three SHNOK life positions here. We can then use a similar system of categorising by OK/not OK to give us equivalent variations to describe our behaviour and emotions as follows.

Our behaviour shows on the disposition diamond in terms of whether we appear to act in a superior, inferior or pessimistic way. I'm OK, You're Not OK behaviour consists of telling other people what to do and generally pushing them around. The old autocratic style of management worked like this. The I'm not OK, You're OK mode indicates a willingness to be controlled by others, and to let them push us around. I'm not OK, You're not OK behaviour is probably the most frustrating to others; it encompasses actions that

Figure 3.3: Disposition Diamond

demonstrate a lack of faith in your own and anyone else's abilities. In this stance, we pour a lot of cold water onto any attempts to improve the situation.

The emotional, or psychological, level is usually hidden from others. We know how we feel but may well go to some lengths to hide it. Inside us, however, the damage is being done. I'm OK, You're not OK feelings include righteousness, triumph, smugness. I'm not OK, You're OK emotions are to do with embarrassment, shame, guilt. I'm not OK, You're not OK feelings relate to despair, hopelessness and a sensation of being unloved. Genuine feelings of gladness, sadness, madness (anger) and scaredness have somehow been repressed and temporarily lost to us when we are locked into one of the unhelpful emotional conditions.

When we are operating in the here-and-now, whether we think of that as I'm OK You're OK, or as I am, You are, our attitudes, behaviour and emotions are in tune and we are outside the confines of the diamond. If we map onto the disposition diamond the various combinations of not okayness, we have 27 possible variations. There is a suggestion, which has not been proven but sounds plausible, that we are in fact likely to have a different position in each space on the diamond. In that case, the number of combinations drops to six. Using plus and minus signs to denote positions (+ signifies OK, - signifies not OK), the options are as shown in Figure 3.4.

Figure 3.4: Disposition Combinations

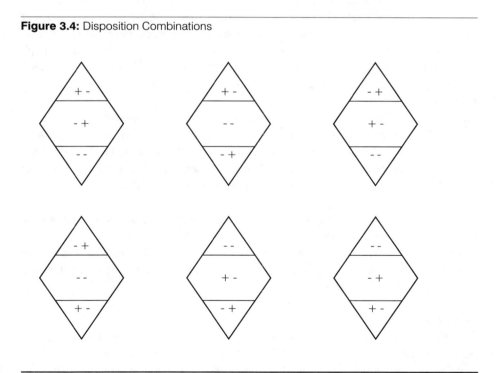

We can now speculate about the characteristics of people who might have each of these combinations. Note that I have given each 'type' a label. This is intended as gentle fun and a memory aid and NOT as any kind of formal psychological diagnosis.

The Martyr

Attitude + - Behaviour - + Emotion - - is a typical pattern for people who feel compelled to engage in counselling. We believe that we know better than most when it comes to understanding people and relationships, the areas that people ask us about. We then behave in a way that implies that we are here to help them, regardless of any plans we might have had of our own. Staying around late to listen patiently to a course member when we should be preparing or resting is an example of this. We give the impression of being wise and caring, if somewhat of a martyr. Psychologically, however, we may well be feeling despair when it becomes clear that we lack the skill and they lack the willpower to change.

Note that we are not in the disposition diamond when we have a realistic view of the potential impact of counselling, agree to counsel at a time that suits us and the client, have adequate counselling skills, and recognise that the client is responsible for their own actions.

The Moaner

With *Attitude + - Behaviour - - Emotion - +*, again we believe we know best. However, we feel that we are inadequate in some way. We are likely to behave, therefore, as if we do not expect to be listened to. We probably grumble about how stupid people are to ignore what we think is the obvious solution to a problem. "No-one takes any notice of me, even though I've seen it all before. I've told them what to do but they're incapable of acting on advice!"

The Bully

The *Attitude - + Behaviour + - Emotion - -* pattern matches the archetypal bully. We believe we are less able in some way than others. We feel despair. So we camouflage these underlying doubts by behaving as if we know it all. We tell others how to behave; if challenged we become even more autocratic and unreasonable. Outside our awareness, we are digging in for fear that our weaknesses will be exposed.

Some trainers are like this. They are scared of being found wanting in technical knowledge so bluster and blame the students when the class activities go wrong. Teaching is run on school lines, with expectations that participants will be like children who have to be kept in order. Anyone foolish enough to ask a question is made to feel it is their own fault they cannot understand the lesson.

The Sufferer

If we have *Attitude - + Behaviour - - Emotion + -*, we behave as if we are hurt but cannot be helped. We develop an aura of suffering but signal to others that they are so unfeeling that they could not possibly offer us comfort. We believe that we are less capable or intelligent than others but that we experience more genuine emotions. We feel, therefore, that our own emotional needs should take precedence over the feelings of others. Indeed, we may be so 'emotional' that we fail to recognise that other people have any feelings.

The Do-Gooder

Attitude - - Behaviour + - Emotion - + means we will secretly believe that no-one knows what they are doing. The world is probably doomed. However, other people's feelings are more important than ours, so we must help them. We set out to save people from themselves. They perceive our behaviour as arrogant, even though they may sense that we are doing it for their own good. We are the typical do-gooder, out to tell everyone how to live their lives better.

We may well campaign for censorship because we believe that all of us must be protected from evil influences as we are incapable of making responsible decisions. At work, we put our energies into setting up procedures so that no-one will make mistakes. We are poor at delegation because we want to save people from their own incompetence.

The No-Hoper

With *Attitude - - Behaviour - + Emotion + -* we again believe that no-one is really capable. In spite of this, we need to deal with our emotions, which are so much more valid to us than the feelings of others. We therefore display our emotions and excuse ourselves by claiming we just can't help feeling as we do. We seek out others to lean on, expecting them to take care of us in some way. We are likely to confide in others and then act as if they are responsible for resolving the situation for us. At an ulterior level, though, we have no real expectation that they will succeed any better than we would.

I include the variation of *Attitude + +* or *IY Behaviour + +* or *IY Emotion + +* or *IY* only to emphasise a point. This grouping is not something you would find on the Disposition Diamond. Once we are into this perception of the world, we are outside the unhelpful confines of the Diamond. We are believing, behaving and feeling in ways that reflect the reality of the situation we are in. We may believe that someone's behaviour is unacceptable without believing also that they are unacceptable as a person. We will behave in ways that imply trust and respect of others, without taking stupid risks or assuming that everyone will respond in the way we hope. And we will experience genuine emotions, of sadness, fear, anger or happiness, in line with whatever is happening in our lives at the current moment. We may also believe that We, They and It are OK; in other words, we are looking through the IOKYOK window on the world instead of the SHNOK ones.

Miniscript

Another useful model for understanding our thinking processes is the miniscript. This is described by Kahler as a 'sequence of behaviour, occurring in a matter of minutes or even seconds, that results in a reinforcement pattern for life'. It is linked to the counterscript messages and script injunctions described later in this chapter, as it is a mental and emotional sequence whereby we reinforce our overall script pattern. We can think of it as a staircase down into deeper and more unpleasant thoughts and feelings.

We begin with a myth – an invalid belief that if we can only behave in just the way we should, everything will be alright. This is our counterscript prescription. As we grew up, we have stored away a message that we will be OK if.... Accompanying this may be a similar belief about other people; they will be OK if.... The 'if' refers to some magical thinking, similar to superstitions. Rather like avoiding stepping of the cracks in the pavement, or holding our collar if we see an ambulance. The difference is that with counterscript we are unaware of the belief so it doesn't get updated (just as some of us are still avoiding pavement cracks without realising we are doing so).

There are five common myths: we have to hurry up, be perfect, please people, try hard, or be strong. I explain each of these in some detail in Chapter 7, Working with Others. For the moment, though, the key point to note is that they are all things we can never quite do enough. However fast we go, we still feel more speed is possible. Human beings will always make some mistakes; absolute perfection is not attainable. People are sometimes displeased with us through no fault of ours; perhaps they are upset by something. Trying hard goes on forever as we can always see yet another aspect needing our attention. And being strong requires us to show no emotions, to have no human needs, to be a robot.

We can go for quite long periods convincing ourselves that we are fulfilling the requirements of these myths. Indeed, the resulting behaviour may well be commented on as a strength. Unfortunately, as long as we fail to 'demythologise' ourselves, we will continue to fall short of the arbitrary standards we are applying to ourselves. We may also set equally unrealistic targets for others.

When we or someone else fails to perform as required, we feel bad. We shift to the script injunction, or stopper, as shown in Figure 3.5. We move from believing I'm OK If, You're OK, or vice versa, into a life position of I'm not OK, You're OK. We feel emotions such as depression, guilt or inadequacy of some kind. If this is our usual life position, we may stay at this point for a while before emerging back at the OK If of the counterscript.

We may however move on. One option is to shift to blaming someone else. We therefore slide into the life position of I'm OK, You're not OK. Now we can justify feelings of anger or triumph, as clearly the other person is at fault. We may or may not accompany our move here with appropriate derogatory comments but we will certainly be concentrating our minds on how incompetent or inept they are. This is our way of fending off the bad feelings that arise when we think, even fleetingly, that we did something wrong.

Not all of us shift to this blamer mode. If I'm OK, You're not OK is our usual life position, we will make the most of our opportunity to remind ourselves how other people are so useless. If it is not our life position, we'll move on quickly or may bypass it altogether.

Figure 3.5: The Miniscript

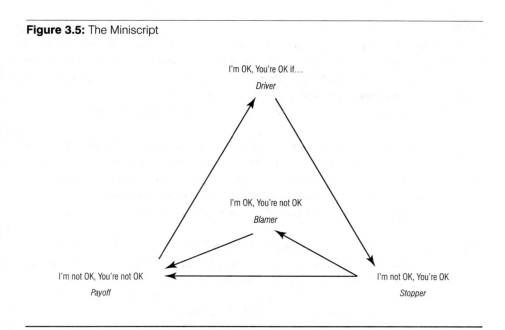

We will then arrive at the final payoff from the sequence. This is where we adopt the life position of I'm not OK, You're not OK. Our feelings here are of being alone, unloved, rejected. We have 'got it wrong' again.

There is a miniscript antidote – an alternative version of the miniscript diagram which shows a positive sequence. The aim is to avoid the counterscript behaviour in the first place. If we can do that , we will not go down the staircase – we will not go around the sequence of feeling bad, possibly blaming, and then feeling even worse. We can give ourselves permissions so we counteract the counterscript.

Those who feel oblige to hurry need to know it is OK to take their time. The perfectionists need to be themselves, and to accept that we all make some mistakes. Those setting out to please others need to respect themselves and pay more attention to their own preferences. Instead of trying so hard, we can just get on and succeed at what we do. And rather than being strong, we need permission to be open about our feelings and to accept that we have a right to take care of ourselves. Equipped with the relevant permissions, we can change the sequence into one of I'm OK, You're OK all the way round, going first to effective action, then to self-affirmation about our competence in the world, and finally to elation about our achievement.

Trainers can influence this process for participants. When we notice that participants are having difficulties with the learning, we can identify which myth is in operation and make a point of emphasising the relevant antidote.

SCRIPT

Being able to influence participants in specific instances needs to be set within our overall aim as trainers – which is to help others develop generally. We need to do this in terms of their skills, their application of knowledge, the way they do their work, so that the organisation will benefit. A holistic approach demands that we also facilitate development in the personal lives of participants; problems outside work are bound to affect performance at work.

In addition to the frameworks already described in this chapter for increasing our understanding of 'what makes people tick', TA gives us theories for understanding motivation, commitment, attitude, and so on as they apply over time. This enables us to take into account these long term influences on the way people learn and develop. We can also interpret specific instances as part of a broader pattern of behaviour and purpose.

The area of TA that is most relevant when we look at longer term career and life planning is that of script analysis. Script itself gives us a way of making sense of what is happening in a person's life. All other TA theories are based on the premise that our everyday actions fall into two categories – they are either script free and autonomous or they are part of the way we live out our script and move on towards its culmination.

The term 'script' in TA is used in the same way as in the theatre; to mean a story that is to be acted out before an audience. Our life script, therefore, is an unconscious plan of how we will get from birth to death. We decide on it when we are small, as a way of making sense of our world. Into its design go a whole range of things – how we perceive the world, our observations of how the big people behave, what they and our peers do and say to us, what we overhear, the stories we are told, even the television programmes we watch. It is fascinating to see how the same themes appear in myths, fairy tales and news stories the world over: only the names of the characters change.

The scripts of most people in organisations tend to be the more mundane variety so they are less noticeable until we know what to look out for. However, we can observe plenty of more 'exciting' scripts, when people seem set on creating problems for themselves or others. Really tragic scripts involve people committing suicide or murder, becoming dictators or martyrs. They may drink themselves to death or work themselves to death. Along the way, they will affect the lives of others too, such as when they company goes bankrupt and people lose their jobs and savings.

As in the best suspense drama, we may keep much of our script secret from the other players although the audience can see what is happening. At work, it is often the uninvolved person who perceives most clearly what is happening, while those engaged in the action are too close to see the total pattern. We observe someone who seems determined to set themselves up to get the sack, and a supervisor who will become the executioner. Yet even though we may try to intervene, the employee seems unable to heed our warnings or act on our advice. This is script in action.

The Story

A major component of our script is the life story that we invent or select. We choose the story when we are quite small, amending it as necessary so that it fits our own circumstances. For some people the selection occurs suddenly, as the result of a particularly traumatic incident such as absence of a loved one. However, most of us probably settle on our story gradually, piecing things together rather like a jigsaw and testing various designs out until we find one that fits. We may no longer remember hearing the original version, having embroidered and embellished it to make it more suitable. If you doubt this, try comparing recollections of fairy stories with your colleagues and see what different versions emerge.

Within our story, we allocate ourselves a role to play. We will not necessarily be the hero or heroine; our character will depend on what we have come to believe about ourselves by the time we make the selection. We may identify most with the lead, with the villain, with one of the supporting roles, or even with one of the bit parts if we have decided to be especially self-effacing.

We will then somehow manage to surround ourselves with the other players that we need to move the story on. We seem to have some psychological mechanism that enables us to identify potential companions in the game, as if we can sniff out people whose stories will dovetail with our own.

Associated with our role in the story will be an attitude towards ourselves, other people and the world in general. We will have opted to be a winner, a loser, a survivor, a fighter, a saviour, a destroyer, or perhaps a mediocrity. We will therefore be operating on a basis of one-up or one-down. Others will be viewed by us as superior or inferior too. The world may seem hostile and threatening, challenging and exciting, boring and dull.

There will also be a somatic component to our role – some feelings within our body that we come to regard as normal. We may tense particular areas such as our neck or shoulders. We may even hold our head in a specific way, as British police officers must to see under their hats. Regular feelings of discomfort in our stomach, frequent migraine-type headaches, nervous indigestion, and similar ailments may form part of our pattern with out us recognising the true cause. This is not to say that such problems may not also arise due physical or genetic reasons; a clue to script is when we accept such symptoms as usual or do nothing to cure them.

Our Choice

Our script will contain more specific elements that determine the way we behave on a day-to-day basis. Although the primary substance of these is provided for us as children by our parents and other caregivers, we still have considerable influence over what is actually incorporated. We listen and observe, then interpret and accept in the light of our previous experiences and our personal proclivities. The same event will be dealt with differently by different children.

Suppose, for example, that mother is tired and feels ill. Her three-year-old is demanding attention and she wants to rest. She has no other adult available at present to take over the childcare while she has a short nap. In response to yet another demand from the child, she angrily tells him to go away. The child does not comprehend the circumstances; he knows only that mother is refusing his request. He therefore interprets this the best way he can, which may be to conclude any of the following:

- she means go away for ever
- she means pester more before she will say yes
- she doesn't love me anymore
- nobody loves me
- it will be alright later on
- if I cry she'll cuddle me
- if I cry she'll punish me
- if I cry she'll beat me
- I'll wait till Daddy comes home
- I'll never ask again.

Almost anything, it seems, but the correct interpretation that she is tired now but still loves him and will play with him again later.

In addition to individual differences in response, our conclusions are affected by what has happened before. If this is the first time mother has been like this, we may be more shocked and therefore react as if to a major tragedy. On the other hand, we may be better able to put the event into perspective. If mother acts this way often, then we may test our alternatives whilst gradually making a decision based on the constant repetitions.

Even children who have been the target of very damaging interactions may still decide to opt for a positive conclusion. However, it is obviously much harder for a small child to remain optimistic if they are severely abused. I am not saying, therefore, that parents should not be held accountable for how they treat their children. Likewise, we should not be blamed if our childhood circumstances were such that we are psychologically damaged and continue to approach the world in the light of our early experiences.

The Components

There are three components that form the day-to-day content of our script story: *counterscript, injunctions* and *attributions*, and *programme*.

As I explained earlier in this chapter under miniscript, our counterscript is a set of ways of behaving that allow us to feel we are functioning effectively. They are characteristic behaviour patterns that enable us to fit in with the expectations of society. By doing so, we reinforce our view of ourselves and others. As we grow, we pay attention to how we can please the big people. They appear to prefer particular habits so these are the ones we develop. These patterns are known as counterscript because they seem to do just that – counter the script.

The five common myths, or themes, are called drivers (see Chapter 5, Working Styles). The term 'driver' refers to the element of compulsion in the patterns; by the time we are grown up we may well feel uncomfortable if we are not behaving in the prescribed way. Each of us develops our own combination of the five themes. Therapists can identify several common mixtures; for our purposes in organisations it is usually enough to concentrate on a person's major driver only.

In each case, we start off by behaving in line with the theme; we may hurry up, be perfect, please people, try hard, or be strong. This usually earns us a correspondingly positive assessment of our performance from ourselves and others. However, we then overdo it so that it turns out badly. This in turn reinforces the underlying message of our script. Perhaps we have an overall script that is due to end in our rejection by others. We may then rehearse this by adopting a please people driver, in which we set out to get the approval of others but are regularly misunderstood because we persist in guessing what they want instead of asking them.

In addition to our counterscript, we also acquire a set of injunctions – things not to do – and attributions – qualities that other people insist we possess. Injunctions are things we are forbidden; we may be told them directly but are also likely to read them into the situation as I have explained already.

The twelve basic injunctions identified by Bob and Mary Goulding include prescriptions against being successful, against being important, against being a child or against growing up, against thinking or against feeling, and even against existing. As with drivers, our own set of injunctions are specific to us.

Injunctions are actually the opposites of the permissions we need to live a full life. The most important permission is to exist; when we arrive in the world we need to experience being wanted and loved. We all receive this permission to some extent although the balance between permission and injunction varies between individuals. Other permissions we need are to be aware of sensations, to feel emotions, to think, to be close to others. Later, we need permissions to grow up and to succeed in the world.

The permissions are transmitted to us in the same ways we acquire the injunctions – through touch, hearing, sight, body language, and through intuition. We pick up some directly when our parents or other caregivers hug us and tell us they love us, just as we may receive some injunctions directly when they chastise us. We also interpret a lot, based on the ways we are treated. The more definitely and clearly our parents communicate positive messages to us, the less script bound we are likely to become.

Attributions are qualities which are attributed to us. In other words, they are the characteristics that we are told we have. We may have attributed to us both negative and positive features, such as being told often when we are small that we are beautiful but clumsy. The attributions are labels, defining how a grown-up has determined we will be. We grow up believing that the attributes are really a part of our personality, and may well adjust our behaviour accordingly.

The process of attributions demonstrates well how scripts are often passed along through generations of a family. We are likely to be told we have the same characteristics as an older member of the family. This form of attributing also saves a lot of time; if we are told we are just like our wicked uncle, we can add the detail ourselves. If wicked uncle drank a lot, got arrested often, washed infrequently, and came to a sticky end, we now know exactly what to do to prove the attribution correct.

Even positive attributions may be a problem. This is because the qualities are being 'forced' on us. Being told we are clever or beautiful or confident, when we may really feel scared and vulnerable, puts us under considerable pressure to pretend. We hide our genuine responses so as not to disappoint the grown-ups, and may eventually lose touch with our true emotions and our spontaneity.

The final component of our story is the programme. This is the way our parents have shown us to carry out the script. It is usually, but not always, modelled for us by our same sex parent. We observe and copy their behaviour, their opinions, their emotional responses, so that we can be like them when we grow up. Included within the overall patterns that we copy will be some significant elements that relate directly to how we will obey our own set of injunctions.

If we have accepted the injunction 'don't be close', we may look to father or mother to show us how to be the strong and silent type. They may model a poker player or a Greta Garbo clone. We will copy the tightly controlled gestures and mannerisms, the stern facial expression, the lack of communication, even the habit of shutting ourselves away in the bedroom or going for solitary walks whenever our partner tries to get too close. We will of course grow up believing that this is the natural way to behave, and will be puzzled if people complain about our remoteness. As far as we are concerned, they are clinging and attempting to invade our privacy.

We can also analyse our script by considering the interactions that we engage in. Significant interaction patterns are our *pastimes*, our *psychological games*, and our *gallows transactions* and *gallows laughs*. Pastimes and games are ways we structure time; these are explained in detail in Chapter 7, Working with Others (games) and Chapter 8, Working in Groups (time structuring).

Gallows transactions and gallows laughs are the ways we reinforce unhealthy aspects of our behaviour by commenting and laughing inappropriately. Berne used gallows as a reference to the way that criminals sometimes joke as they go to the gallows. Thus, a gallows laugh in TA is the laugh we give as we describe how we have done something stupid, or had something unpleasant happen to us. People often laugh with us, increasing the impact. When challenged, we may rationalise the laugh by claiming that it was a harmless release of tension. However, each gallows laugh is psychologically reinforcing this form of self-sabotage.

The Payoffs

We get both major and minor *payoffs* from our script process. The severity of the major payoff will depend on the nature of our own story. If we have opted for a tragic ending, our final payoff may be an untimely death, loss of sanity or physical health, or loss of liberty. For most of us, the ending will be far less dramatic so we may collect a series of payoffs. Maybe we will settle for distress as we retire from our work, as our children leave home, as we are divorced from our partner. Or perhaps we engage in a series of disastrous relationships, with significant payoffs each time a liaison comes to an end.

Our daily interactions will also generate many relatively minor payoffs. We can pick up unpleasant feelings whenever we chat with someone about how bad things are for us. We will collect a definite payoff each time we engage in a psychological game. We can also generate bad feelings for ourselves by engaging in rackets (see Chapter 7, Working with Others), a form of distorted thinking that is often accompanied by manipulative behaviour.

All of these bad feeling payoffs can be recycled via our *stamp collection* (also described in Chapter 7). Berne suggested that we collect bad feelings just as we might collect trading stamps; we save them up until we have enough to cash in for a prize. Whereas real trading stamps are exchanged for real prizes, our psychological stamps are converted into our payoffs. When we have enough, we trade them for temper tantrums, staying away from work, walking out of a meeting, or similar actions. We use the stamps to justify to ourselves that we were right to behave in a way that is not normally acceptable.

As trainers, we are likely to see the effects of scripts even though we may not directly analyse the life plans of our participants. Being aware of the existence of scripts will help us to keep events in perspective. Inevitably, our students will sometimes initiate psychological games with us and with each other. They will also engage in racket-like actions, and seek to offload their stamp collections of bad feelings onto us. Understanding that these processes are outside consciousness will help us to be more tolerant when things go wrong and more skilful at designing training programmes that invite participants to relax and enjoy the learning process. We will then find that we have far fewer 'problem participants' on our courses.

ACTIVITIES
Activity 3.1 Windows on the World

Hand out sheets on which appear the diagram for the windows on the world (see figure 3.1). Suggest participants might like to draw in their 'blob' – an outline shape which reflects the amount of time they believe they spend in each life position.

Invite them to compare their responses in pairs or threes.

Activity 3.2 Impact of Windows on the World

Create small syndicate groups (3-5 people). Brief them to work through whichever of the following questions you select as most relevant for your training session.

How will a person in each of the life positions behave when:
- giving praise, receiving praise
- giving criticism, receiving criticism
- dealing with conflict
- being expected to trust, being trusted
- handling customer complaints
- dealing with more senior or more junior people, inside or outside the organisation
- being expected to show initiative, taking risks, working without supervision
- being involved in emergencies, accidents, crises

Afterwards, review and compare the responses from the groups. Most will be obvious but check their understanding on the I'm OK, You're OK position. This does not mean blind trust, never criticising, always being nice to people. It means recognising that people are to be respected but that they will still sometimes operate from unhealthy life positions. Therefore, trust should be tempered with caution and appropriate safeguards.

Criticism is necessary and needs to be phrased constructively. It may be more appropriate to be assertive when others are behaving badly, firm when they would take advantage, even angry when their actions are outside the norms for a caring society.

Activity 3.3 Windows on the World Questionnaire

The Windows on the World Questionnaire in Appendix 5 can be purchased. Brief the participants that the results are to be treated light-heartedly as an indication of how much time they spend perceiving the world through various windows.

Once individuals have completed and scored their own results, suggest they review in pairs and think about what they might want to change – and how.

Activity 3.4 Disposition Diamond

Create syndicate groups of up to 8 people. Brief them to prepare a role play of one of the variations in the disposition diamond. Ask them to discuss what the person would be like and then to select a typical situation that might occur.

Have them enact the role play in plenary. Then discuss and answer any queries.

Activity 3.5 Your Fairy Story

Invite participants to select a fairy story, or any other story, that they recall was special for them when they were small. Even if they cannot remember having a particular story read to them when they were little, ask them to pretend that they now have to amuse a five-year-old. They can choose anything that resembles a story, such as a TV series or a film that made an impact in the past.

Form groups of 3-5. Each person is to tell their story to the group, taking about 5 minutes. The group should listen and then ask questions to ensure they know the story, its ending, and which character the storyteller is.

Groups then discuss the story so that the storyteller is helped to see its relevance to their life's events. Points to explore include:

- the ending – group members may know different endings to the same story; we often remember an ending that has particular significance for us
- the character selected – the group may well have imagined that the participant was a different character; it can be enlightening to discuss these different perceptions.

Activity 3.6 Script Questionnaire

Suggest that participants answer the following questions individually.

Depending on the group level of trust and openness, you might also suggest they pair up afterwards to review their responses.

1. Describe your favourite fairy story and your role within it (or any other story that appeals to you)
2. What have you been told about your life?
3. What happens to somebody like you?
4. What are your good points?
5. What are your bad points?
6. How do you get what you want?
7. When things are not going well for you, what happens?
8. When things are going well for you, what happens?

After completion, you could add the following explanations for each question.

Question 1 gives an overview of the script story. Treated as a metaphor, participants can consider how events that happen to the character they select may mirror events in their life. The ways they relate as the character to others in the story will also give an indication of their life position.

Question 2 gives information about the social and emotional level roles that the person may occupy. Are they rescuer, persecutor or victim? (See Chapter 7, Working with Others). Or are they expecting a long and happy life?

Question 3 may elicit the script ending, or the lack of negative programming. It may also provide information about permissions or injunctions. In conjunction with Question 1, attributions may also be identified.

Question 4 is intended to identify permissions and positive attributions, even when Question 3 has yielded only injunctions. Question 4 can also be considered in an organisational/working context.

Question 5 gives details of possible injunctions and negative attributions.

Question 6 identifies possible symbiotic adaptations (see Chapter 6, Thinking Styles). It may also result in information about process scripts, and hence about drivers.

Question 7 should provide descriptions of psychological games and rackets (see Chapter 7, Working with Others).

Question 8 gives information about the positive miniscript. This detail is important for planning new strategies and constructive changes in behaviour. This question also ensures that participants finish their review on a positive note.

Activity 3.7 Script and Work
Brief participants to respond individually to the following questions:
- What opinions about success did you pick up?
- What opinions were you given about earning money?
- What were you told that you should do?
- What were you told you would be good at?
- What were you told you would not be good at?
- How was work considered by your family?
- What messages did you receive about work and your sex?
- If you had a job as a child, what were your feelings about it?
- How do your answers above relate to your present job situation?

Afterwards, they may like to review their answers in pairs or small groups.

Activity 3.8 Life Planning
Prepare a handout so that participants can respond individually to the following questions:
- What are you doing about   your personal development?

  your professional development?
- Where do you want to be in   20 year's time?

  10 year's time?

  5 year's time?

  1 year's time?
- How (by what processes) have you developed so far   personally?

  professionally?
- What else do you need to do?

Afterwards, invite them to share their responses in pairs or small groups.

Activity 3.9 Why Are You Here?

Again, this is an exercise for completion by an individual and potentially for sharing in pairs or small groups. It can also be usefully completed at the start of a course, as part of establishing the contracts referred to in Chapter 2, Contracting for Learning. Used in this way, it gives the trainer, and the individual, an opportunity to see the training within a much wider perspective.

- Why are you here today?
- How do you expect to contribute to your personal and professional development by being here?
- How will this training course fit your overall development pattern?
- How might you sabotage this opportunity for development?

NOTES & SOURCES

Hungers are described by Berne – see *Transactional Analysis in Psychotherapy* in the list of books by Berne in Appendix 1.

Life Positions were also introduced by Berne. See also *I'm OK, You're OK* by Thomas Harris, Pan Books, 1973. Franklin Ernst took this idea further when he devised the OK Corral, a model for describing the impact of the life positions on our relationships and interactions with others. He was awarded the Eric Berne Memorial Scientific Award for this in 1981; see Appendix 2 for publication details. The term OK Corral is somewhat outdated, especially as current audiences are not familiar with cowboy films – hence I use windows on the world instead.

Martin Groder's work appears as 'Groder's 5 OK Diagrams' in *Transactional Analysis after Eric Berne*, Ed Graham Barnes, Harper's College Press 1977.

The Disposition Diamond is my name for what Graham Barnes called the Drama Diamond. For more details see *'On Saying Hello: The Script Drama Diamond and Character Role Analysis'* by Graham Barnes in *Transactional Analysis Journal* Jan 1981, 11(1). I have been asked by Graham to point out that he no longer believes his ideas are as useful as I believe them to be.

The Miniscript was developed by Taibi Kahler; the OK Miniscript by Hedges Capers. See *'The Miniscript'* by Taibi Kahler with Hedges Capers in *Transactional Analysis Journal* Jan 1974, 4(1). Kahler received the Eric Berne Memorial Scientific Award for this work in 1977.

The original concept of Scripts that was introduced by Berne was developed considerably by Steiner. See *Scripts People Live* by Claud Steiner, Bantam Books, 1975.

Bob and Mary Goulding received the Eric Berne Memorial Scientific Award in 1975 for their work on Injunctions. See Appendix 2 for publication details.

CHAPTER 4:   INTERPERSONAL STYLES

This chapter covers the major building blocks of TA: *ego states* and *transactional analysis 'proper'*, meaning the analysis of transactions. It is also designed to include details of TA concepts in a way that you can use directly as the basis for your own teaching, as well as the background you need and a range of activities to choose from.

The chapter begins with an introduction to ego states and how these can be likened to wavelengths on which we communicate, or fail to communicate, to others. I then describe five *personal styles* which are the results of our ego states as they show to others, followed by an account of how the same phenomena operating internally may at any moment be at odds with our outward appearance.

Having explained how ego states can be observed and analysed, I go on to show how they form the basis of our transactions with each other – which is where the term transactional analysis originally arose. Having described the different modes of interaction, I work through some typical situations to show how such a framework can help us identify options for improved people skills.

Because I have prepared this chapter on the basis that you will want to teach the material to participants, I have kept separate my ideas on how to relate the concepts to your own work. This is the first of several chapters, therefore, in which I have included a specific section on trainer effectiveness. Here I use the ego state model to analyse what happens in the classroom, and to suggest how you might increase your range of options as a trainer.

Finally, I provide a number of activities to bring theories to life. These cover identification of personal styles and of *internal ego states*, practice at analysing transactions, and ways of relating the frameworks to real situations. Two simple questionnaires are included for use with participants who require that bit of extra structure; many people can identify their ego states without these once they understand the concepts.

PERSONAL STYLES
Ego States

Ego states as a phenomenon were first identified by Eric Berne. His original conception was of two, and subsequently, three ego state systems, which he called Parent, Adult and Child (always written with initial capitals to distinguish them from parent, adult and child as biological descriptors of people). He defined ego states as coherent systems of thought and feeling manifested by corresponding patterns of behaviour. His diagram, shown here as Figure 4.1, has become an internationally recognised symbol and is even registered by the International Transactional Analysis Association as a trademark for use as a logo by Certified Transactional Analysts.

According to Berne, Adult ego state is in evidence when we are operating in the here-and-now; we process information rationally and make decisions about how to act. He defined both Parent and Child as archaic. When in Parent ego state, we are replaying behaviour, thinking and/or feeling that we have learned from someone else in the past. When in Child ego state, we are replaying some of the behaviour, thinking and/or feeling that we ourselves experienced in the past.

Since Berne first proposed this model, various writers have developed and extended his original ideas. This has given us a richer body of information but it has also made the subject more complicated. Currently, there are different models applied by different theorists. Unfortunately, the different models have sometimes been mixed inappropriately, resulting in apparent contradictions. If you already have some knowledge of ego state theory, you may well have been confused by this.

One area that is still contentious is how we deal with Berne's original hypothesis that Parent and Child are always replays from the past. If this is true, then any display of behaviour,

Figure 4.1: The Basic Model of Ego States

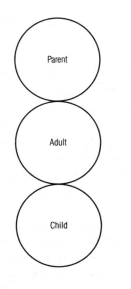

thinking or feeling associated with them means that the person is not in touch with reality. It also implies that the content of these ego states is fixed at some date in our past. Later writers have proposed that these two ego states continue developing. This latter model has more utility for organisational applications. It allows us to understand how people add extra skills into their Parent ego state by working with and copying competent colleagues and managers. It also reinforces the notion that we can continue to extend our Child ego state if we allow ourselves to experience joy, excitement and anger that may have been denied us as small children.

A further source of confusion in the TA books arose when writers took up the idea of using body language and vocabulary to identify which ego state a person was in. Berne stressed that using behavioural clues was only one of the four ways of determining an ego state. Equally important was evidence related to: how other people reacted; how the individual experienced themselves; and what historical antecedents existed. Perhaps because this other evidence is more difficult to obtain, there has been an over-emphasis on behavioural aspects. This has tended to trivialise the concept – lists of words and gestures associated with the outward signs of an ego state have come to be regarded as if they were the final arbiter.

Of course we cannot generally ask a person if their parents behaved as they are now, or even what ego state they believe themselves to be in. We can, however, interpret our observations with caution. We can also pay attention to our own responses. Often, these will be more reliable than the evidence of our eyes and ears, because we will be registering more subtle clues outside our conscious awareness.

To better understand the nature of ego states as they are displayed to others, imagine for a moment that people are radios. An ego state can then be likened to a particular wavelength that a person is tuned in to. Other people pick up the signals that are being broadcast, and in this way they know which wavelength we are on.

Each of us has preferences about the radio stations to which we prefer to listen, and we tune ourselves in accordingly. As we become conscious of the wavelength selected by another person, we make some fairly instantaneous, possibly out-of-awareness, decisions about whether we anticipate having much in common with that person. Are they playing pop music while we like classical? Are they tuned into a documentary while we pay attention to news bulletins? In other words, are they in Parent while we are in Adult? Adult while we are in Child? The particular mix of wavelengths will determine the success or otherwise of any interaction between us.

Skilled communicators are the ones who quickly, and accurately, identify the wavelength of the other person and then ensure that they themselves select a complementary wavelength. Unskilled communicators fail to identify correctly, or select an inappropriate wavelength to adopt for themselves. Poor communicators take no notice of the wavelength of the other person, or simply expect everyone else to fit in with them.

Although we all have basically similar radio equipment available to us, we do not all use it to full effect. Some people tune in to one station more or less permanently. We may well believe that this demonstrates a certain constancy; that people 'know where they are with us'. However, it also severely limits our ability to communicate competently with people. We will only get on well with those who are already in a corresponding wavelength, and those skilled individuals who are willing to make the effort and switch themselves into a complementary mode. Most of us know someone who is like this – who is predictable and inflexible and expects others to accept them as they are.

Another difficulty arises with the person who is not clearly tuned in to one wavelength. Perhaps they change ego states so frequently that we cannot judge which would be best to select for ourselves. One minute they may be serious, the next humorous, then sad…. How can we choose an appropriate way to respond? Can we too switch fast enough to keep up with them? At times the switch may be quite dramatic, as for example when someone who has been asking us a series of rational questions about our opinions on a new company policy suddenly accuses us angrily of lacking commitment or persisting with outdated views.

Sometimes, as with a real radio, a person has set their tuning dial so that it is not correctly on a station. This means that we pick up garbled signals. We can hear more than one wavelength at a time, and neither of them are clear enough to distinguish properly. Again, we are in a quandary over how best to respond.

The other common problem is the individual who stays on one wavelength during an interaction, but who opts for different wavelengths at different times. These are the people that no-one wants to deal with, because you never know what mood they will be in. One time they may be friendly, another time they ignore you. Or perhaps they respond impatiently one day and then want to chat the next time, when you are busy. We find ourselves thinking it would be easier if they stayed in a bad mood all the time – at least then we would know what to expect.

Although I have said the Berne identified three ego state systems, when we consider the behavioural implications of this it is more useful to distinguish between five wavelengths. Figure 4.2 show how we can divide Parent and Child into two different styles each. Adapted Child can be further divided but I will concentrate on the five main styles as they are the ones with the greatest potential for skilful interactions. These five patterns are presented in different amounts by individuals and thus create their own blend of personal styles.

Natural Child

In this ego state, with which we arrive in the world, we display our genuine feelings. We let people know we have needs and we act on our impulses. Our communication as babies is limited to crying and cooing but we still manage most of the time to let the grown-ups know when we want something. Soon, we add a myriad of other emotions, including

Figure 4.2: Personal Styles (Behavioural Ego States)

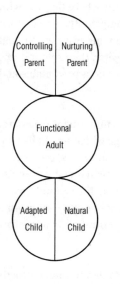

contentment, a sense of humour, and frustration when we cannot get our own way. Curiosity emerges, especially as we become mobile. We begin to show our creativity as we invent toys out of everyday household implements. We may have to be protected from the results of our curiosity and creativity when we want to explore dangerous objects such as electrical outlets.

As small children, we also demonstrate a considerable capacity for friendliness and affection. At this age, we like other people unconditionally; we have not yet learned to be wary. Watch how small children accept each other, strangers and stray dogs alike – they look pleased and excited as others move towards them. As grown-ups, whatever we retain of this open friendliness will be an important facet of our personality.

Natural Child is the wavelength to adopt when we judge it appropriate to let others know how we feel. We will then let them see our genuine pleasure in their company, our friendliness, our excitement about working with them. We will also allow those we trust to know when we are disappointed, or angry that things have not worked out as we hoped. Genuine sadness at unhappy events in our lives will not be hidden.

Natural Child is also the ego state needed for genuine brainstorming as this is when we are at our most creative and can invent ideas that are outside our experience. Other positive aspects are our willingness to ask questions and express our curiosity without feeling the need to pretend to know more than we do.

However, if we spend too much time in this ego state, we risk being labelled immature, childish, over-emotional. People may feel that we are unlikely to settle down to serious work instead of having fun. A surfeit of creativity may be perceived as being out of touch with the real world. Our genuine friendliness may come over as too good to be true; we may be somewhat naïve if we expect everyone to reciprocate.

Adapted Child

As children, we soon sense that the grown-ups have certain expectations of us. We recognise this even before we can talk by the way they hold us and through their tone of voice. Later, they tell us how they require us to behave, and may punish or reward us for specific actions. We come to realise that Natural Child behaviour is not always welcomed. We therefore set about developing an alternative version that will enable us to fit in with the demands of our family and our society.

Depending on our culture, we learn to say please and thank you; to perform simple greeting rituals, to eat with knife, fork, chopsticks, right hand only; to defer to our elders; to help old ladies carry their packages. In other words, we acquire the skills of getting along politely with other people and of behaving in socially acceptable ways.

We may also acquire some of the gender-specific messages that belong in our culture. Often, boys are allowed to show anger but mocked for sadness; they may grow up determined to display only aggression and no tenderness. Girls may well receive the opposite programming, so that as women they become tearful when the genuine response would be anger.

When we are older, we move into Adapted Child when we demonstrate that we know how to behave. By now, much of this is automatic and we are barely conscious of it. If we are British we apologise when someone else bumps into us, we join queues, and we do not talk to strangers. At work, we are especially polite to customers and senior managers. We pay attention to the organisational norms about dress and appearance. We adapt in a variety of ways so that other people will find us acceptable and amenable.

If we overdo it, however, we may be perceived as lacking confidence. We will not then be trusted with responsibility and may have difficulty in resisting unreasonable demands from colleagues or customers. Perhaps we were told that "children should be seen and not heard", so now we sit so quietly at meetings that no-one recalls afterwards that we were there. Alternatively, we may have learned during childhood to overcompensate so that now we appear aggressive and rebellious. In this case, our objections may be dismissed as just another attempt by us to start an argument.

Nurturing Parent

At some point when we are small children we realise that one day we too will be a grown-up. We set out to prepare for this by copying as much as possible of what the big people around us are doing. Much of this has to do with looking after others. They dress us, comfort us when we are hurt, prepare meals for us. So we do the same, as best we can, for our dolls or pets or younger siblings. We may notice that they do similar things for other adults and not just for children; if not we may grow up believing that such nurturing should be restricted to babies.

As adults ourselves, we need our Nurturing Parent ego state at those times when it is appropriate to care for someone else. Perhaps a new member of staff needs to be shown around the building, or someone about to tackle a difficult task needs some reassurance. Sympathy may be called for when bad news has been received. Even a simple thing like getting coffee for a colleague who is overworked and needs to relax.

In many organisations, there is barely enough Nurturing Parent to go around. However, occasionally you meet someone who overuses this wavelength. They are likely to smother you with their concern. They may fuss over you as if you were not capable of managing alone, or even insist on doing the job for you. It is difficult to refuse their assistance when they are so clearly intending to be helpful. When this happens, people are denied the opportunity to develop their own skills.

Controlling Parent

As with Nurturing Parent, we develop this ego state also by mimicking our elders. We observe that one of the ways we can take care of others is by setting down rules and boundaries for them. In this way, we keep them safe and make sure they learn the correct ways to behave. Parents do this for children when they stop them doing dangerous things, warn them against going with strangers, impose curfew times on reluctant teenagers.

This ego state is the one to use when we need to be firm. Many disciplinary hearings in organisations might be avoided if managers were to use Controlling Parent sooner – to spell out clearly what the performance requirements are and how the person must change in order to meet them. Firmness may also be appropriate with colleagues and customers who are trying to take unfair advantage. A firm refusal to do their work for them or to provide services not covered by the contract will be more skilful than resentful compliance.

Overdo this ego state and you will come over as bossy and overbearing. This happens when we insist that the job is done our way, even though there are other options that would work just as well. Imposing rules based on our opinions rather than the true requirements of the task is another area for grievance. Ordering people about as if they were children will not usually fill them with enthusiasm for us or our instructions. Indeed, we are more likely to stimulate rebellion than obedience.

Functional Adult

This ego state is tuned in when we are being logical and rational. As children, we begin to understand cause and effect. We drop a rattle from the pram and observe that people keep picking it up for us. We tip the bottle too far and our drink overflows from the mug; we work out that we need to hold the bottle differently to avoid spilling any more. We learn that compromise may be called for: if I want to ride my brother's bike I will have a better chance if I offer to lend him my computer for a while.

We develop the ability to think rationally on more than one level, so that we can understand both our inner and outer worlds. We acquire the skills of problem solving and decision making. All of this is clearly very relevant to us in later life. We have to balance priorities and decide between conflicting requirements and limited resources. We have to take into account our own feelings and those of others, yet still remember the objectives and practicalities.

A word of caution. If we spend too much time in Functional Adult we will come over as boring and pedantic. It is not always necessary to analyse a situation. Sometimes intuition or past experience will provide a better basis for our decision. Imagine the effect of Functional Adult on someone who is telling jokes, as we keep attempting to analyse the punch lines. Being logical about everything may make us seem like a robot. If we lack the characteristics of the other four ego states, people will find it hard to get to know us.

Choosing our Personal Style

We can also sketch out a histogram, or bar chart, of how much time we spend in each personal style. Figure 4.3 shows a typical example.

The originator of this idea, Dusay, suggests that we have only so much energy to invest. Our 'combined energy total' for the five ego states will therefore remain constant. If we want to decrease our use of an ego state, it is much easier to plan to make a corresponding increase elsewhere. For example, if we set out to spend more time in Natural Child, we are likely to

Figure 4.3: A Typical Egogram

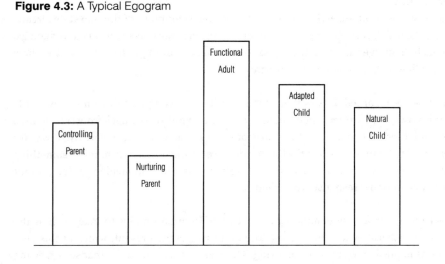

reduce any unwanted peaks in the other ego states. Planning to do something new is usually easier and more effective at changing behaviour than seeking to stop doing something that has become a habit.

Employing the concept of ego states gives us a method for checking our behaviour and consciously selecting the most appropriate option for our current objective. In summary, the key qualities of each are:

Friendliness, creativity	Natural Child
Politeness, courtesy	Adapted Child
Nurturing, caring	Nurturing Parent
Firmness, control	Controlling Parent
Logical, problem solving	Functional Adult

WHAT HAPPENS INSIDE US

So far, I have only described in detail the way ego states are exhibited to others. This concentrates on the identification of an ego state using behavioural clues. For many of our interactions, this will be enough to allow us to analyse the transaction and select our own ego state for good communication.

However, there will be times when this is not so. It will sometimes seem as if the person is in two ego states at once, or the behavioural aspects will feel somehow out of line with our intuitive sense of what is happening. We can use the familiar diagram of three stacked circles to show a set of internal ego states. To distinguish it, in Figure 4.4 I use dotted lines to indicate that these are under the surface – they cannot be observed directly by others although we can speculate about them based on what behaviour and body language that we do see.

Internal Child

As with Natural Child, we arrive in the world with the beginnings of this ego state already in place. Basically, it is our experience of ourselves. We have needs, wants and feelings. These include hunger and thirst, fear, curiosity, anger, wanting to be loved, and a whole range of other feelings that occur as we grow.

All of these are recorded. It is as if our Internal Child is a computer disc on which we file everything away. We are continually adding new data. We also refer back from time to time to the old files. We may do this consciously, as when we are aware that we are remembering. We may have lost the file, as when we try unsuccessfully to recall something we used to know. We may go back without realising, as when an incident in the present triggers an emotional response from the past.

Another metaphor for understanding the nature of Internal Child is to imagine it as the rings of a tree, as shown in Figure 4.5. The outer ring is the present, which at this very moment is being formed into another ring. There are trees in Australia that stop growing during the years of drought. Unfortunately people are not able to do this so our rings may

Figure 4.4: Internal Ego States

well contain some that are not as healthy as they might be. There are likely also to be knots in the tree, representing trauma. However, most of us will also have some healthy rings, plus areas where things went really well for us.

Figure 4.5: Internal Child

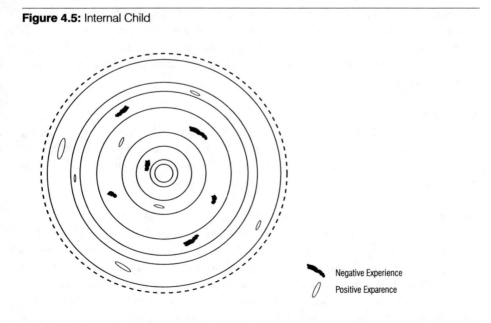

A common example of reverting without intending to is when we meet someone who treats us as a teacher used to. Perhaps they say our name in a way we no longer expect. For men, this may involve being addressed by your last name only – not Mr Smith, just Smith – said in a tone that sounds ominous. For women, it is perhaps the use of your full first name rather than its shortened version. The result is often an instantaneous reaction of feeling like a small child who is back at school. In my case, I momentarily expect to be told I have to stay behind after classes. Then I realise that I am really a grown-up. We have rubber-banded, or snapped back, to an earlier ring in the tree, and maybe to a knot.

The same thing happens if we actually meet our teacher again. In spite of being adult now, and perhaps having children of our own, we still get an overwhelming urge to relate to them in the way we did years ago. On a training course, we may well experience the same response to the trainer even though they have never been a school teacher and do not behave like one. See what happens when the trainer leans over you to look at your work. You are quite likely to want to hide it with your arm in case they criticise you, whereas they are more interested in finding out whether they have taught the topic successfully.

Every day, we add new recordings to our Internal Child. We react in a variety of ways to what is going on around us; in the future these responses will have become our memories. For now, though, they are our current sensations. They are new rings being formed in our tree. We feel them internally and can then choose whether to display them through Natural Child. We may decide that this would be inappropriate; in that case we select a different way to behave.

We may go for Adapted Child and hope that people remain unaware of our real feelings. We may use Functional Adult to describe or explain our feelings, and perhaps to review how their behaviour affects us. We may use Controlling Parent to insist on a change in their behaviour. Our Nurturing Parent might shift the focus onto someone else's feelings. In the right circumstances, however, we will react spontaneously and let others know how we really feel.

Internal Parent

I have already said that Controlling and Nurturing Parent are learned by copying the big people. Internal Parent is our storage system for all of these copies. Included are the opinions, beliefs and value systems that go with the behaviours. As with Internal Child, at any moment we may pull out an old recording or lay down a new one.

We can diagram Internal Parent as shown in Figure 4.6 by showing lots of little behavioural ego state diagrams to which we add arms and legs. Our copies are replicas of the behaviours of all the people we have ever been in contact with. Of course, some who we met only occasionally may be very small versions and tucked away in the background but our primary care-givers and other significant people in our lives will have numerous 'slices' of their behaviour copied into our Internal Parent. Size of the copies may also vary as a factor of intensity: one very impactful interaction may occupy as much space

Figure 4.6: Internal Parent

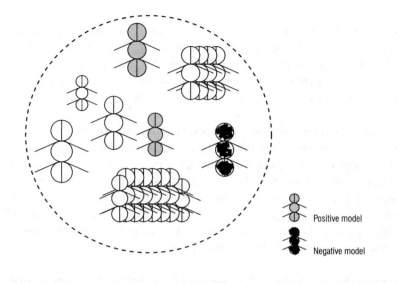

Positive model

Negative model

(metaphorically) as several copies of someone we interacted with more often but with less excitement. Whether our interactions were positive or negative will also affect the intensity of the recordings.

Old recordings, or copies, emerge when we catch ourselves repeating what our parents told us years ago. This may be a problem if things have changed since then. Beliefs about nutrition, for example, are very different nowadays. We may share our parents' political views without question and yet be leading a life that depends on economic policies they would disapprove of. Racial prejudices are often the result of old recordings from a time when people had insufficient information and exposure to other cultures.

Our development as individuals requires that we can update our Internal Parent. We need to pull out the contents of the file for scrutiny. Then we can archive those aspects which are no longer relevant. As we meet more people, we can observe and copy the things they do that are effective. We can add these new options to a part of our filing system where they will be readily accessible. We can then choose when to 'reproduce' a role model, when to adjust or combine different copies, and when we will be better served by devising some new way to behave.

Internal Adult

Our Internal Adult is like a computer programme that we use to access our disks and to process and store new data. It takes in information from the outside world, such as who is talking to us and how. It monitors our reactions in Internal Child and checks whether these seem relevant to the situation. It scans through our Internal Parent for any recorded ways of responding that would be appropriate now.

I draw this as shown in Figure 4.7, with the zig-zag line to represent some fairly instantaneous processing. An external stimulus is perceived; we check our Internal Child reactions to ensure they are here-and-now and not a rubber-band to a previous occasion; we check that our Internal Parent responses are also relevant now and not out-dated; and then we decide which behavioural ego state would be the most useful to display.

Or perhaps we process the current situation and realise that we have a healthy portion of tree that was formed some time ago in our Internal Child – and that it would be appropriate to choose now to feel the same way again. For instance, our confidence when skiing might be just the right way to feel when we are making a presentation to senior management. We then access a copy within Internal Parent of someone who was reassuring us – and choose to replay that experience as well so that we 'parent' ourself as we prepare to start the presentation. This drawing on internal resources to suit the present circumstances is made possible by maintaining our Internal Adult in the here-and-now.

When our Internal Adult is functioning well, we are continually making choices about what to do. These selections may take only fractions of a second, yet we manage to weigh up probabilities and make balanced decisions. Doing this does not prevent us from behaving instinctively; rather it paves the way for more spontaneity by ensuring that we have considered the consequences first.

Figure 4.7: Internal Adult

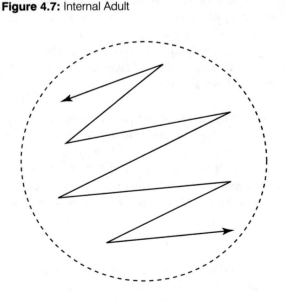

CHANNELS OF COMMUNICATION
Transactional Analysis

Although this book is written about a whole field of theories that form part of a general field of Transactional Analysis, the term was originally used by Berne in a far more specific way. Transactional analysis 'proper' refers to the analysis of transactions between people. It is the process of considering which ego state in one person is interacting with which ego state in another person.

In many of our transactions, this analysis can concentrate only on the behavioural aspects. This will be satisfactory when our internal ego state matches the one displayed externally. It will also be adequate when we are in Internal Adult and are therefore operating in the here-and-now. We will, however, need to analyse at two levels when we interact with someone whose behaviour does not reflect their internal ego state.

Berne identified three types of transactions and three corresponding 'rules of communication'. *Complementary* and *crossed* transactions require analysis at behavioural level only. *Ulterior* transactions involve hidden agendas at the psychological level; to deal skilfully with these we must also take into account the internal ego states that are involved.

I add a fourth type of transaction: the *refracted* transaction occurs when one or more parties has such fixed expectations that they imagine (incorrectly) which ego state is being presented to them.

Complementary and Crossed Transactions

Complementary transactions occur when the ego state addressed is the ego state which responds. If I use Controlling Parent to address your Adapted Child, and you reply from Adapted Child to my Controlling Parent, we have a complementary transaction. If you opted instead to respond from Functional Adult, and sought to interact with my Functional Adult ego state, we would have a crossed transaction. Figures 4.8 and 4.9 give examples of each type of transaction.

The rule for a complementary transaction is that the communication can continue indefinitely. The rule for a crossed transaction is that a break in communication will occur. This does not mean that complementary is good and crossed is bad!

Perhaps your complementary transaction is a highly unsatisfactory one, with an angry colleague shouting at you from Controlling Parent about a mistake you have made. You have begun with a complementary transaction by apologising from Adapted Child. However, your colleague is ignoring your apology and is still shouting at you. It will not be appropriate to keep apologising while the shouting continues. You need the break in communication that a crossed transaction would provide; shift to Functional Adult-Functional Adult for some problem-solving discussion, or use your own Controlling Parent to tell their Adapted Child firmly not to talk to you like that.

Figure 4.8: A Complementary Transaction

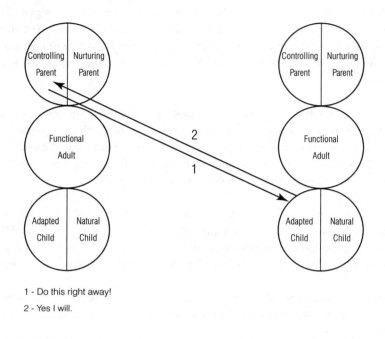

1 - Do this right away!

2 - Yes I will.

Whether we have to cross a transaction or not, we will still need to attain some matching of ego states for the communication to proceed at any length. Our process of choosing an ego state should therefore include consideration of the effect we want to have on the other person.

Although in theory you can pair any ego state with any other, in practice there are four channels that are especially likely to result in good relationships.

Functional Adult - Functional Adult | problem-solving
Nurturing Parent – Natural Child | nurturing
Natural Child – Natural Child | having fun, being creative
Controlling Parent – Adapted Child | giving instructions

Each of us has a preferred channel. We will probably be reasonably comfortable with one or two of the others, and somewhat uncomfortable with the fourth. Our interactions will be successful more often if we can match the channel to the recipient. Paying attention to the ego state selected customarily by the other person can give us a good idea of the best way to respond.

There are other options that will enable us to communicate adequately but these will not necessarily have the added benefit of building a close working relationship through using the preferred channels.

Figure 4.9: A Crossed Transaction

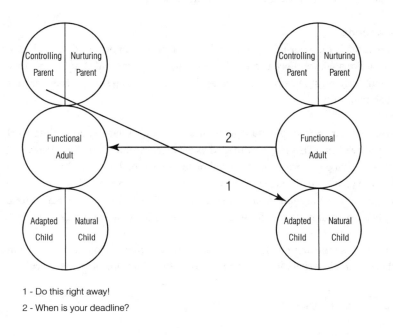

1 - Do this right away!
2 - When is your deadline?

Nurturing Parent – Nurturing Parent - discussing how to care for others, as when two managers review a subordinate's progress – the risk here is that they may be overlooking the fact that the subordinate is not a child – and should be part of the decision making process.

Controlling Parent – Controlling Parent - agreeing on what rules should apply to others – again, the risk is that this will only be effective if they have the authority to impose the rules.

Adapted Child – Adapted Child - being compliant or rebellious together – unfortunately someone in Controlling Parent may then decide to take charge.

Some combinations of ego states are likely to lead to poor communication. Miscommunication is likely to occur if we use Functional Adult to address someone in any of the Parent or Child ego states. Conversely, we are unlikely to get an appropriate response if we use Parent or Child with someone who is clearly tuned into Functional Adult and expecting a logical discussion.

Such crossed transactions are only useful when you want to make a significant change to the communication. Even then, you are more likely to be successful if you first select one of the four preferred channels before you attempt the change. By doing this, you will establish an initial contact in the way the recipient expects. They will then be more likely to switch ego states in order to maintain communication with you.

Ulterior Transactions

By combining the models for external and internal ego states, we can now understand what happens in transactions where there is a hidden message. Our Internal Child is intuitive and will pick up underlying signals from someone else's internal ego states whatever they may be doing behaviourally.

Take the example in Figure 4.10 of the manager who asks a subordinate whether the report will be ready by the deadline. This may be phrased as a logical, rational question. However, the manager may really be convinced that the subordinate will be late with the report, as has happened in the past. The manager's Internal Parent is therefore holding some fairly derogatory thoughts about the subordinate's performance. These are liable to 'leak'; there will be small indicators of them through the manager's body language and tone of voice.

A reasonably intuitive subordinate will pick up these small signals through the excellent antennae attached to their Internal Child. They may choose to say nothing but will now believe

Figure 4.10: An Ulterior Transaction

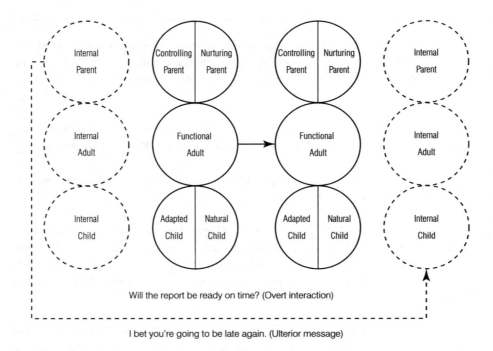

Will the report be ready on time? (Overt interaction)

I bet you're going to be late again. (Ulterior message)

that the manager does not trust them. This can be enough for them to justify a late report – why bother if it's not expected on time anyway? Or they may respond directly to the signals and accuse the manager of lacking trust. This is more likely if the comment has reactivated the stored feelings in Internal Child that they acquired during previous bad experiences.

Berne's 'rule' of communication for ulterior transactions says that the behavioural outcome will be determined by the psychological, or ulterior, level of the interaction. The unspoken intent will have more impact than the overt, social comment. Whenever our inner and outer messages conflict in this way, the secret agenda will carry the most weight, even if we both pretend it does not exist. It will be difficult to build effective relationships with people unless we address their underlying concerns.

Refracted Transactions
Refracted transactions, as shown in Figure 4.11, are often seen in organisations, especially when a new employee arrives:

1. The manager tells the employee what to do – Controlling Parent to Adapted Child.
2. The employee is new and keen to learn so asks the manager why it is done that way – Functional Adult to Functional Adult.

Figure 4.11: A Refracted Transaction

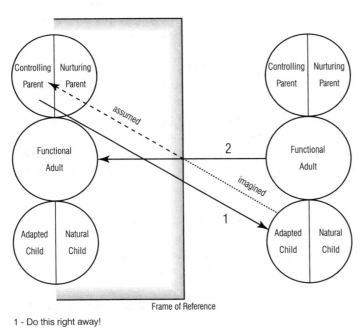

Frame of Reference

1 - Do this right away!

2 - Why do we do it like that?

3. The manager 'refracts' the transaction and imagines it is coming from the employee's Adapted Child – and hence it sounds rebellious, as if a child is challenging a parent figure.
4. The manager therefore emphasises the use of Controlling Parent and simply insists that this is the way things are done – no explanation is forthcoming.
5. The employee concludes that asking questions is a waste of time and thereafter simply follows orders.

The 'refraction' is like the way that water affects the direction of light, so that we see an object underwater and think it is in a different position to where it actually is. In our interactions, our frame of reference (or our distorting beliefs) may act like the surface of the water. Refracted transactions are powerful contributors to the problem of hierarchal symbiosis, which is described later in this chapter.

PEOPLE SKILLS

There are many ways in which we can apply TA models to enhance our skills with people. I have selected three examples that regularly feature on training courses when participants are asked to identify typical instances of the communication problems faced in their organisations: conflict, complaints, and manager/subordinate interactions in a hierarchy.

Handling Conflict

Figure 4.12 shows how a conflict develops. Often, this sequence will begin with an ulterior transaction; sometimes an individual's frame of reference will lead to them believing there is an ulterior when none was intended. The result may be the same.

Chris picks up or imagines that Pat is criticising. Chris's Internal Child makes contact with an old experience of being criticised, and feels threatened. Chris's Internal Child then does what any small child does when scared – goes to fetch Mother. In this case, Mother is handily stored away as a copy in Chris's Internal Parent. Chris simply sifts through to find the best version of Mother when she was telling someone else to leave her child alone. Chris's Internal Adult has been bypassed in this process so Chris is not considering any other options. Instead, Chris selects a copy of Mother and uses external Controlling Parent to criticise Pat.

At this point, Pat does the same as Chris has done. Pat goes back into an old experience, feels scared, fetches Mother, puts a copy of Mother into Controlling Parent, and zaps Chris. And so it goes on, with each 'mother' becoming increasingly aggressive on behalf of her offspring and each 'child' feeling even more scared.

Knowing about internal ego states can help us to avoid conflict. As we are criticised, we can make a point of investing extra energy into Internal Adult. Count to ten and keep thinking. Remind ourselves that we are likely to react by re-experiencing an old hurt. Check how much of the pain is really related to the current comment. Consider the consequences of responding angrily. Review what other options we have.

Figure 4.12 : Stages of Conflict

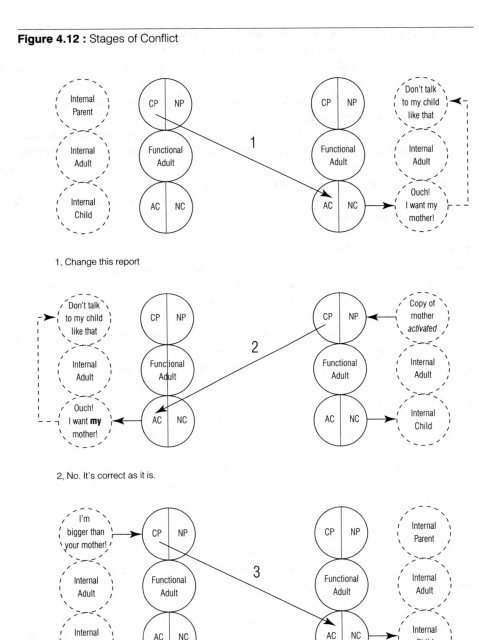

1, Change this report

2, No. It's correct as it is.

3, I insist that you change it

- Natural Child could be used to let them know that we are hurt by the criticism. They may not have realised they have said something unkind.
- Adapted Child could accept the criticism as justified and ask how they want us to be different.
- Functional Adult could be employed to question the basis of the criticism and discuss what we might decide to change.
- Controlling Parent could tell them firmly that they are criticising unjustly or unhelpfully.
- Nurturing Parent could reassure them that our action will not cause a problem for them.

Several of these options are aimed at the internal ego state in the other person. Used in a genuine attempt to avoid conflict, they are likely to be perceived as constructive and will help build a closer relationship.

Dealing with Complaints

The way we deal with conflict can also give us ideas for handling complaints. This is, after all, the sort of situation which often finishes in conflict. Any of the suggestions above may be better than getting annoyed with a customer or colleague.

There is also a specific sequence of behaviours which can be particularly effective, as shown in Figure 4.13. This takes account of the probable dynamics of the person who is complaining. Although there may be times when you judge that an alternative method would be more appropriate, the steps outlined below will serve to defuse most conflict and complaint situations.

Imagine the other person is in angry Controlling Parent, telling you off. So:

Response Part 1 You need a polite Adapted Child response to make an initial connection with them. Any other ego state will be perceived as inappropriate by them and you will not make any contact. Make sure this is an honest comment, such as "I'm sorry you are not satisfied, Sir/Madam."

Inside, they are in scared Internal Child because they are afraid you may refuse to deal with their complaint. Perhaps someone at home will tell them they should have known better than to spend money on your goods. So:

Response Part 2 You now need a reassuring comment from Nurturing Parent to soothe their Internal Child. Do not commit yourself to specific action at this stage. Tell them that you are sure you will be able to sort things out.

With luck, they are now ready to solve the problem. So:

Response Part 3 Use your Functional Adult to ask for details of the problem. Make it something straightforward and factual to start with, such as asking to see the item.

Figure 4.13 : A Complaint Handling Sequence

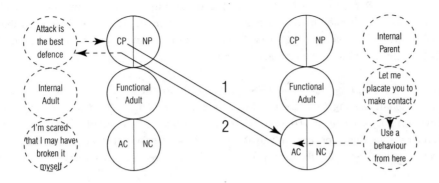

1, I demand a refund.
2, I'm sorry you're not satisfied. Sir/Madam.

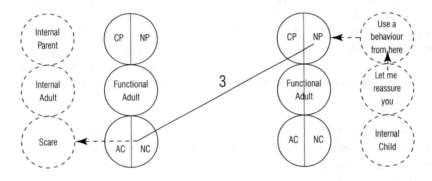

3, I'm sure we can sort this out.

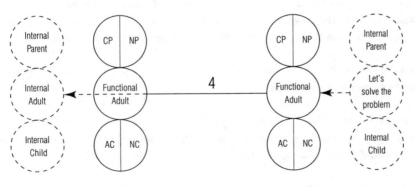

4, Where is the broken part?

It is essential to use this sequence without pausing – polite response, reassurance, problem-solving question. If they are still angry, repeat the sequence. Sometimes when we are very upset we fail to even hear what the other person says to us. It is as if we knock the olive branch from their hand before we realise what it is. Somehow, it never seems feasible to pick it up at that stage, although we will often wish they would offer it again. If they do, we will usually accept it on the second occasion.

However, if you have repeated the sequence with no effect, perhaps they have no real investment in solving the problem. Maybe today is one of their 'off-days', those days we all have sometimes when we wake up feeling cross with the whole world. If you suspect that is the case, let them continue to yell at you until they run out of steam. Meanwhile, have an internal conversation in which your Internal Parent reassures your Internal Child that this is not your fault.

HIERARCHICAL SYMBIOSIS

Within organisations there is a tendency for a common, generally unhelpful, pattern of ego states to occur. This is particularly likely when there is a strong hierarchical structure. What happens is that managers use mostly Controlling Parent ego state while subordinates opt for Adapted Child. In other words, the managers tell the workers what to do, and the workers do it. This communication format is repeated through the different levels of the hierarchy; senior managers tell junior managers what to do, and junior managers tell first-line supervisors.

This conjures up the amusing, but unfortunate, vision shown in Figure 4.14 – those in the middle doing an about-face in ego state terms as they move from junior to senior contacts. They control and instruct those below them – then go in to be controlled and instructed by those above them in the hierarchy.

This creates a *hierarchical symbiosis*. Symbiosis is a natural phenomenon whereby two entities come together to meet each others needs, such as birds eating tics from the back of a rhinoceros. The birds get a meal and the rhino gets cleaned of parasites.

In TA the term symbiosis is also used to indicate the ways that people come together and share just one set of ego states.

A functional symbiosis is when the two parties have agreed to share out the tasks so that, for example, one cooks and the other cleans. This is fine as long as neither believes they are incapable of undertaking the other task if that becomes necessary.

When in a hierarchy, there will often be an unhelpful symbiosis. The manager acts as if only they can operate in Parent mode and expects the subordinate to function only in Child. You will see from Figure 4.14 that the other ego states are not being activated, so each party is not operating to their full potential.

Figure 4.14: A Hierarchy of Ego States

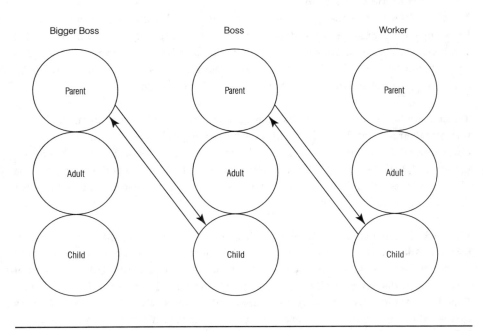

What has happened is that we have held onto patterns of behaving that we learned at home and at school. When we were real children, we spent a lot of time in Adapted Child, doing as the grown-ups told us. Generally, this made sense because they were older than us and knew more of the world. (This was not always true, and even when it was we did not always believe it but we acted as if we did.) At work, we subconsciously put managers into the slot we have reserved for those who know more, and so we expect them to tell us what to do just as our parents and teachers did. (Again, we may not believe it but we act as if we do.) When we in turn get promoted, we simply switch across to the Parent ego state side of this equation.

Effective managers and competent subordinates do not fit into this pattern. They recognise that we need all of our ego states in use for the range of situations we will face. They realise that a subordinate using only Adapted Child will not display the creativity of Natural Child nor the problem solving ability of Functional Adult. They are unlikely to be firm when faced with unreasonable demands, and may commit themselves inadvisedly. Their lack of nurturing may give a poor image of the organisation.

Managers who use only Controlling Parent will be perceived as uncaring. Lack of Functional Adult ego state will limit their consideration of options when problems arise. Lack of Natural Child will cause them to appear unfeeling, with no sense of humour. They are unlikely to motivate and enthuse their subordinates; rather they will encourage staff to avoid risks and to check first instead of using initiative.

TRAINER EFFECTIVENESS
Ego States in the Classroom

Too often, the pattern in the classroom matches that I have described for the organisational hierarchy – trainer in Parent and students in Child. The danger of this is reinforced by the way being in a classroom triggers memories of school, with a corresponding shift into the ego state most experienced during those year of our life. Sit us behind a desk, looking up at a trainer/teacher standing in front of us, and we feel like children again.

Trainers are lured into believing that they in their turn should be copying the behaviour they saw their own teachers adopt. This may happen regardless of our current view of the effectiveness of our teachers. It is rather like when we swore we would never act as our parents did, and then find ourselves treating our own children in just the same way. The likelihood of us falling into this trap is increased when our participants make it so clear that they expect to be told what to do.

We need our participants to have all their ego states available to them for maximum learning. Adapted Child is useful to ensure an adequate level of courtesy towards us and the rest of the group, and it does at least get them listening to us. Natural Child is essential if they are to display curiosity about the subject, and ask questions to find out more. Functional Adult is needed if they are to discuss the subject rationally and ask questions to check they can use what they are learning. Nurturing Parent ensures they are willing to help and encourage each other. Controlling Parent enables them to share in setting the pace at which they can learn.

Used inappropriately, each ego state can cause its own set of problems for the trainer. Participants who are stuck in Adapted Child may be so polite that you cannot tell they are failing to learn. Worse, those who had a bad time at school may have decided then to cope by being rebellious. They will now behave like an obnoxious child during your session, tempting you to use your Controlling Parent ego state in an unhelpful way to tell them off. Other participants note your reaction and become afraid you will treat them in the same way.

Participants in Natural Child may have come prepared to have fun but not to do any work. They join in the activities you suggest but make no effort to review the learning afterwards. Perhaps they are nervous of being observed or filmed; if unchecked their Natural Child may simply refuse to take part. This may seem to you to be too much like the action of a spoiled child; again you may be hooked into Parent. Go for Controlling Parent and you seem like an ogre. Select Nurturing Parent and you risk being so sympathetic that they manage to avoid the exercise altogether, along with the learning they should have gained.

Functional Adult may seem like a useful ego state for a participant to apply. Watch out for the ones who use it to search for flaws in your logic. If you are training in people skills, you may find it difficult to convince someone who stays mostly in Functional Adult that the other facets of a human being are important. They may well dismiss emotions as being irrational and therefore of no value.

Too much Nurturing Parent means a participant who keeps trying to look after the rest of the class. Set up something challenging and they may sabotage it by making it easy for the others to do. Given the opportunity, they will take care of the trainer too. They will leave group activities in order to fetch coffee for you. Or they may 'help' you by distributing the handouts before you intended. They will certainly create some interesting group dynamics through acting as if you cannot function without their reassurance.

Controlling Parent may boss you around, boss the other participants around, or generate conflict. Bad cases will do all three. They will tell you firmly that you are wrong. You are likely to be tempted to argue simply because of the ego state they use to tell you. This will be even worse when you really are wrong. In syndicate work, they will insist that their interpretation of the group task is the correct one. Others will shift into their own Controlling Parent in order to retaliate in kind, or into rebellious or submissive Adapted Child.

Trainer Tips

Know your own ego states. Work through the activities at the end of this chapter and make sure you have all ego states in good working order. Talk over your results with colleagues to add to your awareness. Use video or audio recordings where possible so you can review yourself in action. Practice until you are comfortable using each ego state during training sessions.

Use Functional Adult to stimulate healthy discussion of your input. Plan sessions in which participants are encouraged to work things out for themselves. Join in with them as an equal and not as someone who knows the answers already. Sit down sometimes so that they are not always looking up at you. Come out from behind the desk so that you eliminate this typical teacher's barrier.

Use Controlling Parent to set clear boundaries and to enforce them. Tell participants what your rules are about programme times, and then start and finish when you said you would. Decline to be drawn into deviations from the programme that you judge to be unhelpful. Deal firmly with participants who cause problems for others.

Use Nurturing Parent to reassure participants about the training methods you will be using. Use it also to welcome them to the course, and to take care of their needs for breaks and refreshments. Find time to listen to individuals who have problems.

Use Natural Child to bring fun and excitement into your sessions. Be creative with what you do. Even if you are not good at telling jokes, you can still introduce humour and laughter. People relax and learn better when they are enjoying themselves. Use yourself as a model to demonstrate to participants that this is a course where they can allow their own Natural Child to come out and play.

Use Adapted Child to be polite and courteous to your participants. Treat them with respect. Make it clear that you regard them as experts in their own right, and that you are willing to take account of their experience. Use Adapted Child yourself so they will realise it is inappropriate for them to stay in that particular ego state the whole time.

Finally, keep up the process of identifying your own weak spots as far as ego states are concerned, and of doing something about it. Plan opportunities to increase your range of options. After training sessions, review what happened. Select one or two incidents you were not totally satisfied with. Analyse the transaction. Consider what other ego states you might have used. Work out what the likely effects would have been. Decide which offers the most scope for the future. Resolve to handle it more skilfully next time it happens.

ACTIVITIES
Activity 4.1 Personal Style Identification
Brief participants to recall a time when they now recognise they were in a specific ego state. Ask them to do this for each of the five personal styles.

As they recall an incident, they should replay their memory of it, identifying their behaviour, how they felt at the time, what they were hearing and seeing, what they were saying and doing, etc. The aim is to 'log' the experience so that they will be better able to identify what ego states they are adopting in the future.

You may want to prepare a briefing sheet with examples, as follows:
Controlling Parent: recall an occasion when you have directed another person to behave in a particular way, e.g. saying "you should do it like this..." or advising them of the correct procedure.
Nurturing Parent: describe a situation when you have 'looked after' or cared for another person, e.g. getting them a cup of tea when they are tired, being sympathetic or encouraging over a problem.
Functional Adult: think of a time when you gathered information on which you based a decision, e.g. choosing a training course to attend, buying a car.
Adapted Child: identify something you do because other people expect it or take it for granted, e.g. holding open a door, making polite conversation.
Natural Child: how do you relax and enjoy yourself, what aspects of your work are the most fun to do?

Pair up participants to review their answers. Reassure them that any 'missing' ego state examples will soon be identified once they start comparing notes.

Deal with any questions. Suggest they might like to think about the effect on their psychological health if they have found out that some ego states are rarely engaged at work. People in particularly uninspiring jobs may need to look outside the organisation for opportunities to exercise Natural Child; those with little seniority in autocratic organisations may find scope for using Parent ego states in volunteer associations.

You may find it helpful to re-read the section in this chapter on ego states in a hierarchy before you use this activity.

Activity 4.2 Personal Styles Questionnaire

The Personal Styles Questionnaire in Appendix 6 can be purchased for use by participants. It is intended as a fairly light-hearted exercise to give participants some idea of their likely ego state balance. Stress to them that it is only a short sampling of their behaviour so they should use their common sense when interpreting the results. Emphasise that the purpose is not to fit them into a set of labels; it is to stimulate their awareness about the behavioural aspects of ego states as they show them to other people.

After they have completed the questionnaire, let them use the marking guide to calculate their own scores.

Suggest then that they pair up to share their results and consider the implications for their effectiveness with others. Review as described for Activity 4.1.

Activity 4.3 Egograms

Invite individuals to draw their own egograms, as in the example shown in Figure 4.3. These may be based on their own estimates or be a reflection of feedback from others. Most people can draw their own fairly accurate egogram; if a group know each other then they can compare these with how others perceive them.

Figure 4.3 shows a single-sided egogram. Participants can also draw a double-sided version, with positive uses of ego states above the line and negative use below the line.

Activity 4.4 Ego States and Behavioural Clues

An activity for small groups of 3 to 8.

Brief groups to produce lists of behavioural clues for each ego state.

You may need to remind the group that they are considering only behaviour – i.e. what can be observed. An individual may be experiencing a different ego state internally to the one they exhibit. (See the section in this chapter on What happens inside us).

Typical clues (there are many more):

Controlling Parent: standing over someone, wagging finger in parental ways, legs apart and arms folded across chest, looking over top of spectacles, words such as 'should' and 'must', expressing opinions, pompous, firm.

Nurturing Parent: standing over someone but leaning forward, arm or hand on person's shoulder, encouraging expression, soothing sounds, "let me do it for you", "you poor thing", caring, sympathetic, fussing.

Functional Adult: standing or sitting to obtain level eye contact, relaxed, asking questions, discussing probabilities, calm, rational, uninvolved, analytical.

Adapted Child: sitting very still, or fidgeting nervously, eyes downcast, looking out from under eyelashes, inattentive or very attentive, words like "want", "wish", "please", "thank you", swearing, polite, restrained, rebellious, withdrawn.

Natural Child: unselfconscious, sitting comfortably, curious, head on one side while thinking, enthusiastic, excited, happy, sad.

Afterwards, compare the results and discuss in plenary.

Activity 4.5 Ego States and Body Language
This is a fun activity. Invite the group to tell the trainer what body language to adopt for each ego state. As they give the instructions, act it out. Add in appropriate dialogue for extra impact.

See Activity 4.4 for ideas on what body language is appropriate.

This is a particularly good opportunity to demonstrate how participants feel drawn into Internal Child replays of being at school when you lean over to look at their written work.

Activity 4.6 Internal Ego State Questionnaire
As with Activity 4.2, the Internal Ego State Questionnaire in Appendix 7 can be purchased for use with participants. It should be treated as a light-hearted exercise in giving participants some self-awareness.

Have them complete the questionnaire, score it, and discuss it in pairs. Review any questions and comments.

Activity 4.7 Internal Egograms
Use the approach described in Activity 4.3 but for internal ego states. Ask participants to consider:

For Internal Adult – how much of the time are they aware of thinking logically about their own opinions (Internal Parent), how they feel (Internal Child), and what they want to achieve in relation to a current situation? Do they take all internal ego states into account or are they ignoring valuable past experiences and current emotional reactions?

For Internal Parent – how much do they draw on previous experiences, identify 'filed copies' of positive role models, and process this through Internal Adult, versus how frequently do they realise afterwards that they have been holding opinions without considering any alternatives, or even caught themselves forming judgements based on things said to them years ago by their parents, teachers or previous managers?

For Internal Child – how often are they in touch with genuine emotions, and then choose via Internal Adult to exhibit such emotions versus how often do they just react emotionally to something and forget to consider the potential consequences of their actions? How often do they feel like a small child again, and do they enjoy it, regret it or hide it?

Activity 4.8 Transactional Analysis

Form groups of five to eight. Brief them to prepare role plays, selecting from the suggestions below. Decide how many role plays to allocate each group, depending on how many groups you have, the time available, and their need to become familiar with the concepts.

Afterwards, have groups perform role plays in plenary, ask other participants to identify ego states, and deal with any queries.

First Set of options – allocate by type of transaction: ask for a typical scene at work that illustrates a complementary, a crossed and an ulterior transaction (and maybe a refracted transaction).

Second Set of options – allocate by ego state combinations: ask for typical scenes that demonstrate Functional Adult-Functional Adult, Nurturing Parent-Natural Child, Natural Child-Natural Child, Controlling Parent-Adapted Child, Nurturing Parent-Nurturing Parent, Controlling Parent-Controlling Parent, Adapted Child-Adapted Child.

Third Set of options – allocate your own scenes and leave the group to identify the ego states. Examples are: boss (male)-subordinate, boss (female)-subordinate, policeman and woman driver caught speeding, policewoman and man driver caught speeding, traffic warden and culprit (any mix of sexes), angry customer and service agent (any mix of sexes and also of ages).

Activity 4.9 Solving People Problems

An excellent way to bring ego states to life is to have participants design and conduct role plays of typical interactions at work. If possible, have at least two groups of four or more people.

Brief them to:
1. select a common situation where communication is unsatisfactory (preferably a situation one of them has actually experienced);
2. write down what happens and rehearse a role play;
3. analyse the transactions in terms of ego states;
4. select one party in the role play to bring about a more constructive result;
5. consider the likely effects of that person using a different ego state;
6. repeat this until each ego state has been considered;
7. select the best option and rehearse the new role play
8. make a note of the analysis of this version.

Groups then present their role plays to each other. Use the following process for maximum involvement and learning:

1. first group presents only their first version role play i.e. of the unsatisfactory interaction;
2. second group provides the analysis by identifying which ego states they have observed (remember to allow for the effects of poor acting);
3. first group then presents their role play of the interaction going well;
4. second group provides the analysis again.

The entire group discusses the two role plays and how they might use what they have learned. This process is repeated for each set of role plays.

Activity 4.10 A Committee of Ego States

Aim for groups of five if possible. Each group is to have a meeting for 30 minutes. During the meeting, they will practice using each behavioural ego state/personal style in turn for five minutes. Ask them to allocate the five ego states between themselves, and to rotate after each five minute slot. Give them a topic that requires no prior specialist knowledge and incorporates a potential mix of organisation (work) and fun (pleasure). Examples are planning a charity fund raising event or designing an outdoor training experience.

Afterwards, review to draw out:

- how they felt in each ego state
- which were hardest to adopt
- which were liked/not liked most by others
- what each ego state contributed
- what more could each ego state have contributed
- how each ego state caused problems
- how else might each ego state have caused problems
- what real life instances can they now understand better
- how they can apply the learning

Problems may include:

Controlling Parent – being bossy, insisting on doing it their way.
Nurturing Parent – fussing, worrying about taking care of everyone.
Functional Adult – dispassionately demolishing every idea.
Natural Child – being silly, preventing others from working.
Adapted Child – not participating, waiting to be asked.

Contributions and/or newly identified options may include:

Controlling Parent – structuring the meeting, controlling interruptions, ensuring any plans have control mechanisms built in.
Nurturing Parent – making sure everyone is heard, including aspects of nurturing in the plans.

Functional Adult – problem solving, identifying compromises, checking that plans seem logical.

Natural Child – humour, encouraging enjoyment of the task, creative ideas to include in the plans.

Adapted Child – being courteous, not interrupting, consideration of how acceptable plans will be to people outside the meeting.

NOTES & SOURCES

Ego states and transactional analysis (proper) were developed originally by Eric Berne. See the annotated booklist in Appendix 1.

Berne referred to structural analysis and functional analysis of ego states. Structural analysis concerns our development as individuals of a set of ego state systems. Functional analysis concerns how we use those systems.

This may be easier to understand if you think of the heart. The structure is about the physical state of the organ – is it healthy or diseased? Are the arteries closed? We may also be interested in knowing how any damage came about if we need to prescribe remedial activity. The functional is about how the heart operates – is it beating at an appropriate rate? Does it murmur, or skip occasional beats, or race? What is the blood flow like? We may be interested in what external events (e.g. exercise, stress) cause what variations in heart functioning. Of course, without a minimal level of structure and function, the heart stops beating and the owner is dead. Hence, we can only improve functioning to the level allowed by the structural soundness.

The internal and external sets of ego states I have described in this chapter are both aspects of the functional model. Structural will be addressed more in Chapter 10, Working with Change.

Somewhat confusingly, Berne used the same diagram of three stacked circles for both structural and functional. I have chosen to retain his model for behavioural ego states/personal styles (see below re changes of ego state labels) and to introduce a version with dotted lines to indicate internal ego states. Dotted lines were chosen because Berne used these to diagram ulterior transactions, which are 'under the surface' and cannot be observed directly.

I have written about our internal ego states as if they exist separately to us. This is only to illustrate the concept. They are more correctly processes that occur. Similarly, our behavioural or external ego states are in fact a series of snapshots of our behaviour.

If you or your participants read the TA literature, you are likely to encounter different labels for ego states. Controlling Parent is often referred to as Critical Parent or Prejudicial Parent. I dislike these terms because of their negative connotations. Free Child is an alternative label for Natural Child. I prefer Natural as a reminder that this ego state contains and generates sad and angry emotions as well as happy, carefree feelings.

Functional Adult is the term I have introduced to distinguish this style of behaviour from the 'Adult' described by Berne as being in the here-and-now.

Likewise, I have introduced the terms Internal Adult, Internal Parent and Internal Child to indicate that these are defined differently to similar labels within the TA literature.

'Little Professor' is a label Berne used originally to refer to the kind of thinking that infants do, before they develop true logical processes. It was a catchy name and has often been used as if it were an ego state in its own right. Strictly, it is part of the Internal Child and cannot be observed except through behaviour. There is more information about it in Chapter 10, Creativity and Innovation.

John Dusay was given the Eric Berne Memorial Scientific Award for the concept of egograms – see Appendix 2 for details.

CHAPTER 5:   WORKING STYLES

In this chapter I show how the TA concept of 'drivers', or sets of compulsive behaviours, can generate a simple but compelling framework for analysing our characteristic styles of working.

After describing the five styles that can be identified, I give ideas on how we can obtain the benefits of each whilst at the same time avoiding some of the pitfalls. Because our *working styles* affect so much of what we do, I have included sections on how they impact on our relationships as well as considering time management.

The time management aspects are covered in two ways: generally and specifically in terms of using a time management system. This is because the model adds considerably to our understanding of why people fail to use time management techniques even though they recognise that they should.

To increase trainer effectiveness, I explain how participants' different working styles are likely to show up in the classroom, followed by a description of the likely effects of the trainers' own style.

The activities section includes a mix of fun exercises and some that are more business-like. In addition to those related to working styles in general, I have included one that can be used for time management training. I have also included two questionnaires.

WORKING STYLES

There are a number of ways in which a framework about working styles can be of use. Our working styles affect everything we do: the way we organise our work, manage our time, how we function alongside others, our contribution to the team, our style of communication, even our sentence patterns. Our customary style has an impact whether we are alone or with others. Greater awareness can help us build on the strengths of our style and minimise any problems. It will also enable us to develop alternative modes so that our range of options is increased.

Several non-TA models for assessing or improving working styles exist but these are often related to specific situations, such as roles adopted in teams. Alternatively, there are approaches that focus on techniques and procedures for better control and organisation. They may also incorporate ideas for dealing with the people who interrupt us or cause our potential work overload. However, such procedural frameworks often overlook the importance of motivation and preferences. One time management system is unlikely to be suitable for everyone. One technique will not be used easily by everyone, nor will it work with everyone we apply it to.

DRIVERS

The TA concept of drivers provides an easy-to-use model of working styles that is readily recognised and applied in ways to suit different people. Based on original work by Taibi Kahler, it has been developed over the years into a relatively simple set of five characteristic styles. These were called drivers to reflect the 'driven', or compulsive, quality of them when we are under stress. Identified first in therapy settings, the styles can still be recognised in somewhat less extreme forms in each of us. They are subconscious attempts by us to behave in ways that will gain us the recognition we need from others; they are also programmed responses to the messages we carry in our heads from important people in the past.

The drivers have simple names that are descriptive of their characteristics: Hurry Up, Be Perfect, Please People, Try Hard and Be Strong. The same labels can therefore be used for the associated working styles. Participants accept the concept more readily when they hear that each style has advantages as well as drawbacks. They are more likely to admit to recognising themselves if they can lay claim to strengths as well as weaknesses. In this way, they increase their self-awareness; an essential first step towards identifying options for growth, increasing effectiveness and reducing levels of stress.

A driver is rather like a superstition. A part of us believes that if we avoid passing on the stairs, or cross our fingers when we are afraid, then we will be spared from some awful impending occurrence. In the same way, we operate as if a certain style of behaviour will ward off problems and earn us the respect of others. Unfortunately, this is a myth; the reality is that we can never do quite enough of whatever our driver calls for. In seeking to be more and more as we believe we should, we create problems. These in turn lead to us feeling more stressed, so we put even more energy into our driver behaviour, create more difficulties, and get yet more stressed. And so a vicious cycle is created.

On the other hand, our driver characteristics are often the things we did when children because they seemed to satisfy the grown-ups. When our stress levels are acceptable, the driver will appear as a strength. It is probable, therefore, that we will be known to others in terms of our style and how effective it is. If they have a different style, they may wish they were more like us (put them under pressure, however, and they may see only the negative aspects after all). If they share the same style, they will probably regard us even more highly. Bosses are likely to value subordinates more when there is a good match of working styles.

One important point to note is that drivers occur outside our awareness. Other people can infer that we are in driver mode by observing our behaviour. Even then, they would be wise to check for several indications before they decided this with certainty. The actual driver process is something which has been internalised over the years as we were growing up. We can identify our own drivers in a similar way, by checking for evidence from our behaviour. We can also examine our beliefs and compare them with the beliefs that other people hold. Where we have views which are not generally shared, then we can suspect a link with a driver.

In practice, identifying drivers is not as difficult as it might seem. Given a brief description of typical behaviour patterns, most of us can readily identify people who fit the stereotype for each. Provided we hear the advantages as well as the drawbacks, we will also happily admit to which drivers show up most in our own behaviour. There will usually be a lot of rueful laughter during a session on drivers as participants recognise the truth of the model.

To recap, the five working styles are:

Hurry Up   *Be Perfect*   *Please People*   *Try Hard*   *Be Strong*

They are not listed in any particular order; for organisational training purposes no style is more significant than another.

In the real world, people rarely fit into the neat boxes we finish up with when we simplify models such as this for ease of use. Few of us, therefore, will show all the characteristics of one style only with no signs of the others. Most of us will, however, find that we relate most to one or two of the styles. We will recognise aspects of the others in our behaviour but they will not be as significant for us. We will also be able to think of a few people who are the epitome of a style, and more who represent a combination.

Hurry Up

People with Hurry Up characteristics work quickly and get a lot done in a short time. Our major strength is the amount that we can achieve. We respond particularly well to short deadlines, and our energy peaks under pressure. We actually seem to enjoy having too many things to do. The saying "If you want something done, give it to a busy person" was probably invented with us in mind.

Our underlying motivation is to do things quickly, so we feel good if we can complete tasks in the shortest possible time. Like organisation and methods specialists, we look for the most efficient way to do work in the hope of shaving even a few minutes off each task. These few minutes can add up to significant time savings across the week. We also spend less time preparing than others do, giving us chance to meet more people and contribute more to the team.

However, give us time to spare and we delay starting until the job becomes urgent – then we start work on it. This can backfire because in our haste we make mistakes. Going back to correct the mistakes takes longer than doing the job right first time, so we may miss the deadline after all. At the least, the quality of our work may be poor because we have not left enough time to check it over or improve it. Our urge to save time may be inappropriately applied to everything we do, instead of being reserved for those tasks where it will make a real difference. Our ability to think fast may lead us to appear impatient. We speak rapidly and have a habit of interrupting others. We may even finish their sentences for them, often misunderstanding and getting involved in needless arguments. Our body language reflects our impatience through fidgeting, tapping with our fingers or toes, looking at our watch, and perhaps even sighing or yawning ostentatiously.

Our appointments get planned too close together, so we rush from one to another, arriving late and leaving early. We are likely to turn up at a meeting having left the necessary paperwork in our office; we may even fail to arrive because we didn't stop to check the location of the meeting. When we do arrive, others must wait while we are given a summary of what we missed. Our constant rushing coupled with an emphasis on task efficiency may prevent us from really getting to know people, so that we feel like an outsider.

A typical event for a Hurry Up is the time we approach a door that opens towards us, while we are carrying two cups of coffee. Most people would put one cup down, open the door, go through, put the cup down and then return to fetch the second cup. Not a Hurry Up, though. We juggle! Usually it's quicker. Every so often, it's a lot slower because we have to stop to clean up the coffee we spill. If you never get the coffees, imagine an armful of files to be picked up from the floor, or the pulled muscle from carrying too many bags of groceries in one trip from the car, or the piece of wood that is too short because you didn't check the measurement carefully before you sawed!

Be Perfect

Be Perfect people are as unlike Hurry Up's as can be. Be Perfect characteristics involve a quest for perfection – no errors, everything must be exactly right, first time. Our major strength is our reputation for producing accurate, reliable work. We check the facts carefully, we prepare thoroughly and we pay attention to the details. Our written work will look good because we aim for perfection in layout as well as content.

This working style means we are well organised because we look ahead and plan how to deal with potential problems. In this way, we are not taken by surprise but have contingency plans ready to put into effect. Our projects run smoothly and efficiently, with effective co-ordination and monitoring of progress.

Unfortunately, we cannot be relied on to produce work on time because we need to check it so carefully for mistakes, and this checking takes time. Because of our concentration on how something looks, we are likely to call for a whole series of relatively minor changes to layouts. Our concern about being seen to be wrong means we are reluctant to issue a draft rather than the final version, so opportunities for incorporating the ideas of others may be lost.

We are also likely to misjudge the level of detail required. We include too much information and have the effect of confusing the recipient. Our reports become lengthy; our sentence patterns also suffer whether we are writing or speaking. We have a tendency (as demonstrated here) to add in extra bits of information in parentheses; not so difficult for the reader (who can always glance at it again) but hard for a listener to follow. We choose our words carefully and may therefore use long, less familiar words or technical terms that others do not understand.

There is a danger that we end up doing everything ourselves because we do not trust others to do it right. We apply our high expectations constantly and fail to recognise when a lower standard would be appropriate and acceptable. This makes us poor delegators and may earn us a reputation for demotivating criticism. On the other hand, when we recognise the errors in our own work we may well feel worthless and not good enough even though others are satisfied with our performance.

The Be Perfect carries the coffees on a tray! The really Be Perfect even has a napkin on the tray to mop up any spills. And they never saw the wood too short; they check the measurements several times with a range of different measuring tapes, find they get different results, and postpone cutting the wood at all while they write to complain to the manufacturers of the measures!

Please People

Please people are the good team members. We enjoy being with other people and show a genuine interest in them. Our aim is to please other people without asking. We work out what they would like and then provide it. This working style means we are nice to have around because we are so understanding and empathic. We use intuition a lot and will notice body language and other signals that others may overlook.

We encourage harmony within the group and work at drawing the team closer together. We are the one most likely to invite the quieter members into the discussion so that their views are shared. This is especially useful when someone is not airing their concerns and might otherwise remain psychologically outside the group. At the same time, we are considerate of others' feelings and will not embarrass or belittle them.

Unfortunately, this style can have serious drawbacks because of our avoidance of the slightest risk of upsetting someone. We may worry so much about earning approval that we are reluctant to challenge anyone's ideas even when we know they are wrong. We may be so cautious with criticism that our information is ignored. Our own opinions and suggestions are so wrapped around with qualifying words that we seem to lack commitment to them.

We spend a lot of time smiling and nodding at people to indicate our agreement with them. Our own views are presented as questions only, with us ready to back off if they do not like what we are saying. Our facial expression is often questioning, with raised eyebrows and an anxious smile. We may be seen as lacking assertiveness, lacking critical faculties, lacking the courage of our convictions. When criticised by others, we may take it personally and get upset even when the comments are worded constructively.

Because we are reluctant to say no, we let people interrupt us and we are likely to accept work from them instead of concentrating on our own priorities. We hesitate to ask questions because we feel we should somehow know the answer, only to find out later that we've not done it the way they wanted. Our attempts to read people's minds often result only in us feeling misunderstood when they do not like the results.

Please People fetch the coffees frequently. They also open doors for other people who are carrying coffees, even those with only one cup to carry who could open the door themselves. Please People open the door long before you reach it with your coffee – or offer to carry the coffee for you anyway. And they want to know if you approve of the way they are about to saw the wood!

Try Hard

The Try Hard working style is all about the effort put into the task, so we tackle things enthusiastically. Our energy peaks with something new to do. People value our motivation and the way we have of getting things off the ground. We may be popular with colleagues in other sections, and with customers or clients, because of our enthusiastic approach to problem solving. Managers especially appreciate the fact that we often volunteer to take on new tasks.

Because of our interest in anything new and different, we may well be noted for the thorough way in which we follow up on all possibilities. Given a project to undertake, we will identify a whole range of ramifications and implications that should be taken into account. The result is that we pay attention to all aspects of a task, including some that other people may have overlooked.

However, we may be more committed to trying than to succeeding. Our initial interest wears off before we finish the task. Managers begin to realise that we are still volunteering for new projects even though we have not completed any of those tasks given to us previously. Our colleagues may come to resent the fact that we do the early, exciting parts of a project but then expect others to finish off the boring, mundane, detailed work.

We may fail to finish also because we spread our interest over too broad a range. Our attention to so many aspects makes the job impossibly large. Even if we complete most of it, we may still think up yet another angle to pursue before we can really agree that the job is done. Thus a small straightforward task may be turned into a major exercise, creating havoc with the time schedule. We miss the deadline or hand in a report full of items that are largely irrelevant. It is as if we are secretly making sure we do not succeed, so that we can just keep on trying.

Our communication with others may be pained and strained, as we frown a lot while we try to follow them. Our own sentences are likely to go off at tangents because we introduce new thoughts just as they come to mind. The listener becomes confused, both around the constantly changing content and about judging whether we have finished speaking. Sometimes we string questions together so the listener has to 'try' and sort out what to respond to. When asked questions, we may well answer a different question – a skill used deliberately by politicians but not so useful when it is outside our awareness.

Try Hards forget they were going to collect coffees because something more interesting occurs on the way. Or they stop to oil the door when they hear it squeaking – so the coffee gets cold. They change their mind about what the wood was for anyway and they may have several half-built items. Or they decide to redesign the saw or build a better workbench. They end up with lots of unused wood with saw marks!

Be Strong

Be Strong people stay calm under pressure. With this working style, we feel energised when we have to cope. Because we are so good at dealing with stressful situations, we are great to have around in a crisis. We are the ones who will keep on thinking logically when others may be panicking. We seem to be able to stay emotionally detached from the situation, enabling us to problem solve around difficult personal issues and to deal efficiently with people who are angry or distressed. We are able to make 'unpleasant' decisions without torturing ourselves with guilt about the effects of those decisions on others.

Because we are so good at staying calm and dealing with all that the job throws at us, we are seen as consistently reliable, steady workers. Our strong sense of duty ensures we will work steadily even at the unpleasant tasks. As supervisors, we are likely to handle staff firmly and fairly. We will give honest feedback and constructive criticism. We stay even-tempered so that people know what reaction to expect from us.

One problem with this style is that we hate admitting weaknesses – and we regard any failure to cope as a weakness. So we get overloaded rather than asking others for help. We may disguise our difficulties by 'hiding' work away; often our desk looks tidy but correspondence is filed away in a rather large pending tray. We may be highly self-critical about our shortcomings, as well as seeing it as weakness if other people ask for help.

Colleagues may feel uncomfortable about our lack of emotional responses. This may be especially pronounced in those situations where most of us would feel the strain. They may suspect that we are robots rather than human beings. It can be hard to get to know us when we seem to have no feelings.

Occasionally, someone with this style will appear to be very jovial and friendly. However, this will be a mask that prevents anyone from getting to know the real person beneath the superficial layer of jokes.

Our communication may reinforce the barriers to getting to know us. We are likely to use passive rather than active voice – "It occurred to me…" rather than "I thought…". We may depersonalise ourselves – "One often does…" rather than "I often do…". Our voice may be monotonous or dispassionate; our face may be expressionless. The observant person will spot that our smile does not extend from our mouth to our eyes. Deep down, we fear that we are unlovable so we avoid asking for anything lest it be refused.

Be Strongs are very matter-of-fact about having coffee. They get coffee when they are thirsty. They carry only one cup because they get it for themselves. This means opening the door is not a problem. Neither is sawing a piece of wood. Be Strongs never have problems – they specialise in coping with anything. If the saw breaks and cuts them, they apply a tourniquet and finish what they were doing before driving themselves to the hospital!

Getting the Benefits of Working Styles

You may well have recognised bits of yourself in each of the styles. Look more closely, though, and you will probably find that one, or maybe two, of the styles fits more closely. Consider what matters most to you: to be quick, to be perfect, to get on with people, to tackle new tasks, or to be calm. How have you approached the task of reading this chapter about working styles: have you skimmed through in a hurry; considered each slowly and carefully; been most interested in ways to improve your relationships; been keen to see if there are new ideas in it; or wondered what all the fuss is about?

What can you do with your increased awareness? The next step is to set out consciously to obtain the advantages of your preferred working styles(s) without the potential problems. What is needed is a conscious choice of options, followed by a period of practice as we become competent with the new techniques.

If you are Hurry Up:
- plan your work in stages, setting interim target dates
- concentrate on listening carefully to others until they finish speaking
- learn relaxation techniques and then use them regularly

If you are Be Perfect:
- set realistic standards of performance and accuracy
- practice asking yourself what the consequences really are – do this whenever you find a mistake
- make a point of telling others that their mistakes are not serious

If you are Please People:
- start asking people questions to check what they want instead of guessing
- please yourself more often, and ask other people for what you want
- practice telling other people firmly when they are wrong

If you are Try Hard:
- stop volunteering
- make a plan that includes finishing a task – and then stick to that plan through to a conclusion
- check out the parameters of a task so that you do only what is expected

If you are Be Strong:
- keep a task and time log so that you can monitor your workload
- ask other people to help you
- take up a spare-time activity that you can really enjoy

A word of warning, however. When we want to make changes to the way we behave, we need to remember that our boss, colleagues and customers may like us just the way we are. And we get lots of recognition for being like that. When we change we can help ourselves by being aware that we may miss some of the recognition we are used to. Others may resist our changes so we need to plan to deal with these barriers. We need to make sure that we get our new behaviours reinforced by ourselves and other people.

Here are a few ideas:
- Hurry Ups get praised for being quick; so set out to get recognition for accuracy as well.
- Be Perfects get praised for accuracy; look for recognition for meeting deadlines and appropriate levels of detail.
- Everybody thinks Please People are nice; aim for recognition for being assertive.
- Try Hard people score points for enthusiasm; get recognition for finishing tasks – successfully.
- Be Strong people often get low-key recognition for not needing help; watch how relationships improve when you let people help you.

Remember also that it may be useful to acquire some of the other working styles if you recognise you are heavily into one or two only.

WORKING STYLES IN ACTION
Working Styles and Relationships

Different combinations of working styles will have different effects on relationships. We are likely to have a higher regard for people who share our own orientation. We will also find it easier to understand them, and to empathise with their problems. Even our sentence patterns will match. Hurry Ups will talk rapidly to each other, interrupt each other, and make quick decisions together. Be Perfects will speak carefully, with plenty of long words and specialist jargon, and arrive at considered decisions together. Please People will be very polite to each other, keep checking that the other party is comfortable with the discussion, and aim to find compromises. Try Hards will explore many alternatives, go off at tangents, fail to finish their sentences, and make decisions enthusiastically. Be Strongs will resemble poker players, give little away about how they feel, and make pragmatic, logical decisions.

One danger with compatible working styles is omission. We need a variety of styles to compensate for the potential negative elements of each. A Hurry Up will add necessary urgency for a Be Perfect who is in danger of missing a deadline, and prompt a Be Strong to request help to save time. A Be Perfect will stop the Hurry Up from rushing into an expensive mistake, and encourage the Try Hard to finish what they started. Please People will stop the Hurry Up from pushing others into hasty decision. Try Hard will provide Be Strong with the animation they fail to show; stimulate the Hurry Up to consider more options, and respond enthusiastically to the tentative ideas of Please People. Be Strong will highlight the need to complete the mundane tasks that the Try Hard tends to overlook, invite the Hurry Up to be less frenetic, and the Please People to be less anxious.

Unfortunately, we do not always attain the benefits of complementary styles. Instead, we are just as likely to have relationship problems when our styles differ. Our incompatibility generates stress; stress sends us more deeply into driver behaviour; the more locked in we get, the more stressed we get. The more stressed we are, the less we are able to tolerate the differences in others. The scene is then set for problems.

Consider a Hurry Up boss who has a Be Perfect subordinate. The subordinate is producing a report. The deadline has arrived (it was a short deadline anyway because the Hurry Up boss did not think the job should take long). The Be Perfect has not finished the report. Indeed, they would like another week to double-check some of the data in the appendices, to amend the layout and run off a reprint, to have the diagrams produced professionally and to consider options for how the report might be bound. The boss was expecting a draft report, which will be combined with the work of others to form a final proposal to a customer. There is a meeting tomorrow at which senior managers will determine the content of the final document.

Imagine the conversation which takes place: the boss asking impatiently for the report; interrupting when the subordinate tries to explain the need for more time; complaining that it has taken too long already; and finally demolishing the subordinate by pointing out that only a rough draft is needed. The subordinate, meanwhile, is deciding that the boss clearly has no interest in quality; is incapable of allocating a realistic time to an important task; is bad-mannered and refuses to listen to a reasonable request for more time; and, horror of horrors, is proposing to show imperfect work to senior managers who will get a totally wrong picture of the standards of the subordinate.

Other examples of problem areas include Try Hards wondering why Be Strongs show so little enthusiasm; Please People types trying desperately to read the minds of Be Strongs so that they can please them; Be Strongs observing uncomprehendingly the anxiety of Please People types about not upsetting anyone; Be Perfect's frustration at the tendency of Try Hards to leave jobs unfinished; Try Hard's resentment at Be Perfects who insist they do the boring part of the task.

WORKING STYLES AND TIME MANAGEMENT

The five working styles give us invaluable insights into what happens to our management of time. We can then identify specific actions to redress the balance. It may be that we need to select from more than one style to create our own time management plan. Remember that each style will have its advantages as well as its pitfalls.

If we are Hurry Up, to avoid mistakes we need to plan sufficient time for tasks, especially the preparation which we are so inclined to skimp. To avoid appearing impatient, we should consciously slow down so that other people have time to absorb the information. We must stop interrupting them and concentrate on listening. It can be very helpful to remember to ask about their needs instead of making assumptions, and to paraphrase back to check our understanding. If we feel we lack real contact with others, we could plan our arrival or departure times to allow us to join in the socialising that goes on before and after meetings.

If we are Be Perfect, we need to relax more and accept that human beings, including ourselves, are not capable of total perfection. Making mistakes is an important source of learning. Prioritising is required so that we can decide which jobs really warrant such high levels of accuracy. We must also understand that deadlines are important to others and that we should keep sight of the objective. We need to plan to finish on time instead of using too much of the time to plan. Check how much detail is enough; then give the key information and stop before we bury people in facts and figures.

If we are Please People, to avoid being dumped with unrealistic requests and unimportant tasks, we need to learn to say no skilfully. It's important that we set our own limits and our own priorities if we are to be respected by others. How much credibility will our "yes" have if they never hear us say "no"? Basic assertiveness techniques will help us to handle customers and colleagues – a firm refusal, said politely, is often all that is needed to maintain reasonable boundaries.

If we are Try Hard, we need to control our tendency towards boredom with the later stages of projects. We, even more than the other styles, can benefit from positive programming into our diary of all aspects of the task. Once we finish a project, we can usefully spend time enjoying the feeling of success so that we will want to repeat it. Sometimes we can find creative ways of making mundane tasks more exciting. Sometimes we simply need to get on with them in spite of our boredom.

If we are Be Strong, we may have the hardest working style to identify in ourselves. Our potential weaknesses may be well hidden. Before we take on new tasks, we should review the potential requirements and check we have access to the appropriate resources. We also need to recognise that there is nothing wrong with asking for help sometimes. Others may well have relevant skills, knowledge, time or enthusiasm for the tasks we are doing, and will welcome the opportunity to contribute.

Using a Time Management System

Our working styles have a direct bearing on the way we use a time management system.

Hurry Up people are usually too impatient to get the full benefit from such a system. They start using the system before taking time to work out the most appropriate way of setting it up to match their work. Without clear sections, they record items hastily and then cannot find them again. Hurry Ups are also the ones most likely to keep many scraps of paper with notes on that they have been too rushed to transcribe into the system.

Hurry Ups are probably better off with a very simple system that allows them a quick sort into a few categories, with no need to transcribe. Carrying a pad of stick-it sheets means that notes can then be attached simply to the correct page. Computerised systems probably take too long for comfort to log into.

Be Perfect people have 'perfect' time management systems. They keep them so accurately and neatly that it uses up a lot of time just making the entries. One problem is designing the 'ultimate' category system. A Be Perfect will be reluctant to use the system at all until they are certain they have made it foolproof. They may spend an inordinate amount of time on this. If they subsequently realise that their arrangement is not quite perfect, they may feel compelled to start all over again and spend hours transferring their data across.

Be Perfects need to review the available systems before choosing one that fits their needs best. They could also look for a system that allows customising. They will probably enjoy a computerised system that automatically amends and updates every time an entry is made. If a Be Perfect is using a manual system, they need to use a pencil so they can erase when things change.

Please People worry about whether they are using their time management system in the way they are supposed to. They look at other people's systems to check if their own is all right. They have real problems using pre-set pages for anything other than the original intention, so they are limited in how far they can personalise a system.

Please People types need to stop worrying about what other people think is right. They should choose a system only because they like it themselves; not adopt one just because everyone else has. Once they have a system, Please People need to give themselves permission to do just as they like with it. Using coloured pages or affixing adhesive cartoon characteristics will help to reinforce their right to be individualistic.

Try Hard people are likely to go from one time management system to another. Each system lasts only until they lose interest. They may be very enthusiastic at first, demonstrating their great new system to everyone else. However, they somehow keep not quite getting around to the mundane aspects of deciding how to operate the system in detail. So then they discover another, better system and start again, and again...

Try Hard people need variety in their time management system. A system which allows them to add new features from time to time will maintain their interest. They also need a system with the minimum of detailed recording. They will probably benefit from computerised project management systems that prompt them to cover all significant aspects of the task.

Be Strong people are likely to wonder why anyone needs a time management system in the first place. They may secretly believe that a good memory should be enough. If their work is very involved, then a straightforward system will be seen as appropriate. Having got a system, then entries must be made promptly and conscientiously, regardless of the circumstances.

Be Strong people should select a system that is very practical. If manual, they will prefer something in a plain yet serviceable cover. If computerised, they will not want too many enhancements to the basic system. Any instructions for the system must be clear and logical, so that they do not have to ask for any assistance in setting up.

TRAINER EFFECTIVENESS
Working Styles in the Classroom

As a trainer, you will be on the receiving end of the working styles of your participants. Recognising this, you can be prepared for many of the common problems that arise during training sessions. You can make a point of communicating with and recognising the talents of particular participants so that you establish good rapport with them. Finally, you can plan your sessions to avoid unnecessary stress for participants, and hopefully avoid inadvertently inviting them into negative, driver behaviour.

You can often identify Hurry Up participants right at the start of the course – they arrive late. They may have got lost on their way to the course because they left their joining instructions behind. Sometimes they will come and tell you they have to leave early, too, because of prior commitments or because they are so busy that they can only spare a few hours for training. Other times you will notice that they have brought work with them and are writing memos or similar during your lectures. They will talk fast, may be the quickest to answer any questions you ask, will grasp points quickly and want to race ahead, and at the end they may well rate the course as being too long.

Give them extra work to do to use up their spare capacity. Expect them to be able to take the notes for the group, let them operate the video equipment for you, have extra reading available. Encourage them to get as much as they can out of the training, by providing options at a more advanced level. When working alone with them, match their voice speed. Watch out for and correct the misunderstandings when they jump to conclusions. Compliment them on the rate at which they absorb information.

Be Perfects are likely to point out the errors in the joining instructions. They will also notice any mistakes on notice boards. They will let you know about any typing errors in your handouts. When asked to do something, they will check to make sure they have correctly understood your instructions. You may have to repeat things for them, and they may want to repeat whatever they are doing several times before they are satisfied with their own accomplishment.

Be patient and thank them for helping you to correct your joining instructions, notices, handouts, briefings. Use the information they give you to amend your documents so that future Be Perfect participants will be impressed by your accuracy. Resist any temptation to point out that the errors are insignificant. Make it clear that you appreciate their eye for detail. Remember that other participants may be confused by errors but may not tell you so.

Please People may well seem anxious. They will check whether they have arrived for the correct course, at the right time, in the right room. These are the ones who will ask what they should wear for meals on residential programmes. When briefed on activities, they may seek more information on how you want it done; 'how' will be as important to them as 'what'. In syndicate work, they may be torn between doing what they believe you want and going along with the rest of their group. They are the most likely to offer to help you, or to bring you coffee.

Reassure them, repeatedly. When you want them to work something out for themselves, explain that this is a necessary part of the teaching method. Warn them (preferably before they pack for a residential course) if there are any dress requirements, encourage them to help other participants as long as this does not interfere with their own learning, and then thank them for being a good team member.

Try Hard participants may well have volunteered to attend without prompting from their manager. They are likely to have opted for more training courses than their colleagues. Check whether they have put any of that learning into practice. At the end, they may well ask you to suggest even more courses they could attend. During your sessions, they will start enthusiastically but then want to move on to the next topic without finishing each stage.

Respond to their enthusiasm. Be enthusiastic yourself about whatever you are teaching. Make sure, however, that you do not go off on tangents with them. Stick to your prepared programme; offer to cover extra topics individually with them during breaks or only if there is time at the end. Be prepared to give brief answers to questions about unusual aspects of your subject. Let them see that you are excited by their enthusiasm and wish you had more time to follow up their ideas.

You may well identify Be Strongs only by the apparent lack of indicators of other styles. They will appear calm, logical, straightforward. Watch out for signs that they have not understood. They will not tell you so. Check how friendly you feel towards them; if you are neutral it may well be because they are showing few real feelings.

Remember that Be Strongs will not ask for help, so check their work – without making it obvious that you are doing so. Emphasise that people often find certain aspects difficult, so that they can admit that they too are struggling. Make it clear that the trainer is there to help; if it were easy to learn alone you would be out of a job. Behave in a matter-of-fact way, especially when they need assistance.

Note: see also Chapter 2, Contracting for Learning, for ideas on how to use the concept of working styles to review and tighten up on participants' action plans at the end of a course.

Trainer Styles

See if you can spot yourself below.

Hurry Up trainers design things at the last minute. They work from outline notes only. They are always rushing, with too much to do. They expect their students to accomplish far more than is possible in the time available. Every so often, they get the timings wrong and their handouts are not ready in time. Or they don't stop to check their equipment, which then lets them down on the day. Their visual aids are likely to be handwritten, often during the session itself.

Be Perfect trainers prepare, and prepare, and prepare. Their lecture notes are neat and thorough. They take a long time deciding their course content and training methods, and then refuse to change them for anyone. Their sessions are timed to the minute. They overload their students with far too much detailed information. They use long words, and long sentences that participants find hard to follow. Their visual aids are immaculate.

Please People trainers want everyone to be pleased with them. They check their work with the training manager and with their colleagues. They can't wait to see the course evaluation forms, to make sure the students have rated them highly. They are reluctant to give constructive criticism to students in case they become unpopular. They may change the content and structure of a session just because students ask them to, instead of insisting on good teaching practice.

Try Hard trainers include everything remotely connected with the subject. Indeed, if they can they will teach all the different courses available in the training school. They work at a superficial level only, as they tend to become bored with a subject before they can become an expert. Having designed a course, they only want to run it once before moving on or changing it completely. They become extremely enthusiastic, for a short time, about each new training approach.

Be Strong trainers accept a heavy workload so they can suffer in silence. They like to feel that they are coping better than anyone else could. They prefer to work alone and avoid asking the other trainers for help. They seem unapproachable so students do not come to them with problems. They cannot understand why anyone, trainer or student, should feel nervous or worried during a training session.

Of course, these are caricatures. However, there were probably items which resonated for you. The more you become aware of your own style, or mix of styles, the easier you will find it to deal with 'difficult' participants. Keep notes of any problems you have in the classroom. Work out what style you think the participant was exhibiting. Contrast this with your own style. Use the information to plan better ways of handling such interactions in the future.

ACTIVITIES

Activity 5.1 Elephants and Giraffes

This is a children's game that can be used to give participants some idea of their likely drivers. It will only be suitable for people who expect learning to be fun, and who are reasonably relaxed with each other. It requires space for the group to stand in a circle. It is best used only where others cannot hear what is happening in the classroom, as it gets rather noisy and may not be appreciated by those outside the course if you are working in a staid organisation.

The group stands in a circle, with one person in the centre who closes their eyes, spins round, opens their eyes, points at someone and calls "elephant" or "giraffe". Three people should then react. The one pointed at must move their arms to resemble the animal called: one arm up in the air to represent the neck of a giraffe; one arm forwards and curved to form the trunk of an elephant. The people on either side must also move. They put one arm down to represent the leg of a giraffe, or one arm curled round to form the ear of an elephant. Obviously, they must remember to do this with the arm nearest the individual between the two of them.

Whoever of the three moves most slowly, or makes a mistake, is then required to change places with the person in the middle. The process is then repeated several times.

The trainer then explains how to recognise drivers: Hurry Ups want to start playing the game without hearing the rules explained, they make snap decisions on who moved most slowly, and get impatient with people who play too slowly. Be Perfects want to understand the rules exactly, they want the circle to be properly round, and they get annoyed if anyone if flippant about how to play the game. Please People types worry about whether they are doing it right, and they worry about anyone else who does not seem to be enjoying themselves. Try Hards are initially very enthusiastic, then want to play a different game, or to redesign this one (a Try Hard was responsible for adding in penguins once). Be Strongs think the whole business is silly and childish, join in only because to do so is less embarrassing than making a fuss, and are relieved when it is over.

Warning – some participants will simply enjoy the game. Trainers will need to ask them to imagine how they would have responded if they had not felt so comfortable.

Activity 5.2 Planning for Benefits

Provide participants with a handout containing suggested actions, such as the options and reinforcements suggested earlier in this chapter (p102-3). Brief them to prepare individual action plans with the aim of maximising the benefits of their current styles, and acquiring aspects of other styles that they rarely use.

Activity 5.3 Typical Interactions

Ask participants to devise and act out roleplays of typical interactions between various combinations of working styles, e.g. Be Perfect and Hurry Up, Be Strong and Please People. Where appropriate, the trainer could specify that the interactions are between close colleagues, colleagues with different functions, between boss and subordinate, or with customers or clients.

Optionally, require groups to produce two roleplays, to demonstrate an unsuccessful interaction and then to show how one of the parties could behave differently in order to achieve a better result.

Activity 5.4 A Meeting of Styles

With a group of five or six, ask participants to have a meeting. If possible, specify an objective that combines work and social aspects, such as planning an annual departmental event that could involve entertainment and meals together as well as formal lectures and business update sessions. Allow 30 minutes in all. Instruct participants to allocate a different working style to each person. They are to adopt that style for the first five minutes of the meeting. After each five minute segment, styles are rotated so that each participant experiments with each style in turn. If there are six participants, one person in each round is allowed to 'be themselves'.

Review afterwards to draw out;
- how similar to a normal meeting the activity felt (usually it seems very like the real thing, especially to an observer);
- how easy it was to adopt each working style;
- how this might be related to each participant's usual behaviour;
- which styles individuals found hardest to work with;
- what participants can do to increase the range of styles available to them

Activity 5.5 Time Management

Use pen pictures such as those in Appendix 8, without indicating which style is which, to stimulate discussion around time management issues.

Activity 5.6 Working Styles Questionnaire

The questionnaire at Appendix 9 can be purchased for the use with participants. As with the other questionnaires in this book, brief participants that completion is simply to give them a better idea of their styles and is not to be taken as a definitive psychological diagnosis!

Once they have completed and scored the questionnaire shown in Appendix 9, have them review their results in pairs or small groups.

Prompt them to consider what the results indicate for their relationships at work – and to consider any changes they might usefully make. The key outcomes are:

- to value their own most exhibited working style(s)
- to bring it into awareness so they can choose when a working style is appropriate – and avoid slipping into driver
- to develop their ability to use the full range of styles, and thereby increase their ability to interact effectively with a wider range of people.

Activity 5.7 Manager Working Styles Questionnaire

The questionnaire at Appendix 10 is similar to that at Appendix 9 but rewritten so that participants answer the questions about how their manager behaves instead of themselves.

Once completed and scored, they can compare the manager's working styles with their own. This may help them understand the dynamic of their relationship with their manager. They can also consider how they might change the way they interact with the manager so as to better fit in with the manager's preferences – and hence improve the working relationship.

Again, a review in pairs may be helpful, although you may need to take care that the partners do not know the managers under consideration.

NOTES & SOURCES

The content of this chapter is based on work by Taibi Kahler which comes within a topic he calls 'process communication'. Drivers are the unhelpful manifestation of characteristic behaviours. Drivers appear under stress so are generally the prelude to bad feelings. I gave more detail about this unpleasant aspect in Chapter 3, Understanding Attitudes. An early article by Kahler on this topic was *Drivers: The Key to the Process of Scripts* in _Transactional Analysis Journa_l 5:3. July 1975

CHAPTER 6:   THINKING STYLES

The previous two chapters looked mainly at behaviour, with some explanation of what happens inside people. This chapter now focuses on that other dimension – the internal, or intrapersonal, processes that occur within us – and on the impact of these in our problem solving and decision making. This internal functioning can be speculated about, guessed at, planned for, and yet cannot be observed directly.

I begin by developing further the model of *internal ego states*, to show how these operate as filing systems and also jointly as a mechanism for identifying and choosing between options. Included are explanations of internal dialogue, of how some ego states are excluded from our thinking, how we may seek to have someone else do our thinking for us, and how our thinking may be contaminated. Also outlined is a structured decision making sequence that ensures each ego state is involved constructively.

I next introduce the *racket system* – the description of a thinking process that takes us round closed loops so that we find it hard to take a fresh approach to many of the problems we face. I show how this is related to the *life positions* described earlier, to the observable behaviour, and to the responses of others, and give some ideas on how to bring about change.

Discounting is an alternative way of understanding why we limit our thinking. I describe six common patterns of overlooking, or discounting, what is happening and what is possible. For this too I include some suggestions for how to use this concept to be more effective in helping others solve their problems. I will also relate it to the common organisational problem of absenteeism.

In the trainer effectiveness section, I suggest ways that each of the frameworks can be used to understand better the thinking processes of participants and of trainers. Finally, there is the usual selection of activities followed by the notes and sources.

INTERNAL EGO STATES

The simplest TA approach to thinking skills is that of ego states. I have already described this model generally, in Chapter 4 Interpersonal Styles, and I use it again with particular reference to creativity in Chapter 11 Creativity and Innovation. For understanding our thinking and decision making processes, we need to concentrate on the internal set of ego states and the concept of internal dialogues.

The elementary ego state model has three parts, or systems: Internal Parent, Internal Adult and Internal Child. Our thinking is based on the contents and structures of these three plus the interaction that occurs between them, as shown in Figure 6.1

Internal Parent

Our Internal Parent operates as a filing system for the incredible range of things that we know – facts, figures, patterns, beliefs, principles – all our knowledge and experience of the world. Most of this has been 'taught' to us, either directly as rules for living or indirectly as we have observed and copied those around us. Over the years we have moved some of this information to 'archives' because we judge that it is no longer relevant. A great deal still remains readily available to us, providing a basis for decision making.

Many times a day we will make our decisions without noticing we have done so. This happens when we rely on our Internal Parent ego state to contain something relevant already; we merely scan rapidly through our mind's filing system and use the decision we made last time. A major difficulty with this is that our records may be outdated so that our subsequent action is ineffective. A significant advantage is that it saves time if we can recycle an earlier sequence.

When we consciously consider a decision, we have to select from the past which recordings will be most applicable to our current situation. Over the years we have decided what is important to us and what can be disregarded. We also have the facility to update our Parent

Figure 6.1: Internal Ego State Thinking

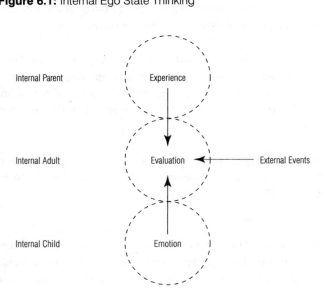

continually; we are likely to do this each time we make a decision that is not based in the past, recording at the same time whether the new decision was successful or not.

Internal Child

Current activity in Internal Child involves our needs, wants and feelings. It provides our emotional responses to each situation. When thinking or decision making, Child's input concerns how we feel about the potential options. There will be internal support for a decision which gets us what we want, takes account of our anxieties, results in a good feeling for us. There will be internal resistance to decisions which might have unpleasant consequences for us. Such consequences might include being left without something we want, incurring the wrath of another person, losing status in the eyes of our colleagues, having to work late instead of going out with friends for the evening – any of the things which are so important to our human spirit.

Our memory banks for Internal Child contain recordings of how we felt in the past. As new situations occur, we may 'rubber-band' back into these old recordings without being aware of it. We will repeat an old emotional response as if it were occurring in the present. This will seriously undermine the effectiveness of our thinking as it will be based on out-of-date feelings.

Internal Adult

Internal Adult ego state has a different quality to Parent or Child. It gives us our ability to think in the sense that separates us from animals; we can think about ourselves thinking. Internal Adult allows us to process information from different sources, to take account of both external and internal considerations, and to know that we are doing so.

In decision making it can be likened to the referee, seeing the events personally by watching the players and checking internally by asking the linespeople for their perspectives. Unlike a referee, however, Internal Adult also takes account of the situation we are in. We take in data from the environment, including noting the reactions or potential reactions of other people to any actions we might take – rather like the referee who calls off the match when the crowd invades the pitch, except that this is an exception for them whereas a well-functioning Internal Adult ego state routinely monitors the external situation. Thus, Internal Adult balances the events around us against our responses in terms of beliefs and feelings, evaluates, and then comes to a conclusion.

For instance, we may spot a potentially workable solution but decide not to pursue it. Perhaps we are short of money and see a way to inflate our expense claim. Although our Internal Adult sees the logic of the situation, our Internal Parent may veto it because it is dishonest. Alternatively, our Internal Parent may raise no objections because we believe our employer is a crook anyway and deserves to be swindled. However, our Internal Child may then object due to a fear of being caught. Our Internal Adult will weigh up the degree of risk before making the final decision.

Internal Dialogues

Imagine yourself standing inside a shop. You are facing a counter on which are several jackets in a style and colour that you find most attractive. You have recently moved house and are now hard pressed to maintain your mortgage payments. In two weeks' time you have to attend an event at which one of these jackets would be most suitable. You hope for promotion soon, with a corresponding increase in salary. Next week is your birthday. The shop you are in is noted for its policy of providing refunds if goods are returned without being worn. You have been working long hours recently and feel that you deserve a reward.

The paragraph above is an example of an internal dialogue. It is a conversation, inside your head, between different ego states. Anyone watching you would see only a silent person standing before a shop counter. We can track and analyse the dialogue:

Internal Child	There are several jackets in a style and colour that you find most attractive. (you want one)
Internal Parent	You have recently moved house and are now hard pressed to maintain your mortgage payments. (you have more important things to spend your money on)
Internal Adult	In two weeks' time you have to attend an event at which one of these jackets would be most suitable. (there is a need for a jacket)
Internal Child	You hope for promotion soon, with a corresponding increase in salary. (you hope so and want to gamble on it)
Internal Adult	The shop you are in is noted for its policy of providing refunds if goods are returned without being worn. (you can take the jacket now and return it if no extra money materialises)
Internal Parent	You have been working long hours recently and deserve a reward. (look after yourself)

What decision would you make?

Much of our thinking consists of internal dialogues, as if we are having a meeting of ego states in our head. The more we apply good meeting techniques, such as letting everyone have a chance to speak and be listened to, the more effective our thinking. Internal paraphrasing and summarising are also useful for making sure our ego states really understand each other.

Exclusions

If we do not listen to ourselves internally, an ego state may be *excluded* from the thinking process. When this happens, we are denied an important part of the input we need for a balanced result. Because exclusion operates as if the ego state does not exist, we will be unaware that we are not operating on the full set.

Exclusion of Internal Parent will mean we lack access to previous relevant experiences and the knowledge that goes with them. We will have to think the situation through as if it had never been encountered before. At the very least, this will waste a lot of time. It will probably also result in significant aspects being overlooked.

This may happen, for instance, when we fail to spot the relevance of some previous occasion to what is happening currently. Managing a project team and managing a family holiday is a typical example. There are many people who happily plan camping holidays where they have to bring together people and resources: tents, cookers, bedding, clothes, food, utensils have to be brought together and loaded into a suitable vehicle in such a way that people can also travel. They then work out an itinerary and get to where they can pitch the tent. They even manage to (mostly) keep the team happy during the holiday, intervene in squabbles, get agreement on what shall we do today, and organise the whole lot safely back home again. And they may well do all of this while it keeps raining!

Ask such a person to lead a project team for the first time and they may well respond with concern... "I've never done anything like that.... Do you think I could.... I've no managerial experience..." In reality, they have done a great deal of it before – planning, organising, co-ordinating, delegating, leadership, motivation, problem solving, decision making, chairing meetings – it's just that we don't use the same labels for family activities.

Exclusion of Internal Child will result in lack of attention to how we feel about the situation. Our decisions may be highly logical but will ignore any emotional responses associated with carrying them out. Decisions that lead to overwork are often made in this mode; our normal feelings of tiredness are repressed.

If we exclude our own Internal Child from decision making, we may well overlook the significance of it as far as other people are concerned. A manager may decide to introduce a new system without recognising that staff may react negatively because it interferes with their enjoyment.

Switching a restaurant from table service to buffet is such an example. Many waiters and waitresses like the contact that they have with the diners, as they take orders, lay out cutlery, and deliver food and beverages to them. Having a buffet eliminates much of this contact. It may be a logical decision financially; it may suit the customer in a hurry better too. However, if staff feelings are not taken into account when the new approach is planned, the best staff may leave or become demotivated while the worst make the most of the excuse not to have to talk to customers.

Exclusion of Internal Adult occurs when our Parent opinions or Child feelings are especially powerful. When this happens, we make our decisions without an adequate evaluation of the current situation and the available options. We may insist on obsolete working practices because they were effective in the past, or opt to spend our money on an expensive new car when we are already in debt.

When I was appointed to manage a unit in a local authority many years ago, I acquired a member of staff who refused to do the work I allocated to him. On realising that here was a 'subordinate' refusing to follow the directions of a 'superior' (a heinous crime then in a local authority), my manager decided that the member of staff must be removed from my section. So he promoted him! That was the way men had always been moved to other sections. I never succeeded in getting the manager to see how illogical that decision was, nor recognise that such moves were meant to be associated with good performance, not bad.

Sometimes it will seem as if only part of an ego state is missing. We may function normally most of the time yet occasionally seem to overlook the obvious. This phenomenon may also be understood as discounting, which is a process whereby we overlook some aspect of a situation or a person (including ourselves). Discounting is explained in more detail later in this chapter.

Symbiotic Thinking

Exclusion may also be the result of an interaction or be a customary style within a relationship. This is similar to the hierarchy of ego states described in Chapter 4 Interpersonal Styles. When exclusion occurs like this, it is known as *symbiosis*, a term used in TA to mean that two people are sharing one set of ego states between them.

We can apply this idea to thinking as well as to interacting. In such a case, one person will provide the 'thinking' from Internal Parent, and possibly Internal Adult although this ego state is often missing altogether. The other person supplies the 'thinking' from Internal Child. The opinions and past experiences of one will be coupled with the feelings and wishes of the other. Each will feel unable to make a decision on their own; together they will engage in symbiotic thinking as shown in Figure 6.2. The Child will generate the need and the Parent will find the solution – for example by providing detailed guidance so that no initiative is required. Note that they are likely to interact in the same behavioural ego states as they are internally – Controlling Parent will tell Adapted Child what to do.

Contamination

Our thinking will be *contaminated* if the detail that belongs in one ego state 'leaks' into another. This occurs with Internal Parent or Internal Child being regarded incorrectly as Internal Adult. We then engage in a distorted thinking process and believe we are being logical.

Figure 6.2: Symbiotic Thinking

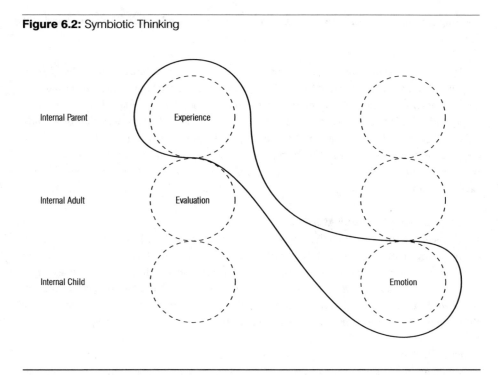

When Internal Parent contaminates Internal Adult, we perceive our opinions as being facts. We fail to recognise the assumptions we are making. We are likely to justify our conclusions by quoting spurious connections, such as arguing that we must be right this time because we were right in the past. Prejudices are contaminations; we may quote from the specific to the general and claim that one negative incident proves that a whole racial group are suspect. We may sound Functional Adult as we make our point and this often misleads people who don't pay enough attention to the content of what gets said.

At a less serious level, my mother provides a good example of Internal Parent contamination. She is convinced that only leading experts write books, and that what is contained in a book is therefore true. (Now you see why I began this book with a comment about impressing her!) What has happened here is that, many years ago, there were fewer books and therefore it was quite feasible that one book on a subject contained all that was known at the time. Nowadays, there are many books, people express different views in them, and there are even books written specifically to summarise and compare competing theories. It is a long time, though, since my mother read textbooks.

When Internal Child contaminates Internal Adult, our emotions cloud our judgement. We believe we are being logical because we have convinced ourselves that everyone must feel as we do. If we were badly treated at school, we cannot see how anyone could enjoy a training course. We justify selfishness because we were denied a share in the past and still feel resentful.

Lest you think I favour one parent, let me use an example here related to my father. When he was a child, food was short, especially the sort of treats that we take for granted nowadays. So, he is inclined to discourage the rest of us from eating all of the cake. He likes to save a piece, which he puts carefully away – and then forgets about! At intervals, a slice of mouldy cake will be found in a tin at the back of the larder and thrown away. His feelings of deprivation from the past are still strong and he believes, therefore, that it is logical to put some cake safely aside for later. He has not updated this belief with the fact that there is now plenty of such food in the house, so his Internal Child still overrides his Internal Adult.

Ego States and Decision Making

I link together thinking, problem solving and decision making because these separate elements are so often generated as part of a process containing all three. Decision making involves selecting a course of action from alternatives (I include doing nothing as a course of action). The stimulus for making a decision is generally the fact that we have a problem to solve. Making our selection requires us to think, so the better we understand our thinking processes the more scope we have to improve our decision making.

Looking back over the last few pages, I realise that it must seem surprising that people make as many good decisions as they do. It is also obvious, I hope, that we have several pitfalls to overcome. There will be many times when the quality of our decision making will improve if we can ensure that all internal ego states are actively involved. This is more likely to happen if we use a structured approach.

Below, I outline a simple decision making process, called NOISICED (or DECISION spelled backwards) after the first letter for each step. Working through such a sequence will considerably improve the process of decision making. I give some ideas for working with a partner also, in the Activities section of this chapter.

Need	Why do I need to make a decision?
	Why now?
Objective	What do I want to achieve:
	in the short term?
	in the long term?
Information	What information do I have:
	about the problem?
	about possible decisions?
	What information do I still lack?
	How can I get it?

Strategies	How can I achieve what I want?
	How else?
	And how else?
	Are these the only options?
Investigate	What is good about each option?
	What are the snags with each option?
	How might I get round the snags?
Choose	Which option is most likely to help me meet my objective?
	Are there clear second and third choices?
Ego States	*Internal Parent* What does my previous experience tell me about each option?
	Internal Child How do I feel about each option?
	Internal Adult What is the probability of success with each option?
Decide	Which action am I most likely to be successful with?
	What action(s) will I take to ensure I reach my objective?

THE RACKET SYSTEM

An alternative model for understanding our thinking processes is the racket system. This is an internal, self-reinforcing system whereby we limit our options. Awareness of the racket system provides a different way of tackling our limitations. Once we identify the closed loop thinking that maintains the system, we can break the cycle at any point and substitute a more realistic frame of reference. I convert the racket system into a simple 3 point model which I call BAR – Beliefs, Actions, Reinforcements. I will describe this after I have explained more about the racket system.

An Internal Sequence

The term 'racket' in TA has several definitions, including: manipulative ways of behaving, power plays, inauthentic feelings, substitute feelings, and repetitive ways of thinking, feeling and behaving (see Chapter 7 Working with Others for more about rackets). The word is used in TA as it was in the days of gangsters and their protection rackets – unless you do as I want I will do something nasty. In everyday life this becomes, for example, unless we see the film I want to see, I'll sulk all evening.

The racket system extends this notion into a sequence that occurs internally but which can be related to our behaviour and our interactions with others as well as to our thinking skills. The same model gives us insights into why we may avoid decisions that require us to be assertive, and what is happening when our problem solving is adversely affected by stress.

Although the system focuses on the internal process, it operates alongside associated behaviour that can be observed by others; we can therefore obtain feedback in an indirect way by noting the responses we appear to generate.

The concept was introduced by Richard Erskine and Marilyn Zalcman, who defined it as a self-reinforcing, distorted system of feelings, thoughts and actions. There are three parts to the system: beliefs, rackety displays, and reinforcing memories. These and the way in which the system operates as a closed loop are shown in Figure 6.3.

Beliefs

Beliefs in this model consist of core beliefs about self, others, and quality of life, together with our emotions and the needs we seek to satisfy. These beliefs influence everything we do. Associated with them are a whole range of more detailed beliefs that form a kind of operating code.

Our core beliefs are known in TA as our life positions. These operate rather like filters, or windows, which may distort our perceptions of the world. This TA concept was explained in detail in Chapter 3, Understanding Attitudes. Here, I will give a description of how these life positions influence our opinions about our own and others' ability to think.

In the genuine I'm OK, You're OK life position, we see things clearly. In Chapter 3, I describe this as looking through the open window with no distortion of reality. We know we are able to think effectively and will therefore expect to be allowed to use our initiative and make decisions. We also respect the thinking ability of others.

Note that I explained previously that I'm OK, You're OK can also be a distorted perception. We may then believe that everybody is OK and will always behave in an OK manner. This is patently untrue and means we are setting ourselves up to be disappointed or taken advantage of.

Figure 6.3: The Racket System

Beliefs	Rackety display	Reinforcing memories
Life position	Behaviour	Reactions of others
Operational beliefs	Internal discomfort	Replay of previous occasions
	Imagining the scene	Comparison with expectations

Looking through the I'm not OK, You're OK window means we believe we are surrounded by people who are much more capable thinkers than us. We will therefore do our best to get them to do our thinking for us. In ego state terms, we will set up a symbiotic relationship so that we do not have to think.

When we spend time in the I'm not OK, You're not OK position, we are at our most pessimistic and cynical. Either we seem incapable of thinking, or we believe that our thinking will not make any difference. We do our best to discourage others from thinking too, by letting them know what a waste of time it will be.

Finally, if we are at the I'm OK, You're not OK window, the view prevents us seeing the good in other people. Only we know the right way to think. Our decisions cannot be challenged as no-one else has our ability to analyse a situation. According to us, the quality of our judgement is unmatched.

Hopefully, we will spend a lot of our time at the I'm OK, You're OK window, seeing that people are generally getting along with each other. However, we will also have a variety of supporting beliefs that we can use to operationalise any of the less helpful views of the world. We will revert to these when we are under stress.

To illustrate this, consider shyness. Perhaps we believe that we are shy. If so, our most likely life position is I'm not OK, You're OK. We probably also believe that many other people are not shy. We believe instead that they are confident and socially skilled. Our belief about our own shyness will have supporting beliefs attached to it, such as that we lack social skills, that no-one wants to talk to us, that we are usually ignored at meetings, that we are not as clever as others, that we have no interesting hobbies to talk about, and so on. This cluster of beliefs will form the basis for our interactions with the world, via our rackety displays.

Rackety Displays

A *rackety display* is the behaviour we exhibit, the internal experience that accompanies it, and the fantasies that we imagine about it. To continue with our example, what happens when we walk into a room full of people while believing that we are shy? Our overt behaviour will probably consist of a 'wallflower act'. We walk in and make for the corner. We keep our eyes downcast. We speak to no-one. In other words, we exhibit the type of behaviour that most people interpret as indicating shyness!

Internally, we are almost certainly experiencing psychosomatic reactions. Our stomach feels knotted and we wish we had visited the bathroom before we came in. We may even have been feeling uncomfortable for some time before we actually entered the room – from the point at which we realised we could not avoid the occasion. If someone speaks to us, we will find it hard to concentrate and respond because we are so conscious of the discomfort in our body.

In our imagination, we are replaying a scene in which no-one speaks to us. We visualise spending the whole time standing alone, trying to look nonchalant. We fantasise that everyone is talking about us and our shyness. Again, we may have started these fantasies beforehand, so that they are well under way by the time we enter the room. The longer we stay in the room, the more vivid and awful are the things we imagine. Each group appears to be deliberately ignoring us, while a glance in our direction is, perversely, interpreted as checking to make sure we are not getting too close.

Reinforcing Memories

We then move into the phase of *reinforcing memories*. These are created from three sources: observing the current reactions of other people; checking back in our memory banks to replay old scenes; and evaluating real-life against our fantasies.

By noting the responses of others we are completing the cycle of a self-fulfilling prophecy. We believed we were shy, we therefore behaved as if we had nothing to say to people, and they therefore did not approach us. Hey presto – we were right to believe as we did.

Dredging out our old memories means that our current feelings are exacerbated; we recall previous occasions when our worst fears were confirmed and re-experience those past feelings as well as the current ones so we feel even worse. This can also be done when people fail to respond as we expected. Should someone actually speak to us (in spite of our rackety display), we will seek to resurrect enough unpleasant memories to override the current experience. We can then decide that this change in response is a fluke as it is so unlike our customary pattern.

Comparison of events against our expectations can be another source of confirmation of our beliefs. If our fantasy was good, we can be disappointed when reality fails to match up to it – and we can castigate ourselves for hoping it might be otherwise. If our fantasy was unpleasant, then we can review the evidence we have collected to prove we were right to be so pessimistic. We may even tell ourselves how things are even worse than we expected

BARs to Success

I teach a simplified version of the racket system as shown in Figure 6.4. This shows how our beliefs lead to our actions which in turn lead to the reinforcements of the beliefs. The use of BAR serves as a memory aid and also means we can liken these to prison bars – they are self-generated bars with which we limit our freedom to behave in ways that are healthy for us. I then draw a person surrounded by such bars and explain that we erect them ourselves so can just as easily dismantle them.

Changing our Thinking

The racket system operates as a closed loop. We believe something, we act in accordance with that belief, we believe that events prove our point, so we have reconfirmed our original belief. As we repeat this loop many times, it becomes more deeply ingrained.

Figure 6.4: BARs to Success

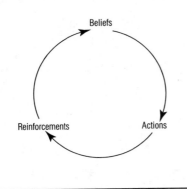

However, the nature of this system means that we have three options because we can interrupt the cycle at any point. If we substitute different beliefs, different behaviours, or different reactions from others, we can change the cycle into a positive one.

Changing our beliefs directly is difficult because they tend to be enmeshed in a network of interlocking values and needs. Indeed, we often shift to an alternative belief if the response from others conflicts with our expectations. If someone shows an interest in us even though we believe we are shy, we may rationalise by deciding that they only did this because no-one will talk to them; they had been told to by our/their manager; they were out to steal our ideas; they were practising their assertiveness techniques and we happened to be handy.

Behaviour change is potentially easier, not least because participants on courses may actually expect to have to do this anyway. If we encourage them to forget their anxieties and to ignore the bodily sensations associated with being nervous, they may well be able to experiment with new ways of behaving. As they do so, the connections back to the old beliefs are being severed. The more they practice, the easier it gets. They begin to recognise that they have indeed acquired the desired skills; this provides them with a new belief to over-ride the old one.

If we are working in a group, the other participants can deliberately change their responses to us so the reinforcement is no longer there. They may do this anyway as the result of our new behaviour. However, they may also do it deliberately even though we have not quite mastered the requisite skill because they know that we need time and encouragement to become more competent. They can also do this in advance of any change from us, simply as an affirmation of their concern to help us. This is the process by which support groups are so powerful.

The alternative to a BAR is PRO, as shown in Figure 6.5, PRO stands for Positive Beliefs leading to Resourceful Actions leading to Okay Outcomes that reinforce the positive beliefs.

Figure 6.5: PRO Success

PRO can be used to explain how we can dismantle a BAR at any point:

■ We may work with someone who challenges us to recognise the flaws in our logic, so that We can adopt more positive beliefs.

■ We can go back into our memory banks to identify some more resourceful actions we could be taking now.

■ We can choose to spend time with people who can be relied upon to respond positively even if we slip back into our old bad habits.

This means that we have three opportunities for breaking the BAR cycle - change our beliefs, change our actions or change the people we interact with.

DISCOUNTING

The final model in this chapter is the TA concept of discounting. This too relates to thinking, but also goes much further into the realms of problem solving. The discounting phenomenon explains why we often overlook potential problems, why we fail to recognise possible courses of action when we are trying to solve problems, and why we fail to implement even the solutions we do identify.

The Discounting Process

Discounting is an internal process whereby we minimise or ignore, without realising it, some aspect of ourselves, others or the situation. In other words, we fail to recognise what is actually there or what is possible. There are three ways in which we may do this; we may overlook the stimulus, the problem, or the options.

If we miss the stimulus, we fail to notice that something is happening. In my youth, I used to infuriate my mother by getting so engrossed in a novel that I would fail to notice that the food on the stove beside me had started to burn. She would rush back to the smoke filled kitchen; once interrupted I would at last put aside my book and register the smell of burning food. Obviously it had to be a very exciting novel for this effect, yet many of us overlook many clues to what is going on. This is especially likely when we have become very used to the stimulus, such as when we don't really listen to what the office bore is telling us.

If we miss the stimulus, we are unlikely to realise there is a problem. However, we may notice the stimulus and still fail to recognise that it indicates a problem. We may see someone pacing up and down but not suspect that they are stressed and anxious. Perhaps we pace when we want exercise so we assume they are doing the same. Or we see how much money is left in the budget but fail to register that we have outstanding payments that still need to be made. We are unaware of the significance of whatever data we have observed.

Finally, we may notice the stimulus, recognise that it signals a problem, but we cannot envisage there being any options for dealing with the situation. For example, a busy supervisor may see that a subordinate looks unwell, by noticing the stimuli of flushed face, sneezing, etc. The supervisor who spots these signs may decide that this represents a problem; it is not just a mild cold which will not interfere with the subordinate's ability to do the work. However, the supervisor may even then believe there is nothing that can be done. They know there is no easy cure for the common cold and it does not occur to them that there are options about what to do now. So they do nothing, when they might have shown concern for the individual, suggested ways of minimising the discomfort, or even considered alternative means of getting the work done.

There are also four levels at which discounting operates. These levels apply whatever way we are discounting. So we may overlook the existence of stimuli, problems or options: we may not recognise the significance of stimuli, problems or options: we may be certain that there are no possibilities for change: or we may believe that we or others lack the personal abilities needed to effect a change. The personal abilities level subdivides into the skills needed, the ability to strategise and the commitment to take action.

Discounting Patterns

The matrix that results from this combining of four levels and three modes is quite complex. However, we can simplify it for organisational purposes because the net effects of some combinations are very similar, so the ways we tend to discount can be grouped into six typical patterns.

Pattern 1	We discount the stimulus; we fail to notice the evidence.
Pattern 2	We are aware of the evidence but do not recognise its significance; we do not realise that it reflects an underlying problem.
Pattern 3	We recognise there is a problem but do not believe that anything could be different; we do not believe that anything can be changed; there are no solutions.

Pattern 4	We accept that things could be different but do not believe that the people involved in our situation could behave any differently; they lack the necessary skills.
Pattern 5	We do not believe that we or others are capable of implementing the potential solution; there are too many other priorities anyway.
Pattern 6	We can identify potential solutions and what needs to be done but do not believe the people involved, including ourselves, are capable of carrying them out; people will somehow 'sabotage' any chances of success.

We can apply these patterns to the common problem of absenteeism in organisations. This also allows us to see that the six patterns are in fact two sequences of three. Patterns 1, 2, 3 involve a lack of awareness of stimulus, problem and options. Patterns 4, 5, 6 repeat this but with the focus on people's abilities – to change the stimulus, to solve the problem, to act on any options.

Pattern 1	We have no attendance records; we have not noticed any absences; you can't expect us to pay attention to details like that.
Pattern 2	We expect everyone to be too ill to attend work for a number of days each year; it's just one of those things; we allow for it when we calculate our costs .
Pattern 3	We know our absence levels are high but they match the average for our industry and location (there is no way to change it).
Pattern 4	We accept there are solutions but they won't work for us (people will always be absent, or managers can't make a difference).
Pattern 5	We can see how it might be done but we have too many other things to worry about (we can't solve the problem right now).
Pattern 6	Our senior management will never 'bite the bullet' (there is no point acting on the options we have).

I take the 6 levels of discounting and show them as a series of steps as in Figure 6.6. These Steps to Success are a useful visual for helping people see how discounting operates.

This can be invaluable when you are planning to persuade. Let's say you have prepared a proposal for dealing with absenteeism. You present it to senior management and they reject it. You have probably been standing on too high a step for them.

Figure 6.6: Steps to Success

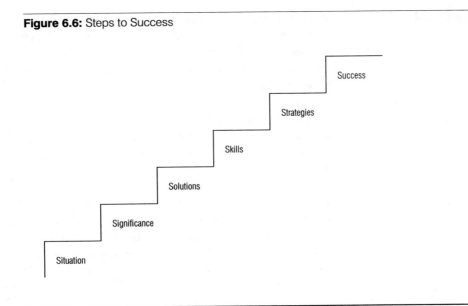

So, if management have already complained about the problem, we can recap their complaint (Step 2 Significance) before helping them to learn about possible options. If they happen to be at Step 5 Strategies, it may be enough to alert them to consider how the success step will elude them unless they are seen to deal with absenteeism by their own personal assistants.

The sensible option is to prepare your presentation so that you begin on the bottom step and only proceed upwards at the pace of the audience. Using the absenteeism example, the structure might be:

Step 1 Situation

Here are the absence records for our employees. You will see that they total XYZ days on average each month.

Step 2 Significance

These represent a problem because:
■ they are twice as high as our competitors' absence levels
■ we end up paying £ABC for people who are not working or for their temporary replacements
■ we upset and even lose customers because queues are so long (or production is so slow…)

Step 3 Solutions

You may think that absenteeism cannot be solved but the following options have been implemented successfully in other organisations. (You will need to say what these are.)

Options X and Y would suit our circumstances

Step 4 Skills

You are probably doubting whether our managers have the skills to use these options. They have all been trained in the necessary competencies as part of their management training OR We can run a course to give them these skills is a couple of days.

Step 5 Strategies

Here is my proposed plan of implementation. The budget for this is £XXX and it should pay for itself in savings on overtime payments, increased sales to happier customers, etc. etc.

Step 6 Success

You will need to be seen to walk the talk. The most obvious absentee in the organisation is 'Mr/Mrs Smith' OR the most obvious absence levels occur in Department M. We must be seen to be tackling these obvious cases – if we are not prepared to do that the initiative will fail because people will not take it seriously.

When I teach this, I add small (unisex, unirace) people on the steps, as in Figure 6.7 to make the point that we need to start on the same step, or even one step below, where someone else is currently discounting.

Discounting is an internal process which serves to maintain our frame of reference. By 'not noticing' things which would conflict with what we believe, or want to believe, we

Figure 6.7: Walking up the Steps

are able to avoid changing our view of the world, of others, and of ourselves. Because the discounting is outside our awareness, it is difficult to spot without feedback from other people. This is why it can be so helpful to talk things over with someone else. Counselling can be thought of as an antidote to discounting; the effective counsellor helps the client to see what they have been overlooking – whether that relates to their awareness of events, their understanding of the significance, or their opportunities to do things differently.

At the root of discounting is a wish that we could leave it to someone else to deal with our problems. As adults, we know that such a wish is inappropriate; however, a part of us would still sometimes like to be free of the responsibility. Discounting is also the mechanism by which we engage in psychological games. By overlooking aspects of our own or others' behaviour, we get into these customary but unhealthy interactions where we can play at being persecutors, rescuers and victims (see Chapter 7 Working with Others for more details about games).

Discounting Behaviour

Although discounting is an internal process, there are several external indications of it. Apart from attempts to 'hook' another person into an ego state that would create the kind of symbiotic thinking described earlier in this chapter, we may exhibit specific behaviours that are not directed at solving problems.

If we consider first our general behaviour, then evidence of discounting might include: doing nothing, as when we do not respond to events or simply look anxious; over-adapting, when we go along with what someone else suggests without even considering whether it is right for us; agitating, as when we pace about, chainsmoke, or otherwise occupy ourselves with repetitive actions which take our energy away from problem solving; and incapacitation, when we get psychosomatically sick so we cannot be expected to do anything about the problem.

Occasionally, we may even become violent as a form of incapacitating ourselves; while others are restraining us we will not be expected to problem solve. I recall employing a less extreme version of this many years ago when I used to storm out and slam the door of my manager's office. This was guaranteed to earn me respite from his bad temper but at the same time I was 'allowed' not to do anything about problem solving because who could expect someone to think when they were as angry as I was. (This approach is not recommended – unless of course you are unfortunate enough to now work for that same unreasonable manager!)

At the micro level, our discounting may show up in our speech patterns. We are likely to be grandiose, claiming that things are 'always' or 'never' so. We make sweeping generalisations based on very skimpy evidence. One example may be used by us as the basis for believing that we have identified a major new trend.

We may also redefine – a process whereby we answer at a tangent or even change the subject completely. Asked if our report will be ready on time, we may respond by complaining about the lack of clerical support. Only later will our questioner realise that they still do not have our answer on whether the report will be ready. Another common example of redefining is that infuriating response "What would you like to do?" said in reply to exactly the same question.

Dealing with redefining is relatively straightforward once we have identified that it is happening. At micro level, we can challenge (politely) the process by repeating the original question, and by querying grandiose statements. We might ask if they really mean always or never. Will they tell us their evidence for generalisations? Can we just make sure their previous experiences are truly relevant in the current situation?

When helping others with their thinking skills and decision making, we can operate to a sequence that relates to the typical patterns and walks them up the steps, checking that:
1. They have noticed what is happening - stimulus.
2. They realise there is a problem - significance.
3. They accept it might be solvable - solutions.
4. They know that people could change - skills.
5. They know that people can solve problems - strategies.
6. They know that people can act on options - success.

There will be no point in asking them to consider aspects further up this sequence than they have reached themselves. Talking about solutions makes no sense to someone who has not even accepted that they have a problem; urging them to draw up action plans is a waste of time if they lack confidence in their ability to change. We need to keep in mind that it is so easy for any of us to spot someone else's discounting even though they are oblivious to it.

TRAINER EFFECTIVENESS
Thinking Styles in the Classroom

I have focused the ideas in this chapter towards providing training in thinking skills and decision making. Such topics feature regularly on training programmes, either in their own right or as part of courses on project planning, creativity, and so on. The concepts are just as relevant applied directly to participants' approaches in the classroom itself.

Although we may have had experience of learning by rote fashion at school, we all know that we learn more if we are required to understand what we are being taught. Understanding allows us to apply the knowledge in a wider range of situations than could ever be dealt with during even a lengthy training course. As trainers, therefore, we need our participants to be able to think, problem solve and make decisions in the classroom. Otherwise, we may as well be programming robots.

The concept of exclusion, for example, can help us understand why participants may act as if they have no valid experience of their own stored in Internal Parent; they anticipate that only 'teacher' will know the right answers. Symbiotic thinking has a similar effect – otherwise perfectly sensible students may look to the trainer to solve even the simplest of problems. Symbiotic participants will call for help from the trainer over trivial problems that they could easily deal with themselves.

The racket system can be helpful in understanding why participants seem to limit themselves. If we have core beliefs about not being as OK as others, we will lack confidence and be reluctant to test out new skills. Our rackety display in the classroom may be a refusal to take part, as when participants are reduced to panic attacks on being expected to perform before a video camera. Few of these would react in the same way towards being filmed for a holiday movie – then the reaction is restricted to a mild embarrassment.

The discounting process is relevant for seeing how participants do their 'overlooking'. Typical examples include:
- the stimulus, such as the way other course members seek to avoid working with them;
- the problem, such as the significance of the manager insisting they attend this course;
- or the options, such as any possibility that they might learn something while they are here.

Trainer Awareness
Developing your self-awareness is just as important as recognising the thinking processes of your participants. You need to think clearly when identifying training needs, designing a programme, and putting it into effect. This is another area where the supervision processes described in Chapter 12, Professional Super-Vision can be so useful.

Check the content of your Internal Parent. This is your store of experience and information about training methods. If it contains only copies of things you have seen done by a small number of other trainers, you may be too limited in your approach. You need access to a supply of new ideas and techniques so that you have a good range of options to select from. Reading, networking, attending conferences and training courses yourself as a participant are all important sources of new thinking.

Your Internal Child will resist using methods that leave you feeling vulnerable. This may be a useful safeguard, as when you refrain from applying a training approach because you are not yet confident that you can handle the likely responses. It may be unhelpful if you are reluctant to try out any new ideas in case you make a mistake. It is no use adding to your knowledge if you do not also build up the skills and confidence you need to put the innovations into practice.

Internal Adult is required to balance the Parent and Child in ways that meet the needs of the situation. For example, your Internal Child has discovered an exciting new training technique and you are keen to try it out. Your Internal Parent experience tells you that the training objectives set by the manager will require at least five days for you to make an impact on the participants. Internal Adult picks up that senior management are looking for cost cutting possibilities and the 'long' training courses are a likely target. Internal Adult is needed to work out the probability of being allowed to run a five day course and the viability of designing a shorter version.

Any symbiotic thinking by a trainer will usually find plenty of reinforcement from participants, who arrive expecting to be told what to think anyway. If you are convinced that only your experience matters, you will miss significant chances to build on the knowledge that students already have. This will slow down your teaching so that you cover less; it will prevent you taking advantage of opportunities to integrate new information firmly with their existing knowledge; and ultimately it will mean that you are limiting your own effectiveness and their learning.

You may have your own BARs specifically related to training. What are your beliefs about training, about participants, about trainers? In Chapter 3 Understanding Attitudes, I invited you to become more aware of your life position, or window on the world. What operational beliefs do you have that support this core attitude? Do you see training as a partnership where trainer and participant each bring their own contribution to the learning?

What about your personal rackety display? Do you get extremely nervous before a training session (extremely rather than a healthy level of tension and energy)? Do you fantasise that this session will be just as bad as the time before when you failed to control the class, or when the participants all arrived late and left early, or whatever other personal disaster you recall? I once worked with someone who regularly got a migraine before certain programmes – the 'coincidence' was quite marked.

For your reinforcing memories, how much are you imagining the responses of participants and how much are you causing the actual responses by your own behaviour? How often do you remind yourself of the failures compared with the successes? What are you doing to ensure you get adequate support from colleagues, and that you develop a healthy, reinforcing sequence of believing in your own competence, behaving confidently and competently, and enjoying the recognition from participants who have learned through your efforts.

Our own discounting is not so easy to unravel. You may need to work with colleagues, asking them to act as a sounding board so you can identify what you unwittingly overlook. Finding out what others would have done when faced with the same stimulus, the same problem, or the same options can be enlightening, especially if you collect several views.

At the micro level, notice whether you make grandiose, sweeping generalisations or have a tendency to redefine by changing the subject instead of responding directly. Are there times when you do nothing in the hope that the problem will go away? Do you over-adapt by letting participants take over and redesign your sessions even though they lack appropriate training expertise? Or do you pace up and down nervously, fiddle with pens, jingle money in your pocket, and otherwise act agitated?

If you notice any of these problems associated with your thinking, use the activities at the end of this chapter to plan appropriate changes. Work with fellow trainers to identify each other's difficulties and, more importantly, to help each other recognise and implement developmental solutions.

ACTIVITIES

Activity 6.1 Structured Decision Making
Brief participants to work individually through the steps shown in the structured decision making process (see page 120), to rework a previous decision or to deal with a current problem.

Activity 6.2 The Stages of Decision Making
Ask participants to select a current problem and to work through the steps of the structured decision making process (see page 120). They are to complete two or three of the steps individually; then to pair up and review each other's responses before moving on.

Brief them as follows:

Step 1   Individually, complete your responses to Need, Objective, Information. In pairs, review each other's replies. Check Information especially to establish what is fact, hearsay, interpretation, assumption. How reliable is it, what are the sources?

Step 2   Individually, complete Strategies and Investigate. Review in pairs.

Step 3   Individually, complete Choose and Ego States. Review in pairs.

Step 4   Individually, complete Decide. Review in pairs or share in plenary.

Activity 6.3 A New Job
In small groups, brief participants to go through the structured decision making process (see page 120) as if one of them was deciding whether to take a new job. The job is a promotion but will mean moving to another location.

You can suggest they appoint one of the group to be the individual offered the new job, or you can describe an imaginary person to them, including details such as whether the person is married, has children at school, cares for dependent elderly relatives who live nearby, does a lot of local voluntary work, and so on. If you select this option, pick a stereotypical person who is relevant to the group you are working with.

Emphasise that the point of the activity is to practice with the framework and not to get the 'right' answer for a fictitious person. Or if a group member volunteers a real case, remind the group not to insist but to prompt that person into increased self awareness.

Activity 6.4 Racket System

This is a light-hearted activity to help participants become familiar with the racket system process. Afterwards, they could be invited to identify the content of part of their own racket system; however they will need to practice first because the system is normally outside our awareness. Encourage them to be as creative as they like as they speculate about the answers to the questions you will raise.

Form small groups (3-5). Give each group a situation to work with or ask them to select their own. Typical situations are: being expected by a colleague to sponsor them for a charity event; being asked by a relative to mind their three children for the afternoon; being required to give a speech at a conference; standing in for the manager at a meeting you have never attended before.

The group should create an imaginary racket system for someone in the selected situation. What do they think the beliefs might be, at the core and the operational level? What might the components of the rackety display be? What might the person be feeling and thinking and how might this affect the way they behave? How might the racket system be reinforced through memories and current reactions of others?

Afterwards, review group results in plenary. Some gentle competition, and more fun, can be introduced if you invite groups to see if they can add enhancements to the results from other groups.

Activity 6.5 BARs and PRO

Ask participants to work in pairs or threes.

Each participant is to think of one of their own BARs. Brief them to choose an everyday example and not anything too serious. Examples of the kind of BAR might be: a sense of discomfort around writing reports, making presentations, speaking up in meetings, etc.

Participants take turns to describe the elements of their selected BAR, with questions and prompts from their partner(s) to ensure they analyse the BAR thoroughly enough to understand how it functions.

The partner(s) then questions and prompts as the participant applies PRO and identifies how the BAR might be disrupted at each of the three stages.

Optional extra: the participant might like to tell the partner(s) what they now plan to do in order to dismantle the BAR and operate a PRO sequence instead.

Activity 6.6 Levels of Discounting

This is similar to the activity above for the racket system. Again, create small groups and encourage them to be creative.

This time, brief them to create an imaginary set of discounting patterns. For the selected situation, how might someone discount the stimulus, the problem or the options, as well as people's abilities to change the stimulus, solve the problem, or act on the options. When they have done this, have them create their own checklists of potential prompts and questions that help others identify their own discounting.

The situations for this activity need to be presented as problems; examples are: high absence levels; low morale; high staff turnover; dissatisfied customers; poor quality control; difficult people to deal with (e.g. patients, Local Authority tenants, prisoners) – or any other topics that are relevant to the group of participants.

NOTES & SOURCES

Ego states, exclusions, and contaminations are all concepts introduced originally by Eric Berne.

Symbiosis is an aspect of material on passivity, for which Aaron Schiff and Jacqui Schiff received the 1974 Eric Berne Memorial Scientific Award – see Appendix 2.

You will see symbiosis drawn to include Parent and Adult versus Child in many TA books, including the original work by Schiff. However, this was because they used a definition of Adult that had it being an adaptive structure (along with Parent and Adapted Child) developed to meet the needs of Natural Child, which they drew as a 4th, separate circle. See Jacqui Lee Schiff et al *Cathexis Reader* Harper & Row 1975.

The Racket System was devised by Richard Erskine and Marilyn Zalcman; this was also the subject of an Eric Berne Memorial Scientific Award, as listed for 1982 in Appendix 2.

Discounting was yet another topic to receive an Eric Berne Memorial Scientific Award, this time to Ken Mellor and Eric Schiff in 1980 – see Appendix 2.

CHAPTER 7:   WORKING WITH OTHERS

In terms of people skills, this chapter fits midway between Chapter 4 Interpersonal Styles and Chapter 8, Working in Groups. 'Working with Others' is the title I picked to be inclusive of those aspects which are more than communicating with others but not quite as complex as working in a team. This chapter therefore focuses on what goes in to building relationships with other people, including an understanding of what motivates, what goes wrong, and why it goes wrong.

To begin with I describe the TA concept of *strokes* – units of recognition – and explain how important recognition is in our lives. I show how it takes various forms, and how we each develop an individual pattern with some common characteristics.

I go on to point out some of the pitfalls and problems that arise because of the way we learn to stroke, and the impact on us of a change in our circumstances that cuts across existing relationships.

In the second section I focus more specifically on what goes wrong in our attempts to build relationships. I describe *psychological games* as interactions that generate powerful negative strokes, explain how we can recognise a game, and give examples of typical games played in organisations. I outline the *drama triangle* as a way of analysing games and list some of the apparent 'advantages', or psychological payoffs, that encourage us to stay with such unhelpful modes of interacting with others. I also describe the *potency pyramid* as an 'antidote' to the drama triangle.

Next I add in two other TA concepts that help explain how we reinforce some of the negative aspects of our interactions. *Rackets* have been mentioned in a previous chapter; here I give more detail to show that they are a form of mini-game that provides repeated negative payoffs. I also use a TA concept based on the notion of *trading stamps* to illustrate how we save up negative feelings until we can justify cashing them in.

The trainer effectiveness section for this chapter is in two parts, to show how both strokes and games affect the relationships between the trainer and the participants.

The activities included relate to strokes, stroking patterns, games and how to deal with them at work, and how to recognise a racket.

BUILDING RELATIONSHIPS

People in organisations have a constant requirement to build relationships. Few of us can work totally alone; generally our technical competence is dependent on our ability to get along with others. As trainers, we may put relationship building under different headings, such as teamwork or motivation, but the underlying dynamics are the same.

Mention teamwork and people tend to think of those settings when a group is physically together – at meetings or attempting some group task. However, teamwork is just as important in those interactions that occur between a couple of individuals. Sometimes, these communications are even more important as they may be the only real contact someone working off-site has with a member of their team.

Mention motivation and people restrict their thinking to something managers are supposed to do to subordinates. Again, this is an unnecessarily limited interpretation. Motivation is also an essential part of how we interact with colleagues and customers. There is also the aspect of self-motivation; some would argue that this is the only true motivation – that other people can only demotivate but cannot create motivation beyond our own self-initiated level.

My preferred TA concepts for these forms of people skills training are stroking, a TA term that stands for acknowledgement and recognition of others, and psychological games, a model for understanding how the stroking is so often misdirected. These two provide frameworks for understanding and for identifying options for improvement in our relationships with others.

Strokes

Stroke is the TA term for a unit of recognition. We all need other human beings to recognise that we exist. Solitary confinement is retained as a severe punishment precisely because we realise how stressful it is to go without human contact. Babies left without attention and stimulation fail to develop normally, as we were regrettably reminded by events in Romania during the late nineteen eighties/early nineties. Although we vary in the amount of recognition we need, we must all get a minimal level of attention from others if we are to function as healthy individuals.

Any form of interaction with others is an exchange of strokes. We may touch someone, speak to them, or simply catch their eye and look away. Even the glance has shown we know of their existence and is therefore a stroke, albeit one of very low recognition power. People who lack sufficient contact with others will respond disproportionately to even a minor stroke, such as when we give a simple greeting to a stranger and then find ourselves listening to their life history.

At the top end of the scale is touching, which research has shown to have major impact even when we are not aware consciously that we have been touched. One candid camera type study found that, if you touched their arm gently, people were far more likely to admit to finding and pocketing your money when it had been left (deliberately) in a telephone box they had used. Those not touched in this way were prone to claim that the money must have gone before they came along.

The term 'stroke' was introduced by Berne as a shorthand for unit of recognition precisely because he was aware of how important physical stroking is to us as babies before we learn to speak. Once we grow older, we learn to accept our strokes in non-physical ways as well. As adults any form of recognition serves as a stroke: catching someone's eye; having a conversation; receiving pay and commission; allocation of a company car. In many cultures we recognise that our society places restrictions on how we touch each other so the majority of strokes at work are conveyed through sight and hearing. We see a smile or a frown; we hear the comments made and questions asked of us. Our strokes via touch tend to be restricted to shaking hands - and not even that in some countries.

As well as varying in their level of intensity and mode of communication, strokes may be positive or negative. Positive strokes invite us to feel OK about ourselves and others. Negative strokes invite us to feel not OK about ourselves, about others, or both.

Positive strokes tend to be thought of as nice comments but this is too much of a simplification. These are indeed positive strokes but so too is constructive criticism even though we may not believe so at the moment we receive it. Constructive criticism carries with it the implication that we are OK – and can therefore do still better than we have – and will only be offered by someone with our best interests in mind.

Complimentary remarks about our work, our appearance, our family, our hobbies, will be positive strokes. Questions are also strokes; paying attention to someone by asking for their opinions, their concerns, their ideas, or their latest news, is a powerful way of recognising their existence as a human being. And constructive criticism adds to our self esteem; I appreciated the time people took to give me feedback on draft chapters of this book. Even though they were suggesting changes I could see that this was enabling me to produce a better result.

Negative strokes, too, are more complex than simply saying something unpleasant. In addition to interactions aimed at inviting us to feel bad in some way, there are also negative strokes involved when we are encouraged to feel superior. Superiority relies on someone else being not OK; this is not a psychologically healthy way to maintain our sense of self-worth. Furthermore, we will also experience strokes that leave us feeling that no-one is OK. These are the cynical comments along the lines of 'Whatever makes you think the idiots will listen to you of all people?'

I am often asked, particularly by young male graduates in the UK, what type of stroke is being given when people are sarcastic to each other. Although it would seem that sarcasm is negative, this form of interaction is used commonly between young men. When they talk in this way to people they like, they are generally exchanging disguised positive strokes. A 'macho' culture inhibits us, especially if we are male, from being too open with our feelings of friendship and caring. We learn to hide behind jokes and comments such as "Oh no, not you again" when we are really pleased to see someone.

One difficulty with sarcasm of this type is that we use a similar technique when we wish to disguise a negative stroke. Perhaps we are angry with someone but feel that it is too risky to tell them so – maybe they are senior to us, or noted for their bad temper. So we make a joke of what we want to say to them. Then, if they react too strongly, we can deny any negative intent and accuse them of lacking a sense of humour. True experts in this manoeuvre can say this in such a hurt tone that the victim finishes up apologising.

As recipient, it is easy to get confused about the true message when sarcasm is employed. We get a mild case of paranoia – did they really mean that as a joke; was there evil intent under the surface? Our communication will be much clearer and our relationships will improve if we take the risk and say in a straightforward way what we really think. If we phrase our comments as positive strokes even our criticisms will be constructive.

Another way of classifying strokes is by whether they are conditional or unconditional: given for doing or given for being. The traditional view of organisations implies a conditional form of stroking – recognition is something that results from performance of the task. Conditional strokes cover the range of things that we can control: how we do our work, how we dress, how we exercise our skills. They may be positive or negative: that was a good report; this needs changing; your shoes are the wrong colour; what a stupid idea. If we are fortunate, we receive a regular diet of positive conditional strokes in a mix which both reinforces our strengths and gives us feedback for our development.

Unconditional strokes add an important dimension; such strokes do not have to be 'earned' through work achievement or appearance. Asking someone about their family or their spare time activities is a powerful form of stroking that involves relating to aspects of them which may otherwise be neglected during worktime. Being told that someone enjoys our company is a potent stimulus to most of us to become energised and enthusiastic. The increasing attention being paid in organisations to the 'whole person' is a reflection of this need for unconditional strokes. We spend too many hours at work to limit ourselves to conditional strokes only.

Stroking patterns

Our personal stroking pattern consists of the strokes that we give and receive. We develop patterns of interactions between us and the people we are in contact with so that we receive a supply of strokes to match our needs. It is not random. We will unwittingly establish relationships with people who are likely to provide the levels and types of strokes that we became used to during our childhood. These have become integral to our way of being in the world; if our customary balance is upset we feel uncomfortable and seek to re-establish it.

We will of course vary in our sources of strokes. Being part of a team means that strokes are available to us from many directions. Working mostly alone yields fewer strokes. Depending on our own preferences, we will therefore opt for the situation that is most likely to produce the pattern we want. You can easily identify your own pattern by noting down who you have contact with and analysing the nature of the interactions. Do they give you positive or negative strokes? How often? What strokes do you give them? Do you have an overall pattern in life or are there distinct trends for work, social, family? Do you rely on a few people for high intensity strokes or a large number of people for low level stroking?

The intensity of a stroke can be measured by the effort the giver puts into it. However, the impact on us will be influenced by the value we place on it. This will depend on the nature of the interaction, our feelings about the stroke giver, and our personal preferences for which aspects of our personality or behaviour get stroked. Some of us like our recognition to be about work performance and achievement; others are more comfortable with strokes about our families and personal relationships; yet others get more of a kick when people show a keen interest in our exciting spare time activities.

The structure of an organisation can have a significant impact on our options for obtaining strokes. For instance, working closely with customers may lead us to rely on the customer instead of our colleagues for our recognition, so that our loyalty to our own organisation is weakened. Each change in our circumstances will cause a corresponding deficit in our stroking pattern until we can re-establish a new source of interaction. Of course, if we are dissatisfied with such a relationship we may welcome the opportunity to begin elsewhere.

Most of us have also developed a tendency to operate a kind of stroke exchange, returning a positive or negative to match whatever we receive. Someone compliments us on our appearance, so we tell them that they look good too. Or they admire some aspect of our performance, only to have us respond with an instant but somewhat artificial remark about the equivalent for them. Done without thinking, this is inauthentic. When it happens, the initiator of the interaction is left feeling that their stroke has somehow been cancelled by a less than satisfactory return stroke.

There is another way in which we appear to swap strokes. In this case, though, we are seeking to maintain our stroke balance by matching the quantity of stroking rather than the subject matter.

Many of us will be used to leaving home in the mornings and greeting a neighbour as we go to our car or the station. Every day without fail, for weeks and months, we say "Good morning" to each other. Nothing more; this may not be someone we wish to become closer to. One morning they are not there. We do not see them for two weeks. Then they reappear, just as before. Only the social incompetent would say "Good morning" again as if nothing had happened.

Instead, we remark on their absence and return. "You're back. Good to see you. Have you been away?" And they tell us about their holiday or their spell in hospital, while we make suitably envious or sympathetic comments. The next morning, we probably pass a few more remarks, such as asking how it was at work on the previous day. So they talk to us briefly about that. On the third day, we are ready to revert to our usual "Good morning" format and so are they. And so it continues until the next time one of us misses a few days.

What has been happening is that we were maintaining our stroking exchange over time. Every day, each of us expects to give and receive one stroke as a contribution to our balance. But if one of us is absent, we miss out. Somewhere mysterious inside us is a special calculator that clicks up the deficit. Two weeks without seeing them, five days per week, so we have missed ten strokes. On day one of their return we manage to exchange about seven strokes by chatting to each other. Our calculator registers that we are now three down from last week, plus we have to catch up with the two days of the current week. So on day two of their return, we need three plus two equals five. Provided we make these up on day two, we can go back to the on-a-day ration from day three.

This type of exchange runs through many of our relationships, with different quantities involved. A good friend that we see once a month will contribute a substantial number of strokes. Miss seeing them one month and we have a lot of catching up to do (and that is often the phrase that we use). We make up the deficit by spending longer with them next time, by telephoning between times, by being a lot more animated when we do meet, or by a mix of all three.

Contrast this with what happens if we bump into them before the month is up. We will spend about the right energy to reflect how long since we last met, and will 'deduct' this at our regular date. If we continue to see each other more frequently, the pattern will gradually adjust. If we continue to miss seeing them, we will probably relegate them to that part of our stroking pattern that handles intermittent contacts. If that happens, we will probably also replace them partially by having increased contact with another friend who is available more often.

Stroking Problems

Because our stroking patterns and preferences are determined largely when we are small, we fall into some common traps. We then grow up with a range of unhelpful beliefs about how stroking should be conducted, and some programmed responses that lead us to react illogically to negative strokes.

To explain some of this, Claude Steiner suggested that we apply some arbitrary 'rules' about strokes. He identified five myths that we are likely to believe to some extent. These are like parent messages inside our heads. Although we may not be consciously aware of them they reflect the views that our parents had about the correct ways to behave. Just as each family is different, so too do individuals vary in the degree to which they operate under each rule.

Don't Give: We may hold back specific comments or strokes in general. Perhaps we worry that the person will become complacent if we praise them, or upset if we criticise. So we see someone achieve a difficult task but act as if nothing unusual has happened, or we claim that there is no need to make a fuss when someone is "just doing the job they get paid for".

Don't Accept: Sometimes you can actually see the movement as a person shrugs off a stroke. At other times the rejection may be verbal, when we make comments about the credit (or blame) belonging elsewhere. Our manager compliments us on an excellent report – and we say that our colleague should really get the praise as they did most of the work (when they didn't).

Don't Reject: We feel obliged to accept whatever is offered, even though it is not what we wanted. We may even come to resent the strokes yet give no clue of this to the giver. Women may smile politely as they accept strokes about their appearance instead of their competence; men may settle for comments about their decisiveness instead of their sensitivity.

Don't Ask: A common difficulty in organisations, where we feel embarrassed to ask for feedback. In personal relationships, we may give this an added twist by declaring that strokes "don't count if I have to ask for them." We feel disappointed and demotivated when our special efforts and skills go unnoticed but we don't know how to draw attention to ourselves without showing vulnerability.

Don't Stroke Yourself: Even more of a problem in organisations. Our fear of being thought boastful prevents us alerting people to our strengths and achievements. This false modesty may lead to us being overlooked for tasks to which we are suited. So we go for a job interview and fail to sell ourselves properly. Or we sit through a poorly structured meeting instead of offering to use our skills to chair it effectively.

Another way in which we build in problems to our stroking patterns is through a propensity to settle for negative stroking. We learn when we are young to accept negative strokes if no positive ones are available. Any stroke, even a negative, is better than being ignored. Imagine a young child, playing on the floor. Few parents would go up to them, interrupt the play, and provide positive strokes for being so good. Instead, most of us would think this was a good opportunity to put the kettle on and have a few moments break from childminding. The small child, therefore, may well come to associate amusing themselves with the momentary absence of the parent. They can behave as parents want them to, but they cannot be sure that positive strokes will follow.

Contrast this with the scene when mother is talking to a neighbour. Small child tries to get her attention, only to be told to go away and play. After a couple more unsuccessful attempts to get positive strokes from mother, the child does indeed go away to play. The plaything selected is something breakable, mother hears the crash, and guess what she does! She promptly leaves the neighbour and rushes in to give the child some negative strokes about breaking things. The child notes that strokes were forthcoming, albeit not nice positive ones.

We all experience these typical scenes when we are small. Many of us come to the 'logical' conclusion: we know how to stimulate negative strokes without fail but there seems little connection between our behaviour and the receipt of positive strokes. Schools obliging continue the pattern: teachers generally pay far more attention to pupils who misbehave than to the average performer. Behave badly enough and you even get to talk directly to the headteacher, a privilege denied to most of your classmates.

Now, as grownups, we can replay the unhelpful sequences when our stroke balance is running low. Organisations know the routine too – managers call in for interview those who perform poorly or have high absence levels, yet take good performance and consistent attendance for granted.

I once heard of an organisation that reversed the pattern and sent congratulatory letters to all staff who had unbroken attendance records over the previous year. The impact was startling; those receiving letters showed them around and absence levels dropped dramatically for a time. Unfortunately, the idea did not catch on, even though everyone I tell the story to recognises the wisdom of it.

Joining a new team

Joining a new team requires a major change to our stroking patterns. This is why it can be so stressful, even when we have initiated the change ourselves. It takes some time to recreate the whole range of patterns across areas such as new boss, new colleagues, new procedures, new customers, new tasks, new products. First, the boss may not know you well and will therefore find it harder to provide the sort of strokes that match your preferences. Do you value most personal contact or recognition through salary and commission? If your usual strokes are for competence and success, there will be a delay until you demonstrate these qualities.

The new team may have well-established stroking patterns between themselves and need time to incorporate you. In the meantime, strokes from your former team may have abruptly ceased, especially if you have changed organisation or location as well. Your new relationships will need working at while trust develops. Learning about new responsibilities can be stimulating, but at the same time strokes for being knowledgeable are denied you.

The time after such a change can be stressful as we go through this period of transition. Knowing our usual stroke patterns gives us a target to aim at. Being aware of the nature of stroking patterns allows us to consider alternative stroke sources while we establish new relationships. Family, friends and previous colleagues will usually be happy to give us extra strokes during that time if we let them know what we need. This will minimise the potential stress associated with the change and give us an easier transition.

A key element in change is whether we have choice. Imposed change forcibly alters our stroking patterns and may also interfere with our options for substitution. In addition to our discomfort at the sudden loss of strokes, we have to begin the process of identifying and establishing new sources. However, if we seek the change we have more control over how we develop new patterns. Indeed, self-initiated change is often a response to an inadequate supply of satisfactory strokes. We may choose to go elsewhere, to find a stroking climate that more closely matches our preferences.

WHAT GOES WRONG

I have already described some of the problems that arise with our stroking patterns and processes. The notion that we will settle for negative strokes is particularly important in understanding why some of our relationships incorporate pain and stress as well as positive aspects. In our attempts to ensure an adequate supply of such negative strokes, we engage in repetitive transactions with others that lead to negative payoffs. The more we need strokes, the more frequently we are likely to engage in such unhelpful interactions.

Psychological Games

These repetitive but unsatisfactory interactions with others are known as psychological games. Although Berne listed good games in his best seller Games People Play, it is rumoured that he did this under pressure from a publisher who thought a book with only bad news would not sell. TA practitioners now generally agree that all games are negative, although our underlying motivation is a failed attempt at establishing closeness.

The time period encompassed by a game is flexible. We may spend minutes only in a interaction which contains the complete sequence: perhaps we start to argue with someone almost as soon as they walk through our door. Games may instead extend over a lengthy period as we move through the steps during a series of contacts. In this case, we may appear to be working well with someone, only to realise later that we have a major misunderstanding.

We can identify several elements of a game; the more of these present the more likely that a game is actually in effect rather than a simple miscommunication.

Repetition - Is the sequence something that we recognise as being common? Do we get the sensation of 'here we (or they) go again'?

Predictability - Can we, or an observer, predict how things will turn out? Is there a certain inevitability in the sequence?

Ulterior transaction - Do we suspect that there is a hidden agenda? Are there unspoken messages beneath the overt behaviour?

Switch - Does there come a moment when the interaction seems to shift? Do those involved switch to addressing the ulterior message instead of the initial subject?

Negative payoff - Do the parties end up feeling bad? Is there an element of win-lose or lose-lose apparent at the end of the interaction?

Out of awareness - This is the most significant aspect of psychological games. We do not realise at the time that we are engaged in such an unhelpful interaction. Indeed, we may not realise afterwards either as we will assume that the negative payoff is a normal part of the pattern of our life. We will have experienced it many times before; we can also see similar unsuccessful episodes happening to everyone around us.

Berne wrote that there were three degrees of games; first degree, which we play in public; second degree which we prefer to play in private; and third degree, where the end result involves serious consequences such as injury or legal penalties. Examples are: first degree – Uproar as an argument in a meeting; second degree – Uproar as a blazing row behind closed doors; third degree – Uproar between manager and subordinate that ends with dismissal.

For organisational application, I find it more helpful to imagine a scale of outcomes from mild to severe. At the less serious end are those games where we end up with little more than a feeling of discomfort. These are the unsuccessful interactions we have with colleagues, for example. Next come games which significantly detract from our performance; people are unwilling to cooperate with us to achieve tasks. Further up the scale are games where the consequences are apparent to third parties; our colleagues complain to the boss about us, perhaps. As the seriousness increases, we move through verbal warnings into disciplinaries. In extreme cases, we get fired or walk off the job. In even more extreme cases, the law is breached and we end up in court. Or we take risks with safety and finish up in a hospital or morgue, or being sued. And all of this happens outside our awareness - we don't realise that we are going through some familiar steps.

Typical Organisational Games

Games are named to capture the essence of the dynamic involved. *Yes, but, Harried, Gotcha!, Uproar, Rebuff* and *Lunch Bag* are examples of psychological games played in the workplace as well as elsewhere.

Yes, but refers to an interaction in which helpful suggestions are countered with reasons against. Typically, someone sighs and mentions a problem they have. When solutions are put forward, they respond by pointing out why each idea would not work, beginning with the words 'Yes, but...'. Eventually, one of the 'players' becomes exasperated and makes derogatory comments about the other person.

The underlying communication here is about who is cleverest. The problem-holder is reinforcing a belief that they have thought of very possible solution, and that they know more about the pitfalls of the job than anyone else. The solution-offerer takes the attitude that they can easily improve on whatever has already been considered. Only one of them can emerge from the interaction feeling they have been proved right.

Harried involves rushing about earning the right to mutiny or collapse as a martyr. Other players are setting themselves up to be disappointed and let down. One of us accepts any work that needs to be done, adding it to an ever increasing array of tasks and responsibilities. If we are a manager, we are likely to be a poor delegator. Our ulterior message here is that we are the only person capable of doing so much work, and doing it properly.

We may have several partners in this game who collude with our efforts to do everything. On the surface, they may well encourage us to further excess by commenting in awe about the prodigious amount of work we absorb. Their secret agenda will be to reassure themselves that no-one is actually that capable, as will be proved when we become ill or intransigent through overwork.

Lunch Bag has similar characteristics to Harried. We bring our lunch to work so that we do not need to take a break for a meal. We then offer to answer the telephones while our colleagues go out to lunch. We refuse their invitation to join them, explaining that we do not want to waste the food we already have with us.

When they return from lunch, feeling rested, we complain in an aggrieved tone about the length of their absence and the number of interruptions we have had to deal with on their behalf. We end up feeling righteous and taken advantage of; they end up feeling guilty and annoyed with us for spoiling their pleasant mood.

Gotcha! is a popular game in meetings. As we explain our ideas, we realise that someone is showing great interest. We feel flattered as they raise many queries and encourage us to expand our comments. Then, just as we are congratulating ourselves on how well the session is going, they pounce on an apparent contradiction in what we have said. We feel confused and embarrassed; the onlookers conclude that our ideas are unsound.

The underlying dynamic in Gotcha! is about being one-up. We have a high opinion of ourselves and are aiming to demonstrate how much more we know than others. If you are the person who takes us on, you have an equally high opinion of your own capabilities and want to make sure the other people see how clever you are. In a sense, we are using cunning in a battle for the hearts and minds of the audience and only one of us can win.

Uproar is a discussion proceeding to a formidable argument. We begin gently enough to have a sensible sharing of views. Gradually, the psychological temperature increases. Eventually, we stop being polite and start telling the other person what we really think of their ideas. Our insults escalate as we really get into an argument. Uproar becomes even more energetic if we involve more than two players, especially if we start taking sides.

Like Gotcha!, Uproar's secret agenda is about winning and losing. If we customarily end up on the losing side of the argument, we may recognise this game better under the alternative title of Kick Me.

Rebuff moves from an apparent invitation into an affronted refusal. This may have sexual connotations, as when we flirt with someone and are then offended if they overstep a boundary which we have not made clear to them. Legislation about sexual harassment has reduced the instances of this, although the dynamic is still available to those who wish to play for higher stakes. The negative payoff of a slapped face has now become litigation.

Rebuff is also played, however, around non-sexual issues. We may offer the services of our section or organisation, only to complain bitterly that we are being taken advantage of when we see the scale of the resulting request. Our colleague or customer is baffled by our reaction – they believed our offer gave them carte blanche.

Our payoff is to retain our cynicism about how people rip you off if you try to help them. Their payoff is to remain cynical about the lack of any genuine desire to help.

The Drama Triangle
An easy way to understand and analyse the dynamics of a game is to use the Drama Triangle devised by Karpman. He saw that psychological games were similar to theatrical drama; the scenes which captured the audience's attention best contained the elements of a game. As in drama, the players also take on the roles of *Persecutor, Rescuer,* or *Victim,* as shown in Figure 7.1.

Take for example the well-known James Bond films. Repetition is there in abundance; the sequence of events repeats itself through each episode in the film, and is even repeated with different villains in different films.

Predictability comes in the form of knowing that whoever is winning (persecuting) now will be losing (victim) later in the film. We also know that James Bond will emerge as victorious persecutor at the end, unless the producers want to show his comeback in a sequel.

Figure 7.1: The Drama Triangle

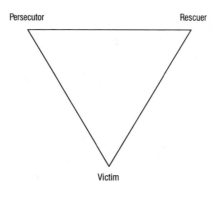

The director makes it easy for us to spot the ulterior transactions. The viewer is allowed to see the hidden agenda because we watch the actors preparing their traps and discussing their motives and their plans with henchmen. James Bond is smarter than the villain; or is the villain smarter than James Bond?

There are many switches in such a film. Indeed, the quicker the switches follow each other, the more exciting is the action. Suddenly the villain is persecutor and gloating openly while Bond the victim swims with sharks, then James Bond regains control and persecutes the villain, then again the villain gains the upper hand. And this happens all the way through the film.

The pay-offs are clear. The villain is punished, maybe by death. Bond is able to relax, with his payoff of smugness and glory, until the next time.

Organisational games may be less extreme but they still follow a pattern around the triangle. Figure 7.2 shows the moves of a typical organisational games of Yes, but....

Lee, victim-like, sighs deeply and complains about workload. If Lee is a very skilled player, there will be no request for help, only a sigh and a comment. Asking someone for help is straightforward and may lead to problem solving rather than a game.

Andy, a keen Rescuer, cannot resist the challenge. Ideas are offered. Lee points out the flaws in each idea as it is presented. This is repeated while several solutions are demolished.

In one version of the ending, Lee gets to the punchline first, by moving to Persecutor and complaining that Andy is making stupid suggestions and wasting time. Andy promptly feels like a Victim.

Figure 7.2: A Game of Yes, but…

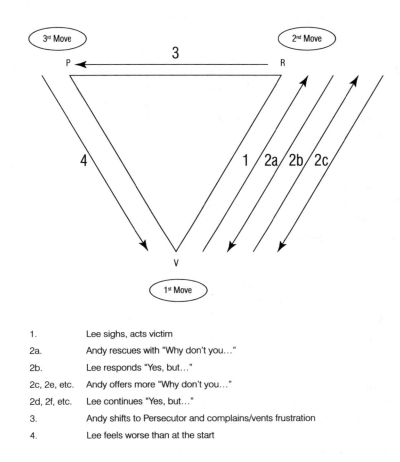

1.	Lee sighs, acts victim
2a.	Andy rescues with "Why don't you…"
2b.	Lee responds "Yes, but…"
2c, 2e, etc.	Andy offers more "Why don't you…"
2d, 2f, etc.	Lee continues "Yes, but…"
3.	Andy shifts to Persecutor and complains/vents frustration
4.	Lee feels worse than at the start

There is an alternative ending, in which Andy delivers the coup de grâce, by moving to Persecutor and accusing Lee of not really wanting to solve the problem, and of dismissing Andy's ideas without bothering to consider them. Lee stays in the Victim role and now feels doubly put down – the problem still exists and now Andy is angry with them.

It takes at least two people for a game to take place. Three handed games also occur, such as when a third party attempts to intervene. This is why the police dread domestic disputes; like arguments at work it is hard to take action without becoming embroiled yourself.

Consider the scene. Husband is beating wife. Neighbour calls police. Police officer attempts to restrain husband. Wife then attacks police officer to stop them hurting husband. In this sequence, the police officer goes from Rescuer to Persecutor to Victim.

The wife goes from Victim to Persecutor of police officer, Rescuer of husband. The husband goes from Persecutor to Victim. For added piquancy, the husband may then switch to Persecutor again, but this time to attack the police officer who is attempting to arrest his wife for assaulting a police officer.

The equivalent scene in industry might involve three colleagues. Two are arguing loudly. One appears to be losing the argument and is being insulted. In wades number 3 on their behalf, making it clear that they will not stand by and listen to the insults to their colleague. Instead of being grateful for the rescue, the insulted party now persecutes by telling them to mind their own business. All three are now arguing loudly and switching rapidly around the triangle, when along comes a fourth person.

'Advantages' of Games

Why do we play psychological games? It seems strange to think that we keep repeating interactions that lead to us feeling bad. A major part of the problem is the lack of awareness; we look around and see everyone else behaving in similar ways and believe that this must be the way life is.

There are also apparent 'advantages' that accrue from playing psychological games. Because of this, we find it hard to stop the repetitive sequences, even when we become aware of them. Knowing what the benefits are, we can plan wider changes than simply altering the transaction. This gives us far more chance of dispensing with the unhelpful sequences and the negative payoffs that accompany them.

Biological advantage - As I mentioned when describing strokes earlier in this chapter, we all need at least a minimal level of attention from other human beings if we are to stay alive. Games generate only negative strokes but these are better than being ignored.

I recall a time when I was working alone, with little contact within the company as my tasks were quite specialised. After a few weeks, I realised that my occasional meetings with my manager were generally argumentative. I had been playing Uproar as a way of getting a large supply of negative strokes during my intermittent visits.

Existential advantage - Existential refers here to our overall attitude towards the world, ourselves and other people. (This concept is described in more detail in Chapter 3 Understanding Attitudes). The outcome of a game reinforces these core beliefs, or life positions. If we believe we are better than others, we will play games where we finish one-up. We play Uproar to win, or Gotcha! to prove the other person is incompetent. If we believe others are better than us, we play Kick Me to get kicked, or Poor Me in which we claim dispensation for failing at tasks because we lack the advantages that others take for granted. If we doubt the value of ourself and others, we play games where no-one wins, such as Yes, but with a payoff of frustration for both players when they cannot solve a problem.

External psychological advantage - There will be something in the current situation that we avoid doing by playing a game. With Yes, but, for example, we do not have to get our work done on time if we can prove to ourself and others that no-one can find a way of doing so. Uproar may be used as justification for storming out of a meeting. Lunch Bag gets us out of going to a smoky pub and pretending to enjoy our colleagues' jokes.

Internal psychological advantage - A game is a way of avoiding an original pain. It is as if we repeat a sequence from the past that we developed then to protect us from something. By doing so, we do not have to deal with the issue in the present. This maintains the psychological stability we have achieved by learning to think and feel in customary ways.

External social advantage - We get to tell our friends all about it! We give a blow-by-blow account of what we said, what the Other person said, what we said them - all to the accompaniment of appropriate commiserations or congratulations from our audience. Games with lots of switches sound especially exciting so we may even be able to establish a reputation as raconteur and so widen our circle of acquaintances - all the while getting strokes as they listen and react to what we are saying.

Internal social advantage - Replaying a game in our heads generates more excitement. We go over the steps again in fantasy, re-experiencing the feelings through a sort of internal pastiming with ourselves. We may repeat the game phrase to ourselves, as when we think "If it weren't for them, I could have ..."

Stopping Game Playing
There are some suggested Activities at the end of this chapter that will help people identify the games they play and plan ways to behave differently.

We can use a 'reversal' of the drama triangle to help with this process. I call this the Potency Pyramid as shown in Figure 7.3.

You will see that I have turned the triangle on its head – this is because it helps to register it visually as a different model to the drama triangle. I have then made the P, R, V stand for healthy options: powerful, responsible, vulnerable.

Powerful – being appropriately powerful, taking action when we should, including on behalf of genuine victims who cannot help themselves

Responsible – taking responsibility only for those things that are truly ours to deal with and not taking over other people's responsibilities

Vulnerable – displaying our own vulnerability and asking for help when we need it – whilst accepting that others have the right to refuse our request.

Figure 7.3: The Potency Pyramid

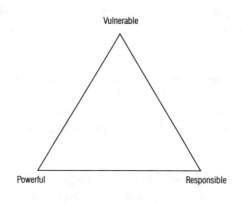

PSYCHOLOGICAL COLLECTIONS

Our psychological collections are our stores of bad feelings. We file away the payoffs from games, and may well review them from time to time as we remember what happened. In addition to playing psychological games, we have some other mechanisms through which we can generate less severe payoffs and milder forms of negative strokes.

Rackets

Berne introduced the term 'racket' into TA in the sense of a protection racket; a form of manipulative behaviour that is designed to force others to do what we want. Gangsters had protection rackets in order to extract money from their victims; we may operate rackets that threaten severe discomfort to others if they fail to modify their behaviour to suit us. For example, we may make it clear that we will sulk if not given first choice about where to go for a holiday, or we may establish a reputation for angry scenes if the work is not completed exactly as we require. Rather than risk these consequences, people may reluctantly comply with our demands.

The word 'racket' has since been used in several ways by different writers. We may have a feeling racket as described above; we may have racket feelings which are substitutes for the appropriate feelings in the particular circumstances; there are thinking rackets such as confusion; we may engage in rackety fantasising as I described as one of the advantages of games; and rackets may be short sequences of behaviours. What these varied definitions have in common is the notion that a racket is essentially an internal psychological process. We can infer the existence of a racket through our observations of behaviour but we cannot actually see the process itself.

Like games, rackets are outside our awareness. Like games, they lead to negative payoffs. Unlike games, we do not need a partner to operate a racket; we can do so alone. If someone fails to speak to us, we can feel upset whether they did so intentionally or not. Indeed, we will often overlook the option of checking with them and will instead tell ourselves that "of course it was deliberate, and I'll feel even worse if I speak to them and they still ignore me."

As substitute feelings, rackets are often responses that we learned as children in order to meet parental exhortations. Small boys are discouraged from showing hurt so substitute anger until they can no longer recognise the underlying emotion and respond aggressively as a habit. Girls are often given the opposite messages, and grow up programmed to burst into tears when a more genuine response would be anger. A common substitution for both sexes is the anger displayed when someone arrives home later than expected; generally this masks the fear we had been experiencing while we worried in case they had been in an accident. Instead of showing our relief and caring, we angrily accuse them of not bothering to let us know where they were.

Rackets may also be thought of as 'artificial' feelings, created in response to the norms of society. For example, we may feel guilty when we forget to send a birthday card on time, instead of sad because the other person may be hurt by our thoughtlessness. The artificiality here refers only to the manufactured nature of the feeling; the feeling itself is no less real in its impact on us. Although genuine emotions consist only of glad, sad, scared, and mad (angry), the range of feelings generated by us in accordance with our beliefs and value systems will be just as vivid.

Rackets as interactions can be classified into three broad groups, based on whether they are by nature concerned with being helpful, being helpless, or being hurtful. Helpful rackets occur when we try to do things for other people that they do not need done for them; they feel obliged to accept our help even though they feel smothered by it. Helpless rackets arise when we act as if we cannot solve problems for ourselves, so that other people feel trapped into dealing with the world on our behalf. Hurtful rackets revolve around passing on our pain to others, as when we blame them for how we feel.

We can identify rackets through some of the clues we use for games; they are repetitive, predictable, we sense a hidden agenda, we end up feeling bad in some way, and they are out of our awareness at the time they occur. It is as if the racket is a watered down version of a game, without the switch that would add extra potency to the negative payoff. The other major difference, as I mentioned above, is that we can experience racket feelings without the involvement of another person.

Stamps

Berne suggested that we save up our bad feelings, from rackets or games, as if they were trading stamps. We paste them into an imaginary book until we have collected enough to claim a prize. We then cash them in for a 'free gift', which will be some form of behaviour that we believe is justified by our collection. The 'straw that broke the camel's back' was a trading stamp.

Serious examples include nervous breakdowns when we have collected enough feelings of stress, or resigning abruptly on grounds of having been passed over for promotion yet again. Less severe, fairly common instances are temper tantrums because we feel that people have persistently been rude to us, or pretending to be sick for a day off because we are unappreciated anyway. We may also cash in our stamps for prizes, such as a special evening out because we deserve it after working so hard, or an extra cake as a reward for all those boring low calorie meals we have eaten.

The stamp collecting process is illustrated well by considering what happens to an airline passenger. Let's suppose this particular passenger is a businessman making a trip to corporate headquarters. He starts his stamp collection as soon as he is summoned to the meeting, as he pastes in a stamp concerning his frustration at being told to make the trip just when he had planned to use the time to catch up on his backlog of work. His next stamp is provided by a secretary who fails to book him on the mid morning flight he wants; now he will have to get up at 5.00 a.m. to reach the airport in time. At home, his wife is annoyed that he will be away for two days, so he pastes in more frustration. He fails to wake in time (more frustration, aimed at the inanimate alarm clock that he forgot to set correctly). He rushes to dress when the taxi driver wakes him, and they reach the airport just in time for check-in. There are no porters to help him, the check-in queue is long, he is too late to get a window seat, the coffee bar is closed, the aircraft is not on a jetty so he has to walk across the tarmac in the rain. He now has a full book of frustration stamps and is looking to cash it in.

At this point, the aircraft steward asks him to put his briefcase under the seat in front of him and not in the aisle. He erupts, complaining bitterly that the airline is incompetent, that there should be more overhead storage, that the steward is rude, that he will not be told what to do like that, and so on. Afterwards, he will wonder ruefully why he behaved like that, when he knows the steward was only reminding him of safety regulations. At the moment, though, he is too intent in cashing in his stamps to think rationally. The immediate outcome will depend on whether the steward understands the concept of trading stamps. If he does, he will recognise that the outburst relates to events beforehand and will tactfully deal with the safety issue. If he does not, he may well use this as an opportunity to cash in his own collection, to which the passenger has obliging provided the final stamp.

There are a number of other similarities between our collection of feelings and the way we deal with trading stamps (nowadays vouchers or coupons). One is the way we may collect only certain kinds of stamps. Just as people will leave stamps behind in shops they visit infrequently, or not bother with school computer vouchers if they have no children of school age, so we vary in the events which generate feeling stamps for us. Perhaps we collect green envy stamps, yellow jealousy stamps, red angry or blue depression stamps. Or we may concentrate on stamps related to people making mistakes, to being kept waiting, to perceived snubs, or to any other specific preferences we have. If an 'impatience' collector is offered a 'mistake', they may not even notice it. Just as in shops, though, a mistake collector standing nearby may take the stamp for their own collection; any mistake is remiss in their eyes, even if they are unaffected by it.

Many of us plan in advance how to spend our collection of stamps. It is as if we look in the catalogue to decide what to save for: we will vary in the size of gift we want; some of us cash in as quickly as we can and settle for relatively small prizes; others save for a long time to have enough stamps for a really big prize. We may go for frequent outbursts of low level misery or wait until we can justify a major disruption in our life. Meanwhile, we may also spend time fantasising about the forthcoming prize, as when we imagine ourselves cashing in. We run a video in our heads as we see ourselves in action; we go over what we will say and do "if someone does that to me just once more".

Another similarity is with the bonus stamp. Just as suppliers offer extra vouchers on certain purchases, so we can collect more bad feelings in some situations. Our rackets may generate only one or two stamps at a time; if our collection is progressing too slowly we may move into psychological games as these will provide enough stamps to fill whole pages in one go.

A final contrast can be drawn about positive prizes. Commercial trading vouchers are cashed in for gifts that have some value to us. Many of our TA stamp collections, however, lead to unhealthy payoffs. Even a collection of gold stamps, exchanged for positive prizes, has its drawbacks. The major problem is the underlying belief that we somehow have to earn the prize. This works against our innate spontaneity.

Psychological health requires that we are free to decide what to do and how to behave. As long as we operate under the illusion that we must collect enough experiences, good or bad, to justify what we want to do, we will be limiting our own potential for autonomous living. Understanding of the TA concept of stamps can enable us to throw away our collections. We can concentrate on dealing with each situation as it arises; if something occurs that we are uncomfortable about, we can recognise this at the time and take appropriate immediate action. Even if we decide to do nothing, we can still avoid the unnecessary stress of carrying unhelpful feelings into the future with us.

TRAINER EFFECTIVENESS
Strokes in the Classroom
Strokes are especially significant in the classroom because of the nature of the relationship between trainer and students. Many participants will feel as if they are back at school, where teacher had the power to distribute very powerful positive or negative strokes. Recognition from the teacher was important for its own sake, but it also had a major impact on how we were perceived by our fellow students. If the courses you run involve feedback to the organisation on student performance, the parallels with taking home a school report to our parents are even more apparent.

If your participants are to relax and enjoy their experience in your session, they need a positive stroking climate. Remember that positive strokes include constructive criticism; it is not necessary to say only 'nice' things to them. What is called for is an atmosphere where people are respected and valued for their experience and potential; not made to feel inadequate because they do not yet know what they have come on the course to learn.

The way you greet participants will help to set the pattern for stroking during the course. Strokes are recognition so they include anything that demonstrates an interest in the other person. Asking questions, and listening to the responses, is a powerful form of stroking. This can be accomplished easily if you schedule in time at the start of a programme for participants to share information about themselves. Asking for brief introductions, about who they are, what their job is, what they do in their spare time, why they are on the course – this all helps to indicate your genuine recognition of them as individuals.

Stroking is also a crucial aspect of giving feedback. Participants need a balance of comments on what they did well and what needs to be improved. Too much focus on what went wrong is depressing; too much emphasis on what they did well denies them the information they require to develop their skills. When using peer feedback, provide participants with a clear structure that encourages them to balance their feedback. For instance, ask them to point out two things their colleague did well, two things which could be improved, and practical suggestions on how to make the changes. This avoids the feedback session degenerating into a series of superficial comments about how well each person did. It also discourages those participants who demonstrate their own superiority by criticising others.

As trainers, we can only provide effective stroking to participants if our own stroking patterns are satisfactory. Otherwise, we are too dependent on our students to provide us with strokes. Even worse, if we cannot get enough positive strokes from them we will revert to a search for negatives, leading us into rackets and games.

Completing the stroking patterns exercise described as Activity 7.3 will yield valuable insights. You may want to repeat the analysis for different areas of your life, so you can add together the results in your working life with colleagues, in your social life with family and friends, and with any time you spend on your own development. This will help you to see if you are relying on course members to meet any deficits. I have known several trainers whose personal lives were so bereft of friends that they relied for strokes on time spent socialising with participants. This created conflicts when they needed to maintain a more neutral stance towards participants.

Games in the Classroom

Some of the games I described earlier in this chapter have variations that are played in the classroom. Gotcha!, Yes, but and Rebuff are common examples. There is also a game called CYG (Can you guess?), and those of us who know about TA may play Transactional Analysis.

Gotcha! in the classroom may involve a student setting up the trainer, or the trainer setting up the student. In the former, the student begins by asking several questions. These become increasingly penetrating; the trainer who is prone to this game will feel pleased that the student is so interested in the subject. The trainer may have a nagging little doubt about whether the material under discussion is becoming too advanced for the rest of the class. However, this doubt will be dismissed because the trainer is enjoying demonstrating just how much they know about the subject. Gradually, the trainer will begin to reach the limits of their knowledge, and will probably be tempted to add facts which they are not totally confident about. Suddenly, the participant pounces, to point out a contradiction or flaw in the trainer's logic. The trainer has been zapped. After a moment of confusion, they are seen to have bluffed and their credibility with the group is diminished.

An alternative version occurs when a trainer feels threatened by the superior competence of a participant. Without being aware of their true feelings, the trainer sets out to 'prove' that the participant is not as clever as they appear. The process will be the same, except that this time the trainer asks the questions and the participant is eventually caught out in an error or discrepancy.

Yes, but occurs when a trainer begins to offer solutions to a participant who has not asked for help. It is very easy to make this mistake when your very reason for being there is to teach and help your participants. An excess of enthusiasm leads us to overlook the fact that some people prefer to stay as they are, and may not even recognise that they have a problem. Perhaps the manager sent them on the course but they still believe that the fault is with the manager and not them.

In this game, the more the trainer tries to find a solution, the more the participant points out the snags. A battle of wills may develop, as the trainer recognises the potential loss of reputation in the eyes of the other participants if the problem is not resolved.

Rebuff is a possibility during courses which run outside normal working hours. Rebuff with sexual connotations is an obvious prospect on residential programmes, or whenever the trainer may be left alone with one participant. Rebuff without sexual elements is also likely whenever work continues outside set session times. The nature of the trainer/student relationship makes it all too easy for the trainer's offers of help to be misinterpreted or taken advantage of. The trainer may then find that their motives are misunderstood, or that they are spending extra hours helping participants with problems that have nothing to do with the course content.

CYG (Can you guess?) is a sort of guessing game, in which the trainer establishes superiority over the class. The trainer begins by asking the group a question, having first neglected to provide them with the full information they would need to answer it. The group respond by calling out as many possible answers as they can, becoming increasingly despondent and frustrated as the trainer keeps telling them encouragingly to continue guessing. They may continue guessing until the trainer switches, or they may refuse to offer any more options and become mutinously silent. In either case, the trainer eventually, and somewhat triumphantly, provides the correct answer. At this point, the participants realise they could not have succeeded because they did not have the necessary information anyway. They feel inadequate, or angry with the trainer for setting them up; the trainer feels one-up over such a slow group.

Transactional Analysis as a game is described in Chapter 1, Applying TA in Organisations, as one of the abuses of TA. Put simply, it involves the trainer using their knowledge of TA concepts to analyse the participant's behaviour without sharing that process with the individual. The trainer typically begins as Rescuer, implying that they can help the participant. To be helped, though, the participant must adopt the role of Victim and act as if they could not help themselves. The trainer then moves to Persecutor, as they point out that the participant does not seem capable of accepting help. This role may extend outside the training room, when the trainer reports back to management that the participant was unwilling to accept feedback.

As with our stroking patterns, our own propensities as trainers will influence which games get played during our courses. We can identify our own games by working through Activity 7.4. This is best done by starting with a general review, as we will probably play variations of the same games whether we are in the classroom or not. Once we have identified potential game preferences, we can then work out how these are likely to show up in interactions with course members. It can be helpful to think about the 'types' of participants that we typically have difficulties with. What repetitive patterns of miscommunication or dissatisfaction occur? Having spotted a game, we can then work out how to behave differently so as to avoid it in future.

ACTIVITIES
Activity 7.1 Written Stroking
This activity requires that the group already know each other, or have spent some time together engaged on group exercises since the course started. It is intended to give practice at giving and receiving strokes.

Each person writes down one positive stroke for each other member of the group. These are then distributed so that each individual receives a collection of strokes.

Alternative formats include:
- any form of positive strokes, with selection determined by the stroke giver
- making the strokes positive but about changes, so that they practice giving constructive criticism in writing
- having participants read out the strokes they have received, to reinforce the impact and get them used to accepting strokes without embarrassment
- allowing people to remain anonymous, although this should only be done as an initial stage prior to requiring them to give strokes directly
- allowing individuals to specify the subject of the strokes they wish to receive (e.g. competence, skill, appearance or more specific aspects such as accuracy, helpfulness, etc.)

Activity 7.2 Verbal Stroking

This activity is similar to Activity 7.1 except that the strokes are spoken instead of written. Participants take it in turns to be the stroke focus and to receive strokes from each other person present.

Activity 7.3 Stroking Patterns

Once you have explained the general concept of strokes, you can invite participants to analyse their own patterns by completing a simple questionnaire. You may like to prepare a ruled sheet to hand out to participants, with appropriate headings. Otherwise, tell them to draw up a sheet divided vertically into five columns, headed with the names of five people they work closely with (for a work-based pattern – for a social pattern put friends). Then divide the sheet horizontally to give space to answer six questions.

Participants will need the following comments on the questions, even if you have already prepared a sheet with headings.

Giving Strokes

1. When did you last give each of them a significant stroke? (i.e. more than a polite greeting).
2. Was it positive or negative? – did it invite them to feel okay about themselves and others or was it some form of put-down of themselves or others?
3. What prompted it? Work, personal, hobbies, appearance, etc – your preferences or theirs?

Getting Strokes

4. When did you last receive a significant stroke from each of them?
5. Positive or negative?
6. What prompted it?

Brief the group to base the exercise on their current work situation, or on their previous post if they have recently changed job. Once they have completed the charts, invite them to consider the following aspects:

- Review your answers and become more aware of the ways in which you give and receive recognition. Consider first your choice of the five people. Are they a good selection or have you included only those people you like most? What interactions do you have with the colleagues you like least. And have you included your boss as someone you work with?
- Next, review your responses in the section on Giving Strokes. How might you appear to others? How much time is spent in put-downs compared to positives? Note that constructive criticism is a positive stroke – it implies that the person can do better and you care enough about them to let them know how. How varied are your reasons for strokes: do you range over work and personal matters or do you only comment on whatever interests you? People who get on well with others target their strokes, making sure that they pay attention to whatever the other person values.

- Finally, consider your pattern for Getting Strokes. Are you getting a reasonable quantity and variety? Do you feel comfortable with your working group? Check for any tendency to swap strokes as this can devalue them. Swapping occurs when we automatically return a compliment, such as when we say "Yours is nice too." The overall effect is to cancel out the original stroke, leaving both parties feeling vaguely dissatisfied or disappointed.

This exercise works well if they complete the sheets individually and then pair up to compare results. Comments and questions can be dealt with afterwards in plenary, giving you chance to expand on the basic input.

Activity 7.4 Game Analysis

Have groups identify situations at work where they now suspect games are being played. Brief them to write a script of the game and produce it as if it were a playlet. When they perform the playlet, have the rest of the class analyse the moves using the drama triangle.

In plenary or in reconvened groups, have participants work out what could be changed by one of the game players so that a satisfactory outcome is achieved.

Note: remind them that games are out of awareness. Spotting one's own involvement in a game is a cause for celebration as you can now change your behaviour. Giving yourself a bad time for engaging in a game is tantamount to playing Kick me inside your head. Rebuking someone else for playing a game amounts to playing a different game, called TA, which is what we are doing when we use our knowledge of the concept to reinforce feelings of superiority over someone who lacks the same knowledge.

Activity 7.5 Game Identification

This activity comes best after participants have gained a reasonable knowledge of the concept of games. It will probably work better if they have already completed the game analysis activity in a group, and accept that games are in fact something that all of us engage in some of the time.

Game identification is an individual activity in which participants identify a game that they play and plan how they might change their behaviour. If the group has established a reasonable level of trust, they could also pair up to compare notes. Brief them to answer the following:

- Think of a repetitive situation that ends with you feeling dissatisfied, uncomfortable or upset in some way.
- How does it begin? Think carefully about the start as it may be before any words are spoken. Perhaps the trigger is the look on someone's face, or an action by you which stimulates a comment.
- What happens next? Note down the sequence of interactions.
- How does it end? What happens to finish the interaction?
- How do you feel when it ends?

- How do you think the other person feels?
- What underlying message are you sending the other person?
- What underlying message do you believe you are you picking up from them?
- How might you behave differently at the beginning to change the dynamics and get a positive outcome?
- What else can you change in your life so that you no longer need the negative strokes that you collect from this game?

Activity 7.6 Dealing with Games

This is a group activity in which participants identify and analyse psychological games, and plan ways to avoid them. Groups can be any size but should be small enough to involve everyone in the discussions (say a maximum of nine). They can choose whether to role play games which involve all of them or which consist of interactions between only two or three of them. Brief them to:

1. Select a typical situation in which they now recognise that a game takes place. To ease any tension, joke with them that they do not have to admit to playing a game themselves; they can pretend they are writing to an agony aunt claiming to have a friend who has a problem.
2. Prepare a role play of the situation.
3. Analyse it using the drama triangle.
4. Identify a more constructive way for one of the parties to behave, so as to eliminate the game. This should be realistic – don't have a 'problem person' suddenly change character – instead, how can another party change how they deal with such a person.
5. Prepare a role play with the new behaviour incorporated, and with an appropriate change in the responses of the other parties.
6. Analyse the new situation using the drama triangle.

Have the groups return and role play in plenary. Use the following steps:

1. One group role plays the game.
2. The rest of the class analyse it. Discuss any discrepancies in the analyses.
3. The group then role plays their new, constructive version.
4. Rest of the class analyse this. Discuss the usefulness of the changed behaviour. Review any other options that exist for a satisfactory interaction.

Repeat the steps with another group.

Activity 7.7 Helpfulness Rackets

Ask participants to select a partner and decide who is A, who is B. A is to be comfortable, not needing anything at the moment. B is to be 'helpful', insisting that there must be something they can do to make A more comfortable.

After about five minutes, they are to switch roles.

When both have experienced both roles, ask them to discuss what happened.

Activity 7.8 Weekend Trip Rackets

In a group of at least four, two are to role play being a couple who are planning a weekend away together. They have quite different views on how they want to spend their time.

The rest of the group are to help them devise a realistic sequence, and then to coach them while they rehearse.

Once the role play is complete, have the group analyse it for games or rackets. This could also be done in plenary.

NOTES & SOURCES

Strokes, games, rackets and stamps are all concepts introduced by Eric Berne. The Stroke Rules were identified by Claude Steiner: see *Scripts People Live* Grove Press 1974 and subsequently Bantam Books (several printings)

Steiner also introduced the terms "warm fuzzies" for positive strokes, and "cold pricklies" for negative strokes, in his Warm Fuzzy Tale in the same book.

I have changed the names of some games because they were misleading and potentially offensive. What I call Rebuff was originally known as Rapo, which had unfortunate connotations of rape being invited by the victim. Gotcha! is my name for NIGYSOB, which stands for *Now I've Got You, You Son of a Bitch* – which nowadays is very non-PC.

CYG (Can You Guess?) was called Argentina by Berne, using a specific example of a teacher asking pupils about that country. I have called it CYG because that better captures the dynamic involved regardless of the topic. And although not mentioned in this chapter, I change Wooden Leg to Millstone.

The Drama Triangle was introduced by Stephen Karpman, who received an Eric Berne Memorial Scientific Award for this concept. See Appendix 2 for the reference.

Advantages of games: Berne described the internal social advantage of games as being similar to the external social advantage, except that the time is spent with intimates rather than acquaintances. However, this uses 'internal' in a way that is inconsistent with the description of the internal psychological advantage. I have therefore based my example on that given by Cowles-Boyd and Boyd in their article 'Play as a time Structure' which I have referenced in Chapter 8, Working in Groups.

Much of the information on rackets was developed by Fanita English. See Appendix 2 for details of the Eric Berne Memorial Scientific Award to her in 1978 for some of this work.

Activity 7.5 Game Identification is based on an original suggestion of a Game Plan devised by John James.

CHAPTER 8:   WORKING IN GROUPS

This chapter complements the previous one on working with others by including some additional dimensions that relate to group processes. The ideas covered are relevant for teambuilding, including those teams that spend time working separately as well as together in meetings.

In the first section I describe seven recognisable ways we have of spending, or structuring, time with others and alone. I show how we move through a sequence as a relationship develops; how a relationship may fail if we omit important parts of the sequence; and how the concepts of *strokes, games* and *rackets* can be linked to the *time structuring* process.

I then present an alternative model, for understanding group processes from the perspective of our individual perceptions. I describe the four stages of development of a group imago, or mental image of a group, with examples of the effects of this on our behaviour. I also compare this to the non-TA model by Tuckman that will be familiar to many trainers.

The Trainer Effectiveness section describes how we can use our knowledge of time structuring and imagoes to facilitate the process by which participants form into a group. Ideas are included on how your own imago as a trainer is likely to affect your interactions with participants. Activities include a fun exercise to demonstrate the impact of time structuring, and two activities to increase self awareness concerning time structuring and group imagoes. I also give a brief account of the non-TA FIRO-B Questionnaire as this provides a useful adjunct to the TA concepts.

TIME STRUCTURING

Berne's concept of time structuring gives us a way of tracking the progress within a group, in much the same way as Tuckman's stages of forming, storming, norming and performing. Time structuring has the advantage of being readily understood and remembered because we go through the same stages whenever we are with people, even though there may be only two or three of us present.

Berne wrote of basic hungers, or needs, that humans have; one of these was for structuring of our time. He suggested that entertainers were paid so much because they filled our time, leaving less for us to have to find a way of structuring. My amended set of time structure categories contains seven options: alone, rituals, pastimes, working, playing, (psychological) games and closeness. (Berne's original list is given at the end of this chapter.)

We can look to the ways we spend our time as a categorisation of the way we exchange strokes. Our natural human desire for recognition from others causes us to move through a sequence of behaviours in order to exchange strokes of ever increasing intensity. The success of our team building is directly related to the ease with which we achieve the forms of time structuring that provide the most satisfying stroking. The seven different ways in which we structure our time form a rough ladder up which we may climb towards a closer relationship.

Alone

Time *alone* may be spent in many places: at the desk planning, in the car driving to appointments, in the swimming pool, sitting in front of the TV. We may be thinking about work or pleasure, be feeling cheerful or sad or angry, be engaged in physical activity or sedentary. We may also be amongst a group of people yet still be alone, as when we daydream or mentally withdraw.

When we structure our time alone, or in what Berne called withdrawal, we are not receiving strokes from others. We may be recycling strokes previously received, or stroking ourselves mentally, but this is not the same as recognition from other human beings. However, all of us need some time alone. It gives us chance to think, relax, and recharge our batteries. Too little time alone may lead to stress and indicate an unhealthy over-reliance on stimulation from others.

Individuals who spend a lot of time alone may be perceived by others as especially self-contained, or even as unfriendly. This can become a problem when the real reason for such minimal contact is a lack of social skills. Someone who does not know how to make small talk may act as if they do not want company whilst secretly longing to socialise more. Similarly, an overly pessimistic or critical view of life may interfere with our ability to make contact with others.

Conversely, those who cannot tolerate withdrawal will become stressed if they lack company. In organisations, they are likely to leave their workplace to go on artificial errands in order to find someone to talk to. Open plan offices are preferred by those who dislike withdrawal, and hated by those who want time to be alone.

Rituals

Rituals include any interactions where we know exactly what socially acceptable remarks are expected from us. In addition to relatively lengthy rituals such as wedding and funeral services, there are the everyday greetings that we exchange. These provide an interesting reflection of cultural differences - depending on our nationality we may bow politely, shake hands, kiss cheeks, or hug. The UK greeting of "How are you?" is fascinating for its illogicality: it would be a major mistake to actually answer the question instead of responding with an echo.

Our ritualised greetings to each other provide fairly low intensity strokes. Our comments are automatic so they involve little real recognition or interest in the other person. We miss them if they are omitted but do not get major reinforcement from them. However, they are an important prelude to more powerful forms of stroking. If rituals are omitted, we may decide that the person is not someone with whom we wish to have further contact.

Rituals form an important part of organisational life. As we meet new people, we are expected to greet them in ways that match the corporate norms. Using a informal mode of address in a formal organisation, for example, may put us at a disadvantage. Forgetting someone's name may undermine the impact of our stroke; the other person may even interpret this as a deliberate negative stroke. Not knowing the hierarchical status of the other person can leave us floundering in some organisations. I recall many years ago, as a junior member of staff, being teased about the way I had chatted casually to someone who turned out to be the Managing Director.

Pastimes

Here we literally 'pass time' with others. *Pastiming* involves small talk, as when we discuss the weather, our holidays, the prices in the shops, and so on. We pastime whenever and wherever we chat socially. Once a subject has been mentioned, we pay sufficient attention to the conversation to be able to add our own views or information. Our conversation is partly ritualised, in that we obey some intuitive rule about not changing the subject until we judge others are ready to do this also. However, it is only the subject that is controlled in this way; within the current topic we are free to say whatever we decide.

The strokes from pastimes are more powerful than from rituals because of the need to pay closer attention to what the other person is saying. If we pick up only the general topic we may inadvertently repeat what they have already said. We have to listen and select our own comments so that the conversation will flow. This deeper listening is experienced as a more intense form of stroking.

Pastiming is often an important prelude to a meeting. We use this time to 'get a feel' for the other people and to establish some rapport. Those who complain about alliances at meetings have often neglected to arrive in time to join in the pastiming. Workaholics who try to move straight into the business of the meeting fail to realise that many people appreciate the opportunity to chat casually beforehand so that they will have some point of contact aside from the task.

Working

Working in this context is performing tasks with others in order to achieve goals and produce results together. We may be discussing needs with a customer, having a meeting, reviewing ideas with a colleague, or any of the many activities we engage in with others on behalf of the organisation. We also work with family and friends, to accomplish objectives such as decorating a house, producing an amateur play, serving as a school governor.

Strokes that arise from working are medium to high intensity. We require a good degree of involvement and attention in order to stroke appropriately when we are working with someone. It is worth remembering that questions are also strokes, and can be very powerful as they indicate a strong interest in what the other person has to say.

Playing

When we *play* we spend time with others engaged in activities that we are doing because we enjoy them. The obvious examples are sports and hobbies (although some of us become so achievement-orientated that we turn these into work). Less obvious instances of play occur when we brainstorm, before we worry about whether the ideas are any use. I describe how to brainstorm properly in Chapter 11 as part of the process of creativity. Genuine brainstorming is play, which we need to follow with work as we review the practicability of our suggestions.

Play-generated strokes are medium to high intensity, depending on the energy that we put into the activity. The more enthusiastic we are, the more impact our strokes will have on each other. Joint laughter is an especially strong contributor to our stroke bank. The effect of play strokes will also be enhanced as we develop deeper friendships.

Playing in organisations is often centred around sports teams or social events. The more these are encouraged by the organisation, the more employees are likely to 'play together' and hence develop closer relationships that will enable them to work together well. An increasingly common form of playing in organisations is the involvement of groups of employees in charitable events; these also stimulate more contact inside the organisation as the arrangements are made and the results are publicised.

Psychological Games

Games were described in some detail in the previous chapter on Working with Others. They are repetitive sequences of interactions, engaged in by two or more people. They are the ways in which we fail to get along well with others; we end up feeling dissatisfied with them or with ourselves. Although psychological games are played out of our awareness, we can sometimes recognise them when we get that "Here I go again!" sensation.

It is likely that games are actually an unconscious substitute for becoming close to others. Unless we have satisfactory relationships with others, we will not receive enough positive strokes. Just as when we were young, we will turn to negative strokes to make up the deficit. Depending on the degree to which we play the game, the strokes thus generated may be very powerful indeed.

Within a team, it is sometimes as if we have special antennae that can identify the very person who is most likely to play a corresponding game hand to our own. As we move through rituals, pastimes, playing and working, we seem to register subtle signals that tell us who wants to be one-up, who one-down, and who will join us in the repetitive, predictable sequence of game moves that we believe to be normal behaviour.

Closeness

As we get to know people, we hope that we will be able to relax and be ourselves when we are with them. Often, we do not believe this is possible so we maintain a façade behind which we shelter our strongest emotions and censor our opinions. *Closeness* occurs when we establish sufficient trust to feel able to share our true feelings and express our views candidly. We are then able to give honest feedback about our likes and dislikes, and we expect them to do the same. Doing this in a caring and respectful way strengthens our relationship and allows us to depend on each other for honesty in our communication.

Closeness yields high intensity strokes which reinforce considerably our sense of well-being. Thoughtful, well-intentioned constructive criticisms are just as valuable to us as direct expressions of love and affection. The significant factor is that we feel truly close to another person, with whom we can be open and trusting. Peck captures the spirit of this in non-TA language when he writes of 'community'. Berne called this way of structuring time 'intimacy'.

I believe that more and more people are now recognising, and demanding, that organisations should be run in ways that enable people to attain closeness with their colleagues. Training courses are often structured specifically to encourage participants to be open and supportive. Management styles are changing to reflect this move. However, it is important to remember that we need to work through the stages from alone, via rituals, pastimes, working and playing, toward closeness. Expecting people to move too quickly into closeness is more likely to lead to game playing.

Time Structuring and Rackets

As I mentioned in the previous chapter, there are several definitions of the TA term racket. One use of the term is as a repetitive, unsatisfactory sequence that leads to us feeling bad. We can relate this concept to each of the ways of structuring time except closeness, which is a way of interacting that is free of rackets or games.

On bad days, when we feel determined to see the world as a cold and unfriendly place, we may slip unknowingly into rackets even when there is no-one around to play a psychological game with. This will interfere with our ability to function well as a team member:

- Alone: The target of our racket response may not even be in contact with us. However, for some reason they come to mind and we imagine them making derogatory comments about us to a third party.
- Rituals: Two people deep in conversation fail to notice us as they hurry by, although we say hello. We conclude that they deliberately chose not to greet us.
- Pastimes: Someone changes the subject when we are telling the group about our new car. They do this because they are so excited by the birth of their grandchild that they cannot wait to break the news. We feel offended and decide they were really signalling boredom with our comments.
- Working: We are asked a genuine question about the progress of our work. We interpret this incorrectly as an expression of dissatisfaction and hear it as a negative stroke.

- Playing: The other person wins the match. We suspect they cheated.
- Games: Rackets can be a mini-game. We have the repetition and predictability of a game, as well as the negative payoff. However, we do not have a switch so the impact will be less. It may be that we escalate to a game when the negative stroke from the racket is not sufficiently powerful.
- Closeness: Now that we are close and trusting, we have no need of our rackety sequences.

GROUP IMAGOES

Group imago is another TA concept that has direct relevance to the ways in which we join and co-operate in teams. This lesser known idea from Berne help us understand even more about the underlying dynamics in groups. We can then see why we like some people and not others, how our preconceptions and prejudices affect our involvement, and how we come to engage in such unhelpful and apparently illogical pursuits as psychological games.

Berne used the term 'imago' to mean a mental image that we have of a group of people, possibly outside conscious awareness, and which influences our actions. Thus, before we enter a room to join a group, we already have in our minds an imago of them and us. This is likely to be based on a mixture of past events, preconceptions, rumour and fantasy. The imago will be personal to each of us, so that we enter a group with different expectations, leading in turn to different perceptions.

Simply knowing that we start our involvement in a team with a pre-existing imago can be useful. Recognising this phenomenon means we can unpack our mental baggage and decide how much of it is relevant, how much is assumption, how much we should discard if we are to meet people with an open mind. However, the concept has additional advantages when we realise that our imago stays with us and is updated as we spend time in the group. Constant monitoring of its content will enable us to relate more effectively to others in the team.

As we become involved in the group, we collect more information about our fellow group members. We are able to develop our imago, with separate slots appearing for individuals as we get to know them and to differentiate between them. We build up increasing amounts of detail in the slots we have for each person.

We can identify four stages in the development of our imago, from the time we first enter the group until the point at which we are as integrated a group as we will become. These phases are not separated by clear boundaries; we gradually move through them. However, the characteristics of each are recognisable and knowledge of them can help us with our teambuilding process.

Anticipatory Group Imago

We begin with an anticipatory mental picture like that in figure 8.1 Typically, this will contain little more than a slot for ourself, a slot on a higher level for the leader, and an

Figure 8.1: Anticipatory Group Imago

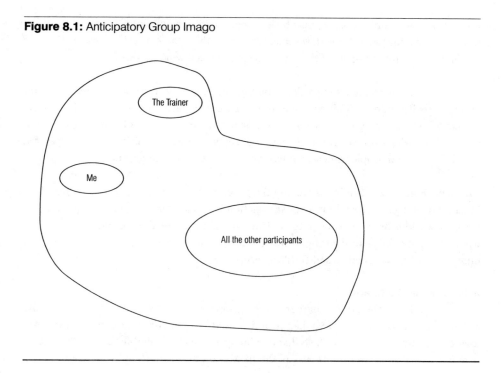

undifferentiated slot for everyone else. If we already know some of the group members, these people are likely to have a slot of their own within our mental picture.

The detail contained within the imago cannot be shown in a diagram on paper. In our head there will be a rich pattern of our ideas, opinions and expectations that make up each slot. Into the slot for ourselves we will have incorporated aspects such as our recollections of previous group experiences, our views of the task, our personal objectives and hidden agendas, and our opinions of our own competence and confidence in such situations.

For the leader, there will be an amalgam of previous leaders we have known, selections from the comments made and rumours put about by others, all merged with any experience we have acquired personally of this current leader. If no formal leader of the group has been announced, we will still have a slot into which we put our attitudes and memories of previous leaders. We will then be waiting for a body to insert into the slot, and will study the group members for likely candidates - or maybe consider whether the leader slot should belong to us.

Slots for other group members will vary depending on what we already know about them. Existing colleagues will be well differentiated, with detail on how we expect them to react based on our observations in the past. Similar to our aim in the board game of Scruples, we will be able to predict their likely responses to a range of events - something we cannot do with new acquaintances. We may be less accurate too in our slot content for those we worked with in the past; although we believe we know them, we may yet be missing changes that have taken place as part of their growth since we last worked together.

Group members we do not know will be compounded together into one conglomerate slot, perhaps labelled in our minds as 'the others'. Or we may have separate, but still relatively undetailed slots, for males versus females, or managers versus staff. Another common division is into departments, as if we believe that anyone from sales will be one sort of person, and different from people from accounts, who are not like those in production, and so on.

Our behaviours and attitudes as we join the group will be structured by our anticipatory imago. We will gain a certain level of satisfaction if we can confirm our anticipations. At least the world is how we expect it to be. However, if our original imago is depressing, we will be hoping to be proved wrong. Unfortunately, we may well invest our pattern with so much power that we create a self-fulfilling prophecy.

Adjusted Group Imago

As we get to know the other members in the group, we update, augment and generally adjust our imago. Gradually we begin to differentiate between individuals who were formerly grouped into one slot, so that our imago comes to resemble that in Figure 8.2. A major contributor to the process is the pastiming and superficial working together

Figure 8.2: Adjusted Group Imago

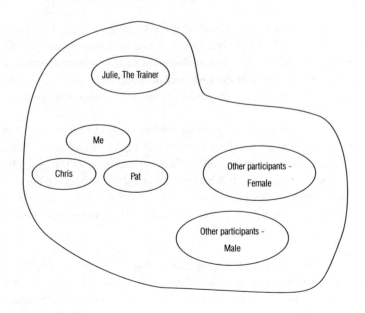

that we do. As we converse, we are collecting data about each other and about how we will fit in.

Our personal approach to rituals, pastimes, playing and working will be important here, as this will be the basis on which others are judging us. If we fail to demonstrate acceptable rituals such as greetings, we may not get beyond the anticipatory imagoes. If we have no small talk to offer, the other group members will become uncomfortable around us. Without realising why, they will react negatively because they cannot acquire the data they need to flesh out a proper slot for us in their imago. After initial attempts to engage us in suitable conversation, they may well retreat and ignore us. We will remain inside an undifferentiated slot, or will perhaps have a slot to ourselves which contains little detail. If we fail generally to respond, it will seem as if we do not belong in the group.

This stage in the life of a group is a time of testing, to see what the others are like, and to think about whether and how we might fit in.

Adapted Group Imago

The third stage as shown in Figure 8.3, concerns our relationship with the leader. We need to sort this out before we can decide how to behave towards other members of the group. We begin to adapt our imago to reflect how we intend to adapt (or not) to the leader and

Figure 8.3: Adapted Group Imago

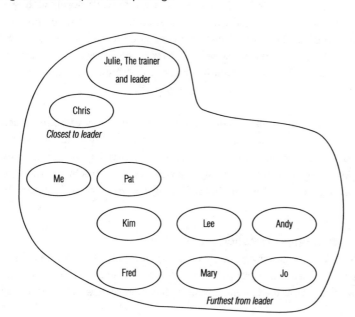

other group members. This is similar to being a child in a family; we needed to know where we stood with our parent(s) in order to deal appropriately with our siblings. Now we interpret the behaviour of our manager as a guide to how we should deal with our colleagues. The position of the slots in our imago, vis-à-vis the leader's slot, take on more significance.

A clear organisational structure will help here, as will consistent indicators from the leader. Power plays are likely to occur at this stage, as we seek to establish the level of control that will apply. In addition to bids for the leadership, we may also be jostling with colleagues to see where we fit in the pecking order.

Whoever is leader will still have a leader slot in their imago. This may be filled with detail about themselves. However, it may instead contain information about other leaders they have known. This will mean that they model their own behaviour to suit a fantasised leader. In effect, they will be transacting with a phantom, with the obvious difficulties that may lead to. They may respond to an internal dialogue with some previous manager or parent figure who must be satisfied, or insists on compliance with outdated requirements.

Within this stage, we will be working at the tasks of the group. We are also likely to engage in psychological games as we move into our habitual patterns for transacting with other people.

Attached (or Alienated) Group Imago
We will enter this stage with a clearer view of individual members of the group. There will be enough detail for us to have decided which people we want to work closely with, who we would prefer to lose from the team, and who we will tolerate provided we do not have to spend much time with them. They will of course have made the same decisions about us. We have also decided the leadership issues, or have determined to continue our struggle for control. Our imago may well look like that in Figure 8.4, although it may also be an alienated version where we do not feel we are in a group at all.

Each of us may have come to different conclusions but now we have some shared expectations about how the group will function. The worst case result will be a group that is sabotaged by psychological games, with conflict and power struggles. The best case will be a group in which we are close, open and trusting and work together to achieve our shared objectives. Either way, our imago now contains sufficient data to guide our interactions with each other.

Forming, Storming, Norming and Performing
At about the time Berne was developing his ideas on group imagoes, Tuckman was writing about the developmental sequence in a group. Tuckman's non-TA ideas are now well known in training for teams and groups as the familiar 'forming, storming, norming and performing'.

Forming relates to the anticipatory group imago. This is the time when the team is deciding who is in or out of the group. The potential members are deciding, on the basis of their

Figure 8.4: Attached Group Imago

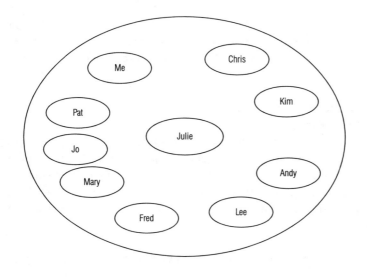

imagoes, whether these are people with whom they wish to form a team, or not. If not, they may opt to withdraw from the group, either physically or psychologically. There may well be confusion in the group as members realise their anticipatory imagoes do not contain enough information for them to make choices about other people.

Storming is similar to the development of the adjusted group imago. Members test each other out, using data from rituals, pastimes and working to determine who will be the appropriate partners when they are ready to play psychological games or engage in closeness. If a number of individuals in the team are intent on playing games, the group will go on to experience a lot of storming and will have difficulty attaining a positive profile for the later stages of the group.

Norming matches the adapted group imago state. Group members are now ready to sort out their relationships with the leader. Everyone aims to settle into their own positions in the pecking order. An effective leader can now act as a facilitator and model positive ways of behaving. An ineffective leader, or one who is prone to game playing, may create norms that generate unhealthy competition within the group. If the issue of leadership is resolved satisfactorily, the group can now establish an element of harmony.

Performing occurs at the final, attached group imago. Team members can now relax and structure time by working and closeness with each other. In a well functioning team, the members will stroke each other positively and obtain much satisfaction from achieving the task via a healthy process of interaction. Unhealthy groups do not reach this stage; the negative aspects of the interaction process take on more priority than the task and an alienated imago is the result.

As with the imagoes, the stages identified by Tuckman are broad patterns only. There is no clear boundary at which a group or an individual moves neatly into the next phase. However, it is possible to recognise the general trends, and to take account of them as the group develops.

TRAINER EFFECTIVENESS
Time Structuring in the Classroom

It is all too easy to overlook the stages of time structuring when we are training a group of people. Often, the trainer is busy setting out the room when people arrive. I have even seen trainers who stay in their own office, or chat with some other trainers, rather than being there to greet arrivals. Some establishments make it difficult for participants to get to know one another; many are hesitant to chat in the classroom but have no other place to meet before the course starts.

It is worth reviewing your training programme and your training environment to see what options you provide:

- Can participants be alone if they want to? Have you allowed sufficient breaks, and is there somewhere else they can go? If not, you increase the likelihood that they will withdraw psychologically. They may still be there physically but they will have stopped listening and learning.
- What rituals do you establish? Do you notice that they read the course documentation studiously as a way of avoiding the need to make contact?
- How much time do you allow for pastiming? Do you suggest that people arrive before the start time so they can chat to each other? Do you include a long enough period within the course for their introductions to include details about who they are, where they work, how they spend their spare time?
- Hopefully there is no shortage of opportunities for working during your courses. The main consideration here is whether it is interspersed with other ways of structuring time, so that people are not overloaded.
- Where does playing fit into your training? Do you regard this as something they only do outside the formal sessions? If so, do you bother to check that they have some options available? Did anyone tell them in advance to bring sports gear or casual clothes with them? Have you realised that training can also be achieved through play? Have you designed activities that are enjoyable and fun?
- Have you read Chapter 7, Working With Others, on how to avoid psychological games?
- Closeness is needed if participants are to be open and trusting about their problems so that you can help them. This will be more likely if you have taken care to provide opportunities for the other ways of time structuring, so that good relationships are established between those present. Setting clear contracts, as described in chapter 2, Contracting for Learning, is also important.

Imagoes in the classroom

Participants will view a training event in the same way as any other group activity, so they will arrive in the classroom with an anticipatory imago. As the course progresses, they will be seeking to develop this mental image through the stages described above. This has obvious implications for their behaviour during the programme.

An individual's anticipatory imago of the training group will have at least a slot for themselves, an undifferentiated slot for other participants, and a slot for the trainer. Each slot will be heavily influenced by previous experiences of training events. A group member may regard themselves as an incompetent participant, as someone who does not need to be on the course, as a star pupil whose role is to work in partnership with the trainer.

Other course members may all be contained in one rather scary slot. They may fantasise that the other participants already work together so they are the only person to know no-one. Prior work contacts may lead them to speculate on a 'departmental personality' as a slot instead of seeing people as individuals. It is not unknown for managers' sins to be visited on the subordinates, so that antagonism exists even before they meet.

Their view of the trainer may well depend substantially on their recollections of teachers at school, as this is an experience that lasted many years for most of us. Some teachers have much to answer for! Encounters with other trainers will have contributed too, and they will expect us to adopt similar styles of teaching. Participants may therefore arrive anticipating lectures when we plan discussion groups, or an academic treatise when we have lighthearted exercises in mind. A further source of their imago content will be the reputation of the trainer and the training. What have previous participants told them about you and the course?

If you are lucky, though, your participants will arrive with a positive view of you and each other, and an expectation that the training will be enjoyable and valuable.

If we run our training in such a way that our students have little direct contact with each other, it will be hard for them to develop the differentiated slots they need in their adjusted imagoes. They will have to rely on observation of participant interactions with the trainer, watching to see who asks or answers questions and so on. This may well involve them making a lot of assumptions about each other, so that the content of the slots may be suspect.

We can make the process easier for them if we allow time for introductions, organise refreshment breaks for casual chatting, and include syndicate and plenary discussions. We can also make these conversations more useful if we establish guidelines for content, such as suggesting they introduce themselves with specific information on their work background or their purpose in attending the course. The more we help participants develop an adjusted imago, the quicker they will complete the testing process and settle down to work together.

The stage of development of the adapted imago has obvious implications for the success or otherwise of the training. However we run our training, we will need to fill the leader slot in the participants' imagoes. If they arrive at a negative view of us, there will be problems in their interactions with us and also with other participants. They need a clear model of respectful and enabling communication, so that they in their turn will interact constructively with each other as well as with us.

If someone else fills the leader slot, participants will become confused about who is really 'in charge'. When groups are in syndicates or working on projects, they will temporarily create imagoes in which another participant may take the leader slot for that session. However, this will usually be seen as still subordinate to the overall leadership of the trainer. Once the session ends, the extra dimension will become part of the slot that represents the participant who led the group. The leader slot as such remains the province of the trainer.

As they move towards their attached imagoes, participants will finally be ready to move into the real work of the group. Provided they have opted for a healthy atmosphere and not a game laden environment, they will be prepared to help each other. Individuals will be willing to admit their weaknesses without fear of ridicule from the group. They will give and receive feedback constructively and generally support each other through the process of learning.

Imagoes and the Trainer

The concept of imagoes gives us a way of understanding how we approach our task of training a group. I have mentioned above that we can include certain activities specifically in order to help participants develop useful imagoes so that their learning is maximised. Awareness of the content of our personal imago will help us reinforce the training design through the way we relate to participants.

Our anticipatory imago will be based on previous experiences. We can check this by consciously reviewing it before a session. Do we have positive expectations of the group we are about to train? Or are we influenced by difficulties in the past, so that we are anticipating problems with a group we have not even met? Perhaps we need to 'clean out' the contents of some of the slots so that we start with an open mind.

We can also consider the nature of our slot for self. What view do we have of ourself as trainer - are we an all-seeing guru, a sparkling entertainer, an eminent academician - or a trainer with a variety of styles to suit the needs of the learners?

What about our prejudices? Imago dissection is an excellent way of identifying these. Do we have separate slots for men and women? Why - does this mean we assume different learning characteristics or abilities? Are there separate slots in our head when we see the skin colours of participants, or when we hear their accents, or even when we read their names on the course list? Perhaps we restrict ourselves to milder discrimination on the grounds of occupation, believing that engineers make better participants than salespeople, or that doctors are less intelligent than pharmacists.

Once we examine the contents of our imago, we can ask ourselves what evidence we have for the various beliefs. If we have reliable data, we can plan how to make our training most relevant. If we have no adequate basis for our assumptions, we can make a conscious decision to set them aside.

We need to get to know our participants in order to develop our adjusted imago. Attempting to do this as we plough through the training itself places a heavy load on us (and on the participants). We can more easily collect the information we need if we use break times to socialise instead of remaining aloof from the participants.

Greater awareness of our own mental processes will also help; the more we understand ourselves the better we can spot the participants who are likely to trigger negative responses from us. Once we accept responsibility for our part in unhelpful interactions, we have the incentive to develop new ways of communicating to avoid similar problems in future.

Our adapted imago will focus on our role as leader. We need to keep in mind that participants will be observing us to see how we behave towards them. They may not do this consciously but they will certainly store the information away into their individual imagoes. They will then respond accordingly, contributing to the session in line with their conclusions about our training style.

If we behave autocratically as the trainer, participants will perceive three options for themselves: keep quiet and hope not to be noticed; behave in a subservient, ingratiating way to keep us sweet; or rebel and challenge us for psychological leadership. If we overdo our desire for democracy and attempt to be just another member of the group, we deny participants the opportunity to develop appropriate detail within their leadership slot. They may well feel cheated and cast around for someone else to fulfil this role. Somehow, we have to balance our style so that we are approachable and encouraging without sacrificing control and structure.

As our attached imago comes into effect, we are hopefully ready to enjoy training the group. The attention we have paid to the earlier stages of our own imago development has enabled us to avoid some of the pitfalls of the past. Through increased self awareness, we have eliminated some of the psychological games we used to play with participants. We are also better able to deal with games that start up between participants.

We accept, realistically, that there will sometimes be participants whose circumstances have conspired to make it difficult for them to develop positive imagoes of the training group. However, we also expect our sessions to be generally worthwhile and affirmative experiences for us and for our course members.

ACTIVITIES

Activity 8.1 Time Structuring

Brief a group of seven to plan a camping trip together. Have each participant attempt to structure the time in a specific way. After each five minute session, they can rotate through the list so as to experience each option in turn. (See table below).

Afterwards, review their experiences during the meeting. How did they feel in each option? Help them relate the way this meeting went to what happens in ordinary meetings, where the range will be less extreme but will still include people who are at different stages.

Person 1	alone	nothing to say
Person 2	rituals	wants to chat, speaks in clichés
Person 3	pastimes	wants to talk about past experiences when camping
Person 4	working	wants to make solid plans, get details all worked out
Person 5	playing	wants to have fun, now
Person 6	rackets/games	wants to feel left out/unwanted or start an argument
Person 7	closeness	wants to share openly their positive and negative responses to the others

Activity 8.2 Time Pattern Pie

This activity helps participants to review the ways in which they currently structure their time, and to plan appropriate alterations if they want to change their stroke patterns.

You will need handouts which consist simply of a large circle drawn on a sheet of paper. Different colours make it more fun and will help them differentiate between the steps of the exercise.

They are going to divide the circle into a pie-chart to show the proportions for each of the ways of structuring time. They will prepare three separate charts as they work through Steps 1 to 3.

Step 1	Chart how they structure time now.
Step 2	Chart how they would like to structure time.
Step 3	Mark up a chart to indicate the areas of change.
Step 4	Plan what specific things they will do to effect the changes identified.

Optional additional step: if participants have recently joined a new team, suggest they first complete a chart showing how they structured their time in their previous situation.

Activity 8.3 Group Imagoes

Having explained the concept of group imagoes, ask participants to draw their own:

- as it was when they arrived on the training course
- As it is now

Suggest they compare notes in pairs.

Remind them to spend a few moments updating and considering the content of their imagoes at intervals throughout the course.

Activity 8.4 FIRO-B Questionnaire

The FIRO-B questionnaire devised by Will Schutz fits well with the stages of imago development. The questionnaire gives participants a measure of how they perceive the second to fourth stages, while the TA theory helps them see why and how these perceptions have come about. The TA provides the understanding necessary to make changing easier.

If you are not already familiar with FIRO-B, the following should allow you to see how it fits with group imagoes. It measures our perceptions on three key elements of our behaviour and preferences in relating to others: inclusion, control and affection, and on two dimensions: expressed and wanted.

Expressed behaviour relates to how much behaviour we feel comfortable exhibiting to others; wanted behaviour refers to how much of the behaviour we want other people to exhibit towards us. It is worth remembering that other people see our expressed rather than our wanted behaviour. They may assume incorrectly that what we want is reflected by what we do to others. This can lead to us being treated in ways that fail to match our real preferences.

Inclusion concerns behaviour related to being included within a group. Our inclusion score will relate to our imago at the second stage of group development, when we are developing our adjusted group imago. It will similarly influence others over the content of their slot for us in their own imago.

A high score on expressed inclusion indicates we are likely to act in ways that get us included in group activities. We are also likely to include others in our activities, and to behave in general as if we value being in the team. A low score on expressed inclusion means we are likely to act as if we do not want to be included in the group. We may offer few invitations to others and take little initiative in communicating.

A high score on wanted inclusion reflects a desire for others to involve us in their activities. We want to be invited to meetings and to be part of a team. A low score on wanted inclusion indicates that we are content to work alone and do not feel the need for others to take the initiative to include us in what they are doing.

Control refers to our propensities to lead and to follow. This relates to the adapted group imago, when we are deciding our relationship with the leader (or our desire to be the leader).

High expressed control means that we are likely to take charge in groups, and seek to control what happens through power and influence. Low expressed control indicates we may well let others take the lead, while we seem content to follow.

High wanted control means we prefer others to take charge. We are willing to let them make the decisions and tell us what to do. Low wanted control reflects that we are unwilling to be controlled by others. Even if we do not seek control ourselves, we may not be prepared to let others direct us.

Affection is about our desire for closeness and sharing. Assuming we have stayed in the group through the issues of inclusion and control, we are now ready to form our attached group imago, with details of who we wish to work closely with.

High expressed affection indicates that we initiate close personal relationships with others. We are willing to be open and trusting, sharing information about ourselves. Low expressed affection means we are likely to keep ourselves somewhat distant from others.

High wanted affection reflects our desire that other people will initiate close and deep relationships with us. We want them to share and be open towards us. Low expressed affection means we prefer that others are not too affectionate towards us. We would rather they maintained a psychological distance from us and did not try to get close.

Awareness of our FIRO-B scores can be very helpful in understanding why we get on well with some people and not with others.

Consider first whether your expressed and wanted scores reflect a consistent pattern. If you express one style but want another, people will be confused about how best to relate to you. They can only interpret your expressed behaviour. If you act, for example, as if you do not value inclusion, they will assume you want to be left alone. If you express high levels of these behaviours, they will respond in kind and keep involving you in their activities when you may prefer more time by yourself.

The other area where a mismatch may occur is in the different patterns preferred by individuals. Someone with high wanted inclusion will feel unwanted around people with low expressed inclusion. Two people with high expressed control may get into conflict, especially if both have low wanted control scores. A person with high expressed affection may seem overwhelming to someone with low wanted affection. Someone with low expressed and wanted control scores may be difficult to work with because they do not want to be the leader, but they are also reluctant to be led by anyone else.

Think about the people you get on well with. On the evidence of their behaviour, can you estimate what their FIRO-B scores might be? Can you now understand why you get on with them?

More importantly, can you now work out why you have unsatisfactory relationships with some people? How might you adjust your own approach to these people in order to develop a better relationship?

NOTES & SOURCES

When Berne first introduced the notion of time structuring, he used the terms withdrawal, rituals, pastiming, activities, psychological games, and intimacy. Playing was added later by Boyd & Boyd - see L Cowles-Boyd & H Boyd 'Play as a Time Structure' in _Transactional Analysis Journal_ 1980, 10(1), pp 5-7.

I have also changed three of Berne's labels to make the model sound less therapeutic and more everyday.

Hence, I use the term 'alone' instead of 'withdrawal'. To match this, I have changed Berne's activities into things done with other people and not any goal-directed behaviour.

I also refer to activities as 'working', to distinguish from 'playing' as this is referred to by most people as activities too. I think playing is an important extra dimension, and serves to remind us that we should pay attention to the whole person if we want to help participants develop as well-balanced individuals.

I substitute 'closeness' for the term 'intimacy' for two reasons. First, because I found that Berne's term was interpreted by participants as being something extremely special and rarely attainable, whereas I want people to realise that this way of structuring time is within their reach fairly readily if they are willing to risk being open. Second, I wearied of having to explain that intimacy did not refer solely to sexual intimacy; sex may be involved in any of the ways of structuring time and is not necessarily part of a close, trusting interaction with another person.

Berne's labels for group imagoes were provisional, adapted, operative and secondarily adjusted.

FIRO-B (not TA) see Will Schutz, _The Truth Option_ Ten Speed Press 1984. Note that accreditation is required to use FIRO; however the themes of inclusion, control and affection can be explained to participants without the use of the questionnaire.

Forming, Storming, Norming, Performing (not TA) see B Tuckman _'Developmental sequence in small groups'_. _Psychological Bulletin_ 1965, 63 pp 384-399 and B Tuckman and M.A.C. Jensen _'Stages of Small-group Development Revisited'_ in Group and Organisational Studies 1977, 2. Pp 419-427

CHAPTER 9:   LEADERSHIP STYLES

In this chapter, I present a framework that brings together many of the TA constructs described in previous chapters. It is very much a simplification but on an everyday basis it gives us a good start at analysing people, working out their probable preferences, and hence choosing ways to interact with them that give us the best chances of successful encounters.

The link with leadership is that effective interactions with a range of people 'types' is exactly what good leaders must be able to achieve. I therefore include within the framework some labels for different leadership styles – and emphasise that the best leaders are those with the flexibility to use all of the styles and the skills to decide which style with whom. Ineffective leaders tend to use their own preferred style only, and then blame others for lack of motivation.

Caveats
Whenever I teach the following material, I always explain that:
- This is a simplification of material that has been developed in great depth by therapists. See my notes about Taibi Kahler at the end of this chapter.
- We can't really fit people into boxes. We do it so we can have a framework to guide us in choosing our own behaviours so we will maximise our chances of getting on with people.
- People are immensely interesting and varied individuals so use the framework tentatively – don't allocate someone to a box and then get annoyed when they don't do everything in the way predicted by that box.

Note also that I have assumed that you, and your participants, will already have basic TA knowledge of *strokes, working styles* (my term for drivers Hay 1996) and channels of communication (*ego states* – and I use Functional Adult (Hay 1995) to distinguish a behavioural ego state from Adult in the various ego state models in current use). These are explained in other chapters but I have taught the following framework without much additional explanation – the terms are fairly self-explanatory.

AP³
This framework is called *AP³* because it consists of 3 dimensions each labelled with an A and a P. Imagine a cube, as shown in Figure 9.1, for which there is height, width and depth. Imagine that these three dimensions are, respectively:

Figure 9.1: AP³

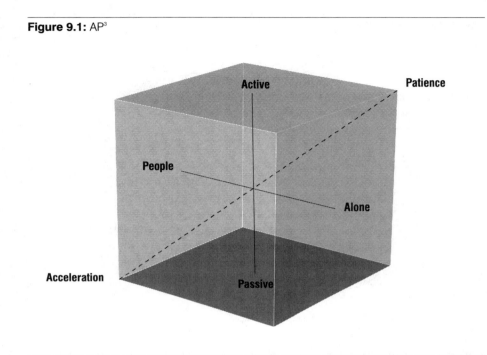

active – passive – do we initiate contact and move towards people and goals – or do we respond to contacts and goals initiated by others?

alone – people – do we prefer to be, or work, alone – or would we rather be functioning within a group of people, perhaps as the central figure?

acceleration – patience – do we prefer to do things quickly, perhaps even with ever-increasing speed – or do we like to take our time, doing things slowly and carefully?

Note that the acceleration – patience dimension runs from the top right-hand corner at the back to the bottom left-hand corner at the front rather than simply from back to front. I will come back to this later.

Identifying the Styles

We will concentrate first on the four AP³ styles that fit within the height and width dimensions of the cube. We can show these as if they are 4 boxes created by the axes, as in Figure 9.2.

The following are some ideas on how you might recognise the different types (and, of course, position yourself!). As you read the descriptions, imagine that the individual (or you) has arrived at a conference. They are expecting this to be mainly work-based but with a significant element of socialising. They arrive before the first formal session is due to start – and come into a large room where people are having coffees or cocktails, chatting

Figure 9.2: The AP³ Quadrant

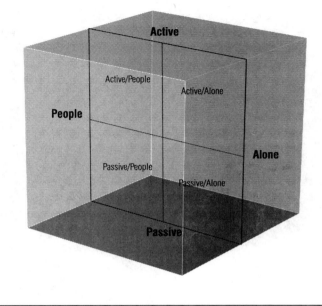

with each other, meeting new contacts or talking to people they already know, and generally passing the time until the official opening event.

Active/Alone

The first thing you'll notice when someone arrives at a conference (or when you meet them anywhere) is their appearance. In particular, you can see what they are wearing and this will be your initial set of clues to their AP³ type.

Active/Alone people are likely to be dressed very neatly, in a classically business orientated style. Everything they wear will be pressed or polished or otherwise in perfect condition. They will be appropriately attired to comply with whatever the cultural norms are for business in the area – and you may well suspect that they are likely to continue to look business-like at all times. These are the people who choose fairly formal outfits even for weekends. Not for them the comfort of casual clothes – they actively dislike dress-down days at work.

Having noticed their clothes, you can next observe their behaviour as they come into the room. Because they are Active, they will probably initiate contact by walking up to people. Because they are Alone, they will prefer to talk to only one or two people at a time.

They will therefore approach one person, or maybe two people who are already together. They will initiate a conversation with them – this will usually be about something work-related. For example, they may introduce themselves with their name and job details, clearly expecting the other person to reply with similar information. Or, if they already know the person, they may begin with a work-based comment such as a query about a current project or a request for information.

As they begin to talk, you get more clues. In addition to the work-based content, you will notice that Active/Alone people speak clearly and concisely. Their words are precise and their sentences are grammatically correct. They will not use slang, they will pause as if for punctuation at the correct points, and they will tend to use long words because these are usually more specific, and therefore more accurate, than shorter, everyday words.

They may also add clauses, or sub-sentences, into their sentences as if in brackets (which they would call parentheses as this is a more specific word) – just as I have done when writing this sentence. You will, I am sure, realise that too much of this makes the sentence rather long, and hence difficult to follow and understand! In their attempts to speak in perfect sentences that include everything, they often merely overload and confuse the listener.

One final clue – Active/Alone people often have horizontal frown lines – generated through all that worrying about getting it right.

When you consider what motivates them, their working style is most likely to be Be Perfect. Their preferred channel of communication will be Functional Adult-Functional Adult and they will respond best to strokes about their work performance.

Active/People

When an Active/People type arrives at our conference, they will be wearing bright colours, interesting fabrics, plenty of jewellery and you'll notice their perfume or aftershave. Women have more scope for this in most cultures, although men will find ways to get round dress codes such as dark suits or plain white robes by wearing rings, cufflinks, decorative watch or identity bracelets, coloured ties, braces, or anything else that can be brighter or more colourful.

These people will not deliberately flout convention but they will opt for colourful and decorative clothing as soon as it becomes generally acceptable. For instance, they would not have been the first men to wear 'Mickey Mouse' ties and socks but may choose them once these are no longer seen as unusual. And Active/People women will choose colourful fashions but not while these are still regarded as avant-garde. They will not want to shock people with their appearance but will want to look pleasing, often in a way that gets them noticed.

As they move into the room, they will usually approach groups. They will initiate contact by moving easily into the group conversation, in a way that establishes them quickly as a significant group member – and often as the 'star' of the group. Somehow, their presence completes the group and they become the focus of attention.

They will be unlikely to do this by talking about work. Instead, they relate to other people at a personal level, perhaps by commenting on their appearance or asking about their family. Active/People types tend to behave in a nurturing way, demonstrating a genuine interest in others and appreciating it when others do the same to them.

Further clues as they talk will come from their speech patterns. They are likely to phrase a lot of what they say as questions, often using an upward, questioning inflexion at the end of comments that are not really questions. For example, they might say "I was just wondering whether you would like to fetch me the file on Project X?" when they really mean "Fetch it!"

Note that they may also use a lot of 'weasel' words (a weasel is a small animal that is noted for its ability to get out of confinement). So they sprinkle terms like 'you know', 'sort of', 'maybe', 'like' – all of which reduce the impact of their comments and allow them to back off if challenged. It is as if they don't want to offend anyone by putting forward their opinion too definitely – and this may mean that they seem weak and undecided. Sometimes, they expect people to mind-read through these sentence patterns and know what they really meant. They may then get annoyed if their vague suggestions are not acted upon.

Another clue to this style is that they are usually smiling, often anxiously and at times when a more serious countenance would be appropriate. And as they speak in questioning style, their eyebrows tend to lift in a quizzical way.

In terms of working styles they are likely to be Please People. They feel most empowered when you use a caring approach and show an interest in them as human beings rather than simply in their work. Their preferred strokes are therefore about them as a person and they will tend to use a Nurturing Parent-Natural Child channel of communication – from either end depending on circumstances.

Passive/People

What you may notice first about a Passive/People type will be that they dress idiosyncratically. They are likely to be wearing something unusual. Even if they have followed organisational norms and dressed in business clothes, you may still spot that something doesn't look right – perhaps they're wearing casual shoes, or an unusual mix of garments.

These will be the types who wear the latest trends before everyone has got used to seeing them – or such old-fashioned outfits that they seem almost eccentric. This is the group of people who first wore the 'Mickey Mouse' ties – before abandoning them to the Active/People types once they became acceptable business wear. They are also the ones most likely to have unusual hairstyles or to wear earrings in one ear only (male or female!).

Remember that this group is at the passive end of the dimension. This does not mean that they do nothing – it means that they generally leave it to others to initiate contact. What they do, therefore, is go and stand near a group. They then wait until someone in the group starts to involve them in the conversation. If they are left waiting for too long, they may join in but will do so in an unusual way – such as by linking what has just been said to something that changes the subject. The people in the group may be momentarily surprised or confused by this.

Once they join the conversation, you may notice that they often seem to change the subject. These are the types who are accused of having butterfly-minds, because they go off at tangents. They are also, of course, the ones most likely to generate creative ideas! And the ones most likely to shift between groups. They may give less than full attention to the group they are in at present because they are scanning to check events in other groups. If another group seems set to become more exciting, they may well disengage themselves and move across.

You may also notice that they don't always finish their sentences. They begin with one topic, which reminds them of another, which reminds them of another, which reminds them of another... and then they just tail off. They will probably sound very enthusiastic about everything that gets mentioned.

In fact, this enthusiasm is likely to be applied to everything. They will greatly enjoy talking about their hobbies, which may change frequently – this week, scuba diving, next week, horse riding, and so on. They often regard their work just as enthusiastically so you can expect them to enjoy discussing their latest projects.

You may be able to see the vertical frown lines that show as they 'struggle' to try and understand or to achieve; in the working styles classifications they are Try Hards. They will respond best to a Natural Child-Natural Child channel of communication and prefer strokes that relate to how they 'play' – inside or outside work.

Passive/Alone

Passive/Alone people will avoid coming to the conference if they can! They prefer to stay on their own. If they do come (generally because they are given no option), you may notice that they seem to pay little attention to their appearance. They may be dressed inappropriately, or their clothes may look unpressed, unpolished, etc. Or perhaps they live with someone who has made sure they start the day looking tidy – but as the day progresses they become steadily more dishevelled because they take no notice of themselves and gradually end up with their shirt hanging out or their make-up smudged.

Once at the conference location, they will enter but wait for others to initiate contact. They may simply stand about, or find an alcove to 'hide' in, or start on some simple tasks (such as putting out leaflets), that will make it less obvious that they are not chatting like everyone else.

These are the people you meet at parties, who wish they were at home but came because their partner insisted. Their partner in such cases is often an Active/People type who is thoroughly enjoying being the centre of attention in a group. If it's your party, you can earn the Passive/Alone's gratitude by finding them something to do that doesn't involve them in initiating conversations (such as clearing the dirty plates or washing the dishes).

Assuming someone does start a conversation with them, a Passive/Alone person will prefer this to be about work – and preferably to involve telling them what to do. They like to be given clear directions and will then go and do whatever is required, conscientiously and calmly, even if it is a task that most people dislike.

Their speech will probably sound fairly monotonous as they are usually fairly matter-of-fact, without much excitement or emphasis in their voice. They may be quite direct, and directive, when it is their turn to tell others what to do – and they will expect firmness from their own managers.

A visual clue to this style is often their lack of expression. Rather like the stiff upper lip of the English, or the deadpan face of the American poker player, they give little away and their smile may not extend to their eyes. Even when told something that shocks them, they can contain their emotions and appear quite calm.

These are the Be Strong working style, who are great in a crisis and prefer to have only minimal amounts of recognition. The usual polite greeting rituals are often enough stroking contact for them and if you want to delegate to them, they will expect you to exercise managerial control so a Controlling Parent-Adapted Child will be the most appropriate channel to use.

Acceleration/Patience

Let's now consider the third dimension. This runs from back to front diagonally, as shown in Figure 9.3. It does not create lots more types. Instead, it blends with the four types already described. What you will see, in terms of appearance and behaviour, will be as we have already described. However, someone at the acceleration end of the scale will do everything very quickly. Someone at the patience end will instead do it all very slowly. This final dimension equates to the Hurry Up working style.

The reason for the distorted shape of the cube is that the Acceleration – Patience characteristics are not evenly spread across the four styles. There are more people with Acceleration in the Passive/People quadrant, and more with Patience in the Active/Alone box. This conclusion is not a theoretical notion; it is based on empirical evidence. We can place Hurry Up in the bottom left hand box, so that it overlaps with Try Hard most, Please People sometimes, and Be Strong and Be Perfect less often. People with a Be Strong/Hurry Up or Be Perfect/Hurry Up combination may well feel more stressed as these working styles pairings have inbuilt conflict - it is much easier to Hurry Up and Try Hard or Hurry Up and Please People.

Figure 9.3: The Third Dimension

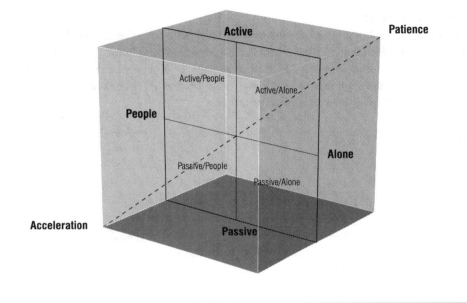

If we now consider the impact of the 3rd dimension on the four types within the quadrant you are most likely to notice:

passive/people/acceleration – dressed unusually, wait for others in groups to initiate contact, always in a hurry so may be very productive.

active/alone/patience – dressed immaculately in business clothes, initiate contact with one or two people, do things slowly and carefully.

You will, of course, also meet people who fit the following patterns:

active/people/acceleration – dressed colourfully, initiate contact and enjoy being in groups, always in a hurry – so manage to nurture or please lots of people.

passive/alone/patience – don't care about appearance, prefer to avoid contact, do things slowly – so great at plodding through essential but boring tasks.

And sometimes you will meet:

active/people/patience – dressed colourfully, initiate contact in groups, take their time with all they do.

passive/alone/acceleration – don't care about appearance, prefer to be alone, rush about.

And infrequently, you will meet:

active/alone/acceleration – dressed in business-like way, initiate contact with one or two people, and always in a hurry so may seem impatient.

passive/people/patience – dressed unusually, wait for others in groups to initiate contact, and spend a lot of time trying, and often failing, to finish things.

Leadership Styles

We can use the AP³ framework to identify the leadership style that is most likely to be successful with each individual. To show this on paper, we need to collapse the cube into two dimensions. I then show the Acceleration to Patience dimension as if it creates a box that 'floats' over the other four boxes. I show it near the bottom left box because there are more people with this particular combination.

Figure 9.4: The ABC of AP³

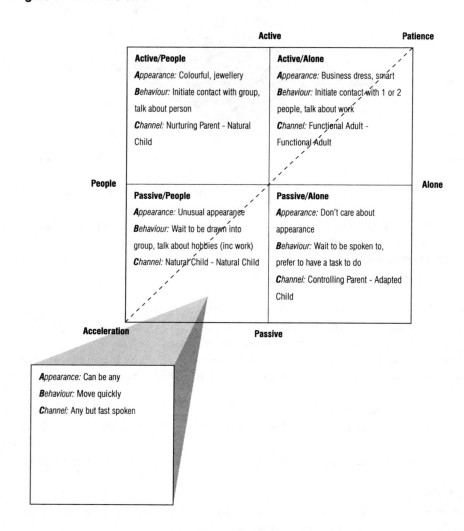

Figure 9.4 shows the ABC of AP³, or what we can observe when we meet someone - their appearance, their behaviour and which channel of communication they prefer. Figure 9.5 shows preferences, as in what kind of strokes will best motivate someone, what working style presents as their strength, and which leadership style is likely to match their own style. This gives us five leadership styles summarised as follows:

Consulting – for Active/Alone: stroke them for their performance, value the positive outcomes of their Be Perfect working style, and lead by consulting. Ask them how they think the work should be done and have rational discussions about it.

Figure 9.5: AP³ Preferences

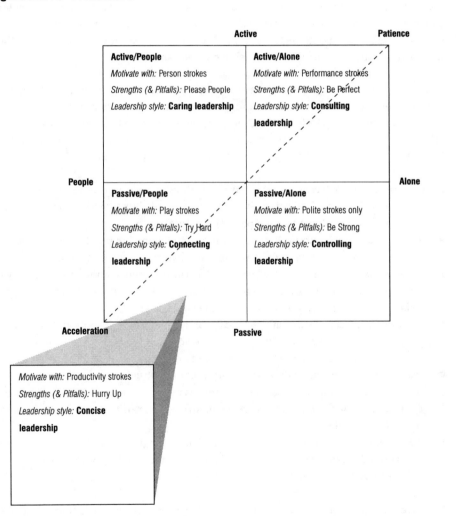

Active | Patience

Active/People
Motivate with: Person strokes
Strengths (& Pitfalls): Please People
Leadership style: **Caring leadership**

Active/Alone
Motivate with: Performance strokes
Strengths (& Pitfalls): Be Perfect
Leadership style: **Consulting leadership**

People | Alone

Passive/People
Motivate with: Play strokes
Strengths (& Pitfalls): Try Hard
Leadership style: **Connecting leadership**

Passive/Alone
Motivate with: Polite strokes only
Strengths (& Pitfalls): Be Strong
Leadership style: **Controlling leadership**

Acceleration | Passive

Motivate with: Productivity strokes
Strengths (& Pitfalls): Hurry Up
Leadership style: **Concise leadership**

Caring – for Active/People: know and stroke them as a person (and don't talk about work until you've asked after their family or noticed how they feel). Value them for the way their Please People working style contributes to a pleasant team spirit. Lead by caring; nurture them and, when appropriate, appreciate the way they nurture you and others.

Connecting – for Passive/People: recognise their Natural Child playfulness and Try Hard enthusiasm, both for work and hobbies. Get enthusiastic with them and lead by connecting. This may mean doing the work alongside them so you seem like playful colleagues rather than a hierarchical relationship.

Controlling – for Passive/Alone: keep your distance. They will prefer to be given clear instructions and left to get on with the task. Strokes can be restricted to polite greetings and matter-of-fact comments and then their Be Strong working style will be evident as they complete tasks that others might have ducked. This type expect a manager to tell them what is required so a controlling leadership style works best.

Concise – for Acceleration: remember they may also show preferences from another box and take that into account. However, for those who are distinctly into the Acceleration 'corner', your leadership style just needs to be concise. You need to interact quickly because otherwise they will have rushed elsewhere before you have finished talking to them. Their Hurry Up style will mean they appreciate strokes for their productivity.

Finally, keep in mind that each of the 'boxes' has drawbacks as well as strengths. A leader needs to be skilful enough to bring out the best in people but sometimes circumstances will work against this. When that happens, the results may be:

- Active/Alone: lock into Be Perfect and refuse to let anyone see their work until it is perfect – so miss deadlines and also miss the chance of feedback from the team.
- Active/People: lock into Please People and become paranoid about upsetting anyone – so agree to do anything asked of them and then miss deadlines that were never going to be feasible – and get upset about letting people down.
- Passive/People: start very enthusiastically on too many new projects and hence fail to complete any of them – and it's hard to say no when they are the only one on your team who is volunteering to take on yet more projects.
- Passive/Alone: may do nothing while they wait for instructions, may then do what you told them even though changed circumstances mean it is no longer appropriate, tend to do tasks as they arrive – and are reluctant to change priorities, and may fail to notice the feelings of others.
- Acceleration: arrive late and leave early so fail to integrate with the team, don't start tasks until deadlines are looming – and then miss the deadline or produce work with many errors due to their haste.

Negative reactions mean there is a stroke deficit, so we need to concentrate on stroking strengths and avoid criticising until the person has moved into I'm OK - Your OK mode.

TRAINER EFFECTIVENESS

The relevance of AP³ to you as a trainer relates to your own leadership role. In any classroom, you are likely to have people from across the range of types and many of them will be looking to you for leadership. Their imago, or mental image of you, may well have you pre-assigned as controlling (see Chapter 8, Working in Groups) because this is what they have experienced from school teachers.

It is therefore important that you have the flexibility to adopt any of the AP³ styles and that you can assess each participant and make an appropriate choice for them. This requires observation skills, practice and enough knowledge of cultural expectations so that you can factor out the impact of local norms on appearance.

Clearly you will also have to take into account that interactions with the group run the risk of being comfortable for some and uncomfortable for others. This is the same problem that leaders have – it is easier to adopt an effective style for one-to-one interactions but not so straightforward when meeting with the team.

Bearing in mind that leadership training is aimed at leaders and potential leaders, you might consider explaining this dilemma briefly when you are creating the initial contract with the participants (see Chapter 2, Contracting for Learning, for more on contracting). Something along the lines of "We are going to be looking at leadership styles – there are several and people vary in their preferences for leading and being led. Participants often expect trainers to behave like leaders. So I will inevitably seem to you to be exhibiting leadership styles and I may not adopt the style you prefer. Please note your reactions to my style and we can use the information to increase the learning available from this workshop."

Another option is to plan so that you exhibit different leadership styles in turn, so that every participant experiences their preferences for some of the time. Again, noting their reactions can lead to significant learning when these are reviewed later in the programme.

ACTIVITIES

Note that activities from previous chapters will also be relevant, e.g. about ego states and transactions, strokes, working styles. The questionnaires in the appendices may also be appropriate.

Activity 9.1 Where am I?

Hand out sheets containing a copy of the basic AP³ framework.

Suggest participants sketch in where they see themselves. Explain that they may be in one box or may 'spread across' more than one. No pattern is any better than any other.

Invite them to compare responses in pairs or threes.

Activity 9.2 Centres of gravity

Hand out sheets containing a copy of the basic AP³ framework.

Suggest participants indicate their own 'centre of gravity' and compare it to those of their colleagues.

Prompt them to think about:
- how close or distant are they from specific colleagues?
- how does this show up in behaviour?
- how do their differences, and similarities, impact on how they work together?
- what might they (the participant) do in order to be able to move closer to specific colleagues and create improved relationships?

Have them review their responses in pairs or small groups.

For groups who work together, suggest they do this activity as a team, i.e. they decide together where to place each person and then discuss the questions above, especially the last one.

Activity 9.3 Improving Relationships

Hand out sheets containing a copy of the basic AP³ framework.

Invite participants to work in pairs or threes. One does the activity below while the other(s) acts as a consultant.

Identify someone that you find hard to deal with; the sort of person that you seem to react negatively to, maybe because you have too much or too little in common.

Analyse them using AP³ – their ABC and their preferences.

Now review how your own position on AP³ contrasts or combines with their's.

Identify two or three action points you can initiate to stimulate a better relationship.

Activity 9.4 Leadership Styles in Action

Hand out sheets containing a copy of the basic AP³ framework. This activity assumes your participants are leaders. Invite them to review the people they lead, using the following prompts:
- where do you think they fit on the AP³ framework?
- why – what evidence do you have of their appearance, behaviour and channels of communication?
- what preferences do you think they have about stroking and working styles and the leadership style they respond best to?
- again, what evidence do you have for their preferences?

- how flexible are you as a leader? Which are your first, second, third preferences? How easily can you switch between leadership styles?
- which people do you get on best with? How?
- are these the people you also lead best? If not, why not?
- which people do you not find it easy to lead? Why?
- plan how you will adjust your leadership styles – with whom specifically and what will you do differently?

NOTES & SOURCES

Many years ago I attended a workshop run by Taibi Kahler where he talked of the assessing quadrant that formed the basis of his two (out-of-print) booklets. Since then, as a Try Hard, I have played with his theory – and as an 'Organisational TA'er' I have simplified it so I can teach it quickly in ways that enable people to apply it and improve their relationships.

The booklets were *Managing with the Process Communication Model* and *Process Therapy in Brief*, both published 1979 by Human Development Publications.

More recently, Kahler's work has been described by Vann Joines and Ian Stewart in *Personality Adaptations*, Life Space Publishing 2002.

And even more recently, Kahler has provided us with *The Process Therapy Model*, published by Taibi Kahler Associates Inc in 2008. In this book, he gives the history of his development of the model and explains the notion of a 'condominium'. In this, we have all six personality types but on different floors and in different orders – my first floor may be your 5th floor and so on.

Kahler's book includes a statement that "Teaching or training of the material in this book requires certification by Taibi Kahler Associates, Inc. or one of its authorised affiliate organisations."

CHAPTER 10: WORKING WITH CHANGE

This chapter starts by looking at the impact of change, both in terms of how the pace of change is increasing in our environment and at how we as individuals typically respond to changes that affect us directly.

I go on to introduce the 'cycles of development' as a TA model for understanding our needs. Drawing on this enables me to show how our childhood pattern of development is repeated throughout our adult life. Knowledge of this helps us to understand our reactions because it is as if we start again from the beginning each time change occurs.

I then link change with cycles of development to demonstrate how the model can generate insights and ideas for handling change better. I approach this first from the perspective of the individual; and, secondly from the point of view of the manager who must lead others through change and may even be required to impose it.

The trainer effectiveness section covers how the impact of changes affecting our participants will show up in the classroom. Included are suggestions for dealing with the resulting problems. I have also related the cycles directly to the individual trainer, both for when change occurs to them and in terms of their own life cycle.

The first activity relates to personal experiences of change. The other is for use with a group within an organisation that is experiencing change.

THE IMPACT OF CHANGE
Our Changing Environment

We are constantly being told that the world has seen more change in the last century than in all the time before. And that the pace of change is accelerating all the time. Handling change has become a growth industry.

Conditions are changing globally. The USA no longer dominates world markets, just as the UK ceased to have its Empire. The barriers between East and West have been removed. Corporations must operate across cultures. Organisations are altering their structures to suit internationalisation. Layers of management are being removed and people allowed to use their initiative. Many of us are now expected to have more than one career, more than one set of skills in our lifetime.

Conditions continue to change locally. Markets change and companies must alter their services to suit. As we position ourselves to better meet customer needs, so we change the shape of jobs, sections, departments. Companies are acquired, merged, divested. Since I drafted this chapter, we have entered a worldwide financial 'meltdown' that will continue to generate change for some time to come. Add to this the changes that occur 'naturally' as people develop new skills, get promoted, or seize opportunities elsewhere, struggle to deal with redundancy, learn new ways of being in the world.

Hence, few of us remain totally unaffected by change. We may enjoy the challenge or dread the results; we may welcome change or have it forced upon us; we are not likely to feel neutral about it. Most of us, therefore, would find it helpful to understand the processes of change and transition. As individuals, this knowledge can be reassuring as we experience normal but worrying reactions to change. As managers, it will enable us to plan change in ways that cause least stress to those affected.

As trainers, we may be asked to provide training to help people deal effectively with change. We are also likely to have in our classes individuals who are suffering the effects of change even as we attempt to train them. This chapter has been written to help you with both situations.

Responses to Change

It can take up to four years before we adjust fully to a significant transition, even one as apparently routine as a job change. An average time for someone to feel in command of a new job is around two years. The pace of change can easily overtake us, so that we move on again without ever reaching full competence.

Given time, we will eventually emerge from the change process whether or not we have been lucky with the responses of other people. We will go through some identifiable phases. Knowledge of these phases can in itself be helpful, as it reassures us that we are behaving as most other human beings would.

The phases that seem to apply most commonly, and their impact on our performance, are summarised in Figure 10.1 The Competence Curve.

During the **first phase** we may well seem to be *immobilised* for a while. In imposed changes particularly, this could even be labelled shock. We need time to absorb the change and to compare our expectations to the new reality. We will appear to be marking time, doing nothing – maybe even not coping. There are several explanations for this:

- we lack information about the new situation
- we are afraid of doing it wrong and appearing stupid
- our fear of the unknown shows up as paralysis
- we may lack the motivation to make the change work.

Figure 10.1: The Competence Curve

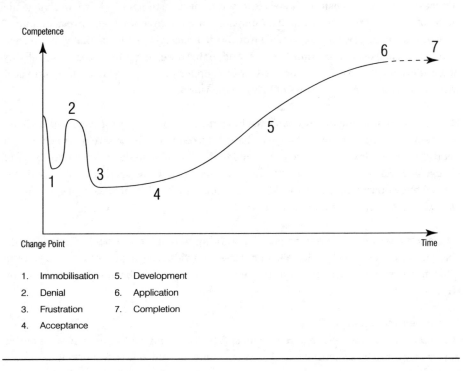

1. Immobilisation
2. Denial
3. Frustration
4. Acceptance
5. Development
6. Application
7. Completion

Even with a change that we chose and planned, a psychologically healthy person needs a short period for simply experiencing being in a new situation – before they are expected to take action.

The **second phase** is one of *denial*. We act as if our behaviour patterns from the past will still be appropriate. Again, even if we have chosen the transition, we hope our existing skills and knowledge will still be useful. Some of them will, but severe problems due to denial can arise because:

■ we feel a threat to our level of competence and skill
■ we are reluctant to experiment
■ we are simply custom bound or in a rut
■ we fear failure
■ we rationalise that it worked okay for us in the past so it should work now
■ we are simply unaware of how we are behaving.

Paradoxically, we may actually appear to be performing better during this phase than in Phase 1. This is because we now start applying our existing skills and knowledge, and are therefore seen to be achieving things. Unfortunately, we will not be using behaviour that relates to the new job; this will gradually become evident.

People will start to question our grasp of reality, or think we are being deliberately obtuse. We, on the other hand, are unaware of our denial and continue to behave in the way that was successful previously. Slowly, we allow our defence systems to weaken and start to notice the need for change.

In **Phase 3** we go through a period of *frustration*. We now recognise we need to behave differently but we don't know how. Our frustration arises because we feel incompetent during our efforts to apply new approaches. Indeed, others too may perceive us as incompetent as we struggle with new skills, new knowledge, new situations – and this means we become even more conscious of our shortcomings. In some cases, we turn our frustration against others, and seek to blame them for our position. Even when we chose the change, we can blame others for not helping us enough, not training us properly beforehand, even for not warning us against the problems we now face.

Feeding into our frustration will be: potential overload due to our genuine need to learn new approaches; fear of losing status through decreased competence; loss of our power base or our network of contacts. So we struggle to work out how we should be different, what new skills do we need, what qualities are required in the new situation.

At **Phase 4** we move into *acceptance*. We let go of the attitudes and behaviours that were comfortable and useful in the past. We now have the answers from Phase 3 and can start the process of acquiring new patterns. We begin to test out new ways of doing things. There will still be occasional moments of frustration, such as when our new skills are not quite practised enough, or we identify yet another area where we lack knowledge.

This phase represents our move, psychologically, into our personal learning cycle. We recognise the reality of our experience – that we are in a new situation and need a new set of behaviours. We review the situation and compare it with the past to identify differences. We analyse the differences and develop frameworks for understanding where we are now. And then we begin to actively experiment. During Phase 4 we may still appear incompetent to a degree. We are working out our identity in the changed situation, so although we have now accepted the change there will still be temporary problems as we try out new approaches.

All being well, we will move on to **Phase 5**: that of *development*. In this phase, we concentrate on developing the skills and knowledge required in the new situation. We become increasingly competent at operating in the changed environment. We make decisions about the most effective techniques and then become skilled at using them. Our knowledge increases so that others come to regard us as the appropriate expert in our field.

In **Phase 6** we move on to *application*. Most importantly, we now consolidate our identity in our changed role. We develop our own views on how the job should be done, how we should relate to others, and how they should relate to us. We resolve in our own minds the questions about our status, our beliefs about the situation, and our view of the organisation. In particular, we work out how we fit in the new scheme of things.

Entering **Phase 7** means we have *completion*. We now feel comfortable and competent once again – so much so that we are no longer conscious of having experienced a transition. We are really into the new situation and have ceased to compare it, favourably or unfavourably, to our position before the change.

In summary, we have progressed through the following stages:

Stage 1 Immobilisation - We seem to do nothing, to withdraw.

Stage 2 Denial - We act as if it hasn't happened and go on as we used to.

Stage 3 Frustration - We know we need to change but don't know how.

Stage 4 Acceptance - We start exploring options that might be appropriate to the new situation.

Stage 5 Development - We develop our new skills and knowledge so as to become a competent performer.

Stage 6 Application - We apply our new skills within our new identity.

Stage 7 Completion - We are through the transition and are no longer consciously aware of the change.

CYCLES OF DEVELOPMENT

Pamela Levin was awarded the Eric Berne Memorial Scientific Award for her work on cycles of development, a TA theory that provides us with fascinating insights into what we do when affected by change. Levin identified seven stages in the human developmental process and, significantly, showed that these occur in cycles throughout our lives. In addition to cycles timed accordingly to our age, we also experience shorter periods triggered by specific events. Levin's model thus bridges the gap between those frameworks that refer to the total life span, such as described in Passages by Gail Sheehey, and those which relate to specific events, such as the normal sequence of reactions to a death outlined by Elizabeth Kubler-Ross.

Life Stages

In each stage of the initial cycle described by Levin, we have certain developmental tasks to complete. Few of us succeed totally. As we recycle through the equivalent period in later life, we have another opportunity for growth. However, we are also at risk of experiencing the same problems as occurred for us before. Unfortunately, we may well then repeat the same strategies that were unsuccessful for us before.

We can envisage this process as a spiral, as shown in Figure 10.2. We complete our first full revolution by the time we are 19 years old. As important events occur in our lives, smaller spirals are started. There may even be smaller spirals within smaller spirals, rather like those sets of Russian dolls where you continue to find a smaller doll inside each one you open.

Figure 10.2: Cycles of Development

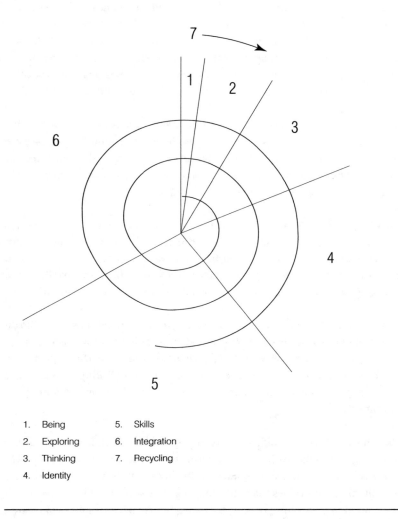

1. Being
2. Exploring
3. Thinking
4. Identity
5. Skills
6. Integration
7. Recycling

If we are very unlucky, we have changes occur in our lives whilst we are at a point on our major spiral that is not comfortable for us. We may even have a series of changes, each sparking off its own limited spiral on the back of another. Loss of job may lead to loss of friends, the next job may require relocation, this may take us away from family, and so on. The accumulation of spirals then adds to our stress.

Even those of us who are at a good stage in life, can be jolted severely by an unexpected change. Pleasant changes will also stimulate new spirals. Marriage, promotion, a new baby in the family, passing an exam – even a break for a holiday can generate a small spiral. Add several together and we see why people get stressed through good news.

Childhood Development

Stage 1 Being - From when we are born until we are about six months old, we need to experience just being in the world. To do this, we need a situation where we feel secure and wanted and loved. This affirmation must be there for us without requiring us to behave in any particular ways; we lack the ability to act on parental wishes at this age. If the people around us cannot provide such an atmosphere, we will grow up needing to rework this stage. Until we do, we may have problems centred around our belief in our right to exist.

Stage 2 Exploring - During the period from six to eighteen months, we want to be doing things. We start by exploring objects with our eyes, hands and mouths. We become increasingly mobile and want to move around. It is still important to us that our caregiver is around to go back to but we need the freedom to do it on our own. If we are thwarted in this stage, as adults we may be reluctant to enter new situations.

Stage 3 Thinking - Eighteen months to three years is our approximate time for developing our thinking ability. We start to reason things out for ourselves and to make our own decisions. We want to choose whether to wear a warm coat or to play in the rain. We object strongly if adults attempt to impose such choices on us. If we are not allowed to develop our thinking skills we will find it hard to form our own opinions in later life.

Stage 4 Identity - From three years to six years we are working out our identity. Who do we intend to be? Whether we are male or female is significant here but we also consider what style to adopt. Will we be sensitive or tough, frivolous or serious? Do we plan to be the cop or the robber, a worker or a layabout, a leader or a follower? Without a clear sense of our identity, we may grow up unsure of our role in life, or with rigid views that limit our potential development.

Stage 5 Skills - Once past six years old, we are ready to spend the next six years acquiring the skills we need to get by in the world. We observe how adults behave and copy whatever fits with the identity we have adopted for ourselves. During this time, we also incorporate a whole range of opinions and values that will enable us to view the world in a structured way. We will be limited as adults insofar as we fail to acquire significant skills or values, so we are very dependent on the quality of our role models.

Stage 6 Integration - Having reached thirteen years old, we seem to start again as if we were babies. However, this time we move at twice the pace. By the time we are nineteen, we will be finishing a repeat of our first thirteen years. At the end of this time, we will have integrated the different aspects into a whole, rather like putting a skin around the facets of our personality: Failure to achieve this will leave us somehow fragmented, as if we have not yet finished growing up.

Stage 7 Recycling - We now start the process of recycling through the stages. As we pass through each stage, we will seek to take care of any needs that we were unable to deal with before. A therapist trained in this approach would be able to judge our age by the issues we raised.

An organisational trainer may not have access to such information but will still notice those people who have significant needs. Perhaps we observe that a participant generally lacks life skills, or does not appear to trust their own thinking. Maybe they seem immature, or are unwilling to explore the computer keyboard without direct supervision. Alternatively, we may come into contact with people who are over-compensating. They insist on investigating alone, or have very rigid views about what training formats they are prepared to accept.

Spirals within Spirals

I have described the stages as they occur over months and years. I also said that we have smaller spirals initiated by events in our lives. Figure 10.3 illustrates this. These may span months and years but they might equally last for minutes and hours only. As you read the following example, keep in mind that we will be experiencing also the impact of the major lifetime spiral, and of any other spirals that may be in effect at the same time. Any problems will be multiplied when stages overlap in which we have 'unfinished business'. Fortunately, the same multiplier effect will occur for any stages in which we are particularly strong.

Let us take a relatively simple change that will happen to most of us at some time – starting a new job. This will generate its own spiral that will last for several weeks. Depending on the complexity of our work, it may be measured in months.

Think about the last time you were in this situation. Assume for our purposes that this job is in a section that is new to you, that you do not already know your future colleagues, and that you will be undertaking different duties from your previous work.

What typically happens? You are probably shown briefly where your new desk or work station is. You may then be shown round and introduced to your new colleagues. Or you are told to start work immediately. In some cases, you attend an induction or skills training programme before you get anywhere near your new place of work. Generally, what happens bears only limited relationship to an effective way of handling such a change.

If we use the cycles of development as our model, then we can predict that a job change will initiate its own spiral. What then would be the ideal process to follow?

First, we need time for a short interval for us to simply get used to being at our new place or work. The reassurance that we are welcomed by our new manager, who is pleased that we are here; and perhaps a chance to absorb our surroundings, look at the view (or lack of), put personal possessions away safely. What we do not want is to be pressured into starting work the instant we arrive. Just a few minutes may be all that is necessary to enable us to feel we have arrived and are wanted.

Figure 10.3: Spirals within Spirals

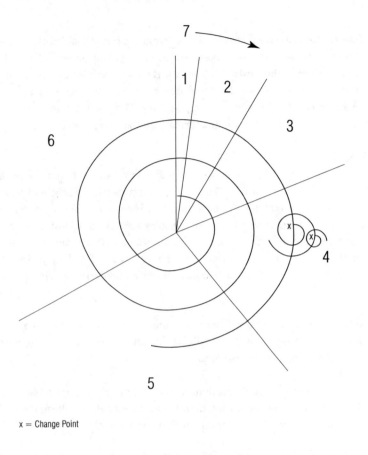

x = Change Point

Second, we want time for exploring. We want to do this at our own pace. We need to walk around the building and register where various amenities are situated. We may take time to visualise our own location on the site. We may appreciate directions but will probably prefer to go alone so we can pay attention to what we see. An important part of this exploration will be the opportunity to meet people and find out what they do. It will help if they have been warned to expect a new face. Introductions will not be as useful if we are escorted to meet a large number of new people in a short time.

Third, we now want to do our own thinking about the job. We need a manager who encourages us to do this, and then is willing to discuss our views. We need information sources such as job descriptions, procedures manual, task instructions. We want to be able to ask others about their views of the job. Then we want to work out how we see our new job. We do not want a manager who tells us we must do the job exactly as they specify. We do want a manager who will answer our questions and listen to our ideas with interest.

Fourth, we move into creating our own identity in the job. In some organisations, this is provided for by having performance standards set jointly by manager and subordinate. We need to believe that we have an element of choice over what sort of worker we will be. This need for self-determination is more often recognised as appropriate for managers, who are expected to have their own management style. It is just as important for those with other types of job. If this choice is denied us, we are likely to accept the decision of the organisation grudgingly and may even become rebellious.

Fifth, we are now ready to learn the skills required to do the job. Organisations that thrust people into training too early will not gain the full benefit. We need to have a good idea of the job itself, and our personal identity within it, if we are to make maximum use of training. Only then can we select what we need to know. Otherwise we must rely on the trainer to predict our training needs instead of working in partnership with them. Motivation to learn is much higher when we know why we are learning.

Sixth, we want to integrate the previous stages. As we undertake the tasks of the job, we are pulling together our prior efforts of exploration, decision making and learning. Gradually, we begin to feel that we are performing as we should. We may rework some of the earlier stages to cover parts we missed. Perhaps we have more people to get to know. Maybe we will change our style now we know the organisation better. If we are prevented from making these adjustments, we will not achieve our full potential.

Seventh, we begin the recycling stage. We have completed our transition into the new job. We will now move through each stage again but with far less impact. The effect of this particular spiral will fade. Soon, we will forget that we changed our job. We will function at our peak level until some other change comes along.

DEALING WITH CHANGE
Change and the Individual
As individuals, we can help ourselves handle change if we keep in mind our needs in accordance with the developmental stages. In a sense, we can act like our own parent figure and make sure that we get the experiences we need for healthy 'growing up'.

Immobilisation/Being: Take time to get used to the idea of change. Arrange for some periods when you can be alone; plan ways to look after yourself so that you relax – a hot bath, your favourite TV programme, a walk in the woods.

Review your previous accomplishments and remind yourself how competent you are. Plan also to be with the sort of friends who will still want your company even if you are anxious about the change.

Denial/Exploring: Be aware that this phase exists. It may be difficult to help yourself through something which is generally outside awareness. Watch out for signs that you may be acting as if your situation is unchanged. Ask someone you trust and respect to give you feedback if they notice you behaving inappropriately.

Actively explore your current circumstances. Make approaches to people and ask them questions. Use this period as a stimulus to making contact with people you do not know. Focus on the opportunities to do things and visit places.

Frustration/Thinking: Recognise that any anger or frustration you feel is normal. Punch a pillow or stick pins in a model instead of saying things to others that you will subsequently regret. Engage in energetic exercise to let off steam.

Talk to someone you respect about how you see your circumstances. Ask others who have been through a similar change about their experiences. Prepare a written plan of what you think needs to happen.

Acceptance/Identity: You will now be starting to come to terms with 'life after change.' Accept that it will require a change in you as a person. See this as a major development opportunity. Take advantage of this chance to decide how you want to be.

Look back over the times you were less effective than you wished. Plan now how to change your behaviour so as to avoid these pitfalls in the future. This is the beginning of the rest of your life, an ideal time to review what is important to you and whether values and beliefs have changed in any way.

Development/Skills: Now you are ready to acquire the skills and knowledge you require for continued success. Look around to see what you can learn from people who are already successful in your new field. Who can you model yourself on, who can you go to for advice, how did they get their expertise?

Check out what training is available, both on-and off-the-job. Prepare a schedule of programmes you need. Remember to cover skills, knowledge and application. Consider other ways of learning, such as through projects, by voluntary work, through self-study.

Application/Integration: Use your new skills wisely. Remember the resolutions you made in the Identity stage about how you now want to appear to others. Apply your learning within your own clear framework of values and beliefs. Monitor your progress and make adjustments as necessary.

Completion/Recycling: Congratulate yourself. You are through this particular change process and may already be looking forward to future change and growth. You can also relax and start to help others deal with change.

We can summarise the stages and our needs as follows:

Stage 1	**Being**	reassurance that people are pleased we are around
Stage 2	**Exploring**	their patience while we find our own way
Stage 3	**Thinking**	their tolerance as we test out our thinking
Stage 4	**Identity**	acceptance as we define our identity
Stage 5	**Skills**	coaching and training
Stage 6	**Integration**	encouragement as we settle into the new situation
Stage 7	**Recycling**	we are on our way

Change and the Manager

If we are the manager, we have a responsibility for the way in which we impose change on others. We can combine what we know about the stages of development with the phases of change to generate ideas for making transitions easier. We can then ensure that the changes we are involved in cause as little pain as possible.

Phase 1, Immobilisation/Being – Those affected by change need time to experience the change. Non-directive counselling approaches are helpful here – letting someone talk, listening to them attentively, reflecting key words back so they feel someone cares. They also need information, although they are probably not in a condition to absorb it. Give them written information that they can retain and study later.

Phase 2, Denial/Exploring – This is probably the most difficult stage for the would-be helper. If the individual denies the change, we can't even discuss it with them. Patience is needed, perhaps accompanied by occasional carefully phrased questions about their objectives and their use of techniques which we recognise as inappropriate in the new situation. If in doubt, keep quiet – too much pushing will only drive them even further into denial. Keep in mind that the denial is subconscious so they are unaware of doing it. Encourage them to explore the sources of information you gave them earlier.

Phase 3, Frustration/Thinking – Here we need lots of tolerance and good humour – especially if they start blaming us for the problems. Empathetic listening is now best, letting them know that we too might be angry and frustrated were we in their position. Remember empathy is not sympathy – we can relate to how they feel and still expect action from them. Avoid any temptation to wallow in mutual misery.

Phase 4, Acceptance/Identity – Now we can start to discuss the new situation with them and expect them to want to start resolving problems. Our comments must, however, be focused on their own recognition of what is needed. Too much advice too soon will interfere with their need to work out their own identity in the new situation.

Phase 5, Development/Skills – This is a much easier phase to deal with. Advice, coaching, teaching are all appropriate now as they start actively to build up their new skills and knowledge. At last, they will be open to comments based on the previous experience of others – now you can say things like "When I did it, I ...." Off-the-job training may also be useful during this phase, and contacts with others who have ideas to offer.

Phase 6, Application/Integration – We may find that our involvement now is greater than during the previous phase, when we perhaps sent them elsewhere for training. Our role is to provide plenty of encouragement and reinforcement as they apply their new skills. It may also be appropriate to remind them of 'old' skills that could now usefully be applied in the new situation.

Phase 7, Completion/Recycling – no more help is needed. The person is now established in the new situation and is ready to begin the process of assisting others to handle change.

TRAINER EFFECTIVENESS
Cycles of Development in the Classroom

People are often sent for training at times when change has occurred in their working lives. This may have affected their personal lives as well. You may therefore encounter participants who are at a difficult time in terms of their major or event-related spirals. Work out where you think they have reached and then adapt the advice given to managers. Broadly, the following will be helpful:

If you suspect immobilisation, remember they need to re-experience the 'being' stage. Make it clear you are pleased to have them on your course. Give them time to settle in. Don't push them to start training too quickly. Make sure any information you give them is written down in case they do not absorb it.

If you suspect denial, get them involved in 'exploring'. Use discovery learning techniques. Let them do things their own way so that they come to recognise that it is inappropriate. Do not insist they do it your way before they are convinced through trial and error that their own way no longer works. Ask questions in order to highlight the differences for them. Draw their attention to the objectives of the training.

If you suspect frustration, recognise they need to be 'thinking'. Give them time to vent their frustration and explain that this is a normal reaction to change. Then invite them to discuss the relevance of the training for them. Encourage them to think through the situation surrounding them and to weigh the pros and cons. Use questions to prompt them to look at events through the perspectives of others, such as their immediate and more senior managers.

If you suspect acceptance, remember they still need to complete the creation of their 'identity'. Use discussion to allow them to build up their own ideas on how they want to perform after the course. Let them review how they expect to put the training to use. Agree the training objectives with them. Encourage maximum input from them about the context in which they will be working.

If they are in the development phase, they will usually be pleased to have the opportunity of being trained. Check that they see the topic as relevant to their needs. If not, ask them to be creative about how they might apply the learning.

If you suspect the application phase, you may want to play down the amount of new learning and spend more time on helping them work out how to use what they know. Give them plenty of practice, the chance to role play, form small groups to discuss applications, and get them to prepare detailed action plans.

In addition to any larger spirals, participants are likely to commence a relatively small spiral as they enter the training room. This is because course attendance represents a change from how they normally spend their time at work. In spite of obvious differences due to childhood experiences, you are still likely to be able to identify the key stages in many of them.

The elements outlined below can provide a useful outline structure for any course.
1. Make sure you greet people when they arrive. Allow time for this. Coffee on arrival also helps. Start the first session with a general welcome to the course. Give out written information to back up whatever you tell them.
2. Get them involved in some kind of exploration. Choose something simple so they will all succeed. For example, let them find out information from each other. Paired introductions can be useful here, with each person getting to know one other participant who they will then introduce to the whole group.
3. Give them something to think about. Begin the presentation of information which they are to learn. Do this in a way which invites student involvement. Encourage them to ask questions and to state their own views on what you are teaching.
4. Allow them an opportunity to consider their identity in terms of what they are learning – perhaps a syndicate group to identify a list of common problems they could resolve using what you are teaching.
5. Now they are ready to acquire skills. This requires practice. Let them use the equipment, or plan role plays if you are teaching people-skills. Add to the knowledge base already provided. Give demonstrations for them to copy.
6. Brief them to consider how they would each use any techniques in line with their own style. Get them to help each other identify opportunities to apply the learning. Have them play devil's advocate for each other, checking that proposed applications seem feasible.
7. Send them back to work with your best wishes.

Change and the Trainer

You too may be at a difficult time in terms of your spirals. Or you may be new to training and have just started a reasonably large spiral associated with your job change. Follow the suggestions given for individuals who must deal with change.

Like participants, you may also generate a smaller spiral each time you enter a class with a new group of participants. Perhaps you are triggered by the need to handle a new topic, or use a different training method. Whichever it is, plan beforehand how you will cope with and make use of your mini-spiral. As the participants are going through a similar experience, whatever you do to help yourself is likely to be appropriate for them too.

Being – build yourself a network of supportive colleagues. Take time out to relax before the start of a course. Set the training room out early so you can join the participants for coffee.

Exploring – make the most of opportunities to meet new people on courses. Get out to visit people to find out what their training needs are. Aim to include a new training method in each course, so that you can try it out and see what happens.

Thinking – discuss your ideas with colleagues and line managers. Draw up plans for training courses showing how you propose to meet the objectives. Produce reports in which you forecast training needs in your organisation.

Identity – agree a job description and annual objectives with your manager. Study the styles of other trainers and select what suits you. Obtain qualifications as a professional trainer.

Skills – be a regular student on other people's courses. Keep updating your skills and knowledge. Read the professional journals. Attend conferences for trainers. Attend the conferences that your participants might attend.

Integration – review your progress regularly. Ask your manager and colleagues for frequent feedback on your performance. Offer to provide training in different situations and on different topics. If you don't already have super-vision arrangements, see Chapter 12 for ideas on this important developmental method.

Recycling – experience the feeling of achievement from knowing you have successfully completed a period of adjustment and are now a competent professional trainer. Start planning your next period of personal development.

ACTIVITIES
Activity 10.1 Personal Experiences
This is a general activity which involves participants in relating theory to personal experience. It can be conducted in plenary or in syndicates which then report back to the main group.

Ask the group to discuss and compare their experiences of change, both in the work context and outside of it. You may want to brief them to answer the following:

- What happened?
- Was the change chosen or imposed?
- What helped?
- What made the experience worse?
- What were the eventual benefits of the change?

Introduce any 'rules' you feel are appropriate in order to take care of confidentiality on individual cases.

The discussion of benefits may be important if you are dealing with a group who have found change generally unpleasant. It will encourage them to recognise that there are usually developmental opportunities associated with change, which may not become apparent to us until some time later.

If you use this exercise before describing the phases of change or the stages of development, you can use their comments as examples to illustrate your input.

Alternatively, use it after describing one or both models and ask the group to relate their experiences to the framework you have provided.

Activity 10.2 Organisations and Change

This activity stimulates participants to consider how the organisation handles change, and to generate ideas for improvement. Again, it may be used in plenary or in syndicates. For a good level of involvement, it is probably best with no more than eight participants.

Brief the group to consider and report back on the following questions:
- How does this organisation operate when change is needed?
- What policies and practices apply that make transitions easier?
- What suggestions do you have for improvements?

For managers, you might add:
- How can you help others deal with change effectively?

You may well want to give examples of the type of changes you have in mind. These will vary in the level of effect they have on people e.g. promotions, transfers, etc; individual redeployments or relocations; organisational restructuring; redundancies; acquisitions, divestments and mergers; bankruptcies.

Do not forget that a range of organisational initiatives spell change to individuals e.g. corporate culture change programmes; customer care campaigns; quality control drives.

NOTES & SOURCES

Cycles of Development: this framework was developed by Pamela Levin, who was awarded the Eric Berne Memorial Scientific Award for it in 1984. (see Appendix 2 for details). She originally published two books on the subject: *Becoming The Way We Are* 1974, 1985, 1988, and now incorporated into *The Cycle of Life: Creating Smooth Passages in Every Life Season*, The Nourishing Company, 2007; and *Cycles of Power: A User's Guide to the Seven Seasons of Life* 1988, now also republished in 2007 by The Nourishing Company. See Pam Levin's web site at www.yourcycleoflife.com.

Other TA concepts which are useful when considering change are:

- strokes: see Chapter 7, Working with Others.
- Life positions: see Chapter 3, Understanding Attitudes.

Change: the following are referred to in this chapter:

Gail Sheehey, *Passages* Dutton, 1976

Elizabeth Kubler-Ross, *On Death and Dying* MacMillan, 1969

Non-directive counselling see Carl Rogers, *Client Centered Therapy* Constable & Co Ltd, London 1951, reprinted 1986.

CHAPTER 11: CREATIVITY AND INNOVATION

This chapter is about creativity and innovation. I have included it because it is currently an increasingly popular topic on training courses, particularly in organisations which have total quality management or similar approaches that encourage new and better ways of working.

I begin with a section on creativity, explaining how we can use a variation of the *ego state* models to understand creative thinking and creative behaviour. I also include a description of how brainstorming should really work.

The second topic is innovation, or applied creativity. I recommend some stages that are needed to generate and develop ideas into practical solutions. I then refer to the *discounting* concept explained in an earlier chapter to explain why we overlook opportunities to innovate. This section ends with ideas on how to increase the level of innovation within an organisation.

The third section covers problem solving – the usual stimulus for creativity and innovation. I describe a non-TA approach for turning creative thinking into practical, workable solutions. Included is an explanation, using various TA concepts, of why this approach is so effective.

The trainer effectiveness part of this chapter contains ideas on how to make your own training more innovative.

The activities begin with a brief explanation of KAI – a non-TA based questionnaire that allows people to identify their style of creative thinking. I include instructions on how to brainstorm effectively and how to use the practical problem solving approach. There are also suggestions about increasing creativity and exercises for practising skills at encouraging creativity in others.

CREATIVITY

I define creativity as 'having an insight which enlarges understanding'. By this I mean we are able to see something that we could not envisage before. There is also a link with problem solving, as this is often the stimulus to creative thinking. The problem itself may be a direct one, as when a process fails to produce the required outputs. It may also be indirect, such as the 'problem' a customer has when no suitable product or service exists yet to satisfy their particular need.

Ego State Systems

The TA concept of ego states provides a useful framework for understanding the psychological aspects of creativity and the behavioural elements of brainstorming. Chapter 4, Interpersonal Styles, contains a detailed account of the basic ego state model as it relates to behaviour and to thinking, and what I call behavioural and internal ego states. Chapter 6, Thinking Styles, picks up the internal ego state theme and relates it specifically to our thinking processes and the links with problem solving and decision making. Now, I am going to extend the information on ego states as they relate to creativity and to brainstorming. For this, I will use a simplification and refer simply to Parent, Adult and Child. This implies a mix of internal and behavioural but I think that extra detail is not needed for this particular topic.

From the time we are small, we are developing our faculties and having an impact on the world around us. At the same time, we are storing away memories of what happens to us and how we respond. Scientists continue to argue about how much of our adult personality is due to genetics (nature) and how much to the way we are brought up (nurture). What they do generally agree on, however, is that both have an effect. We should not be too quick to dismiss ourselves or others as being incapable of creativity. Maybe we were not so lucky in the genetic lottery and failed to get our share of innate creativity. We will still have quite a lot, as you will see if you watch any small child making toys out of whatever is available. There is still plenty of scope for removing some of the inhibiting effects that social conditioning will have had as we grew up.

We can use the three-part ego state model shown in Figure 11.1 for understanding ourselves and increasing our creativity. We have:

- A Child ego state system that contains our creativity, along with our other natural responses to the world and to other people.
- An Adult ego state system that contains our ability to process information, think logically and solve problems, and therefore enables us to be competent.
- A Parent ego state system that contains the 'messages' and opinions which are significant in our lives, and which seeks to ensure that we adopt solutions that conform.

Among other things, our Child ego state is curious and creative. As babies, we rapidly begin to explore our world. We are not satisfied with looking – we want to touch things, hold them, turn them over, put them into our mouths. As we gain mobility, many more objects come within our reach. Left to our own devices, we will find and play happily with almost anything. Cardboard boxes become dens; stones become animals, cars or food for dolls; pans become hats; stuffed toys become fierce dragons. This is our natural creativity in effect.

Unfortunately, many of us experience curbs on our creativity and curiosity. Objects are moved out of reach in case we break them. We are put into a playpen for our own safety but this stops us exploring our surroundings. We may be unlucky enough to reach something dangerous and get burned by the fire or spill something hot over us from the

Figure 11.1: Creativity and Ego States

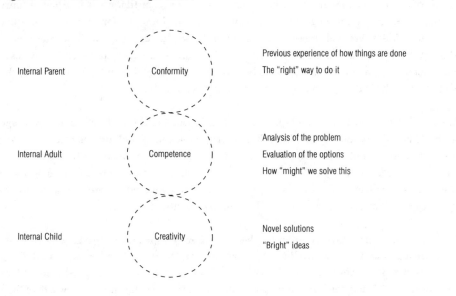

Internal Parent	Conformity	Previous experience of how things are done The "right" way to do it
Internal Adult	Competence	Analysis of the problem Evaluation of the options How "might" we solve this
Internal Child	Creativity	Novel solutions "Bright" ideas

stove. Perhaps our caregiver gets angry, so that we come to associate our actions with fear as we are shouted out, or pain as we are chastised. When we put our creative ideas into effect, we may be ridiculed. In these ways, we learn that it is not always wise to show our natural reactions to the world about us.

Small children have a deep need for love and approval. They will do all they can to please the grown-ups. When getting approval conflicts with showing creativity, the child is faced with a dilemma. If the big people mock our use of a saucepan for a hat, we are torn between fitting in with their expectations or continuing to be creative.

There are also conflicts between our creativity and our need to learn from others. People teach us the 'right' way to do things. We learn that pans are for cooking in and that it is unhygienic to put them on our heads. At school, more of this teaching takes place, as we discover what low marks we get if we make up our own answers to the teacher's questions instead of quoting from the textbook.

Some of us will be lucky enough to be exposed to people who encourage us to be creative. We will learn that it is alright to have bright ideas and to experiment. Those of us who were allowed to take our toys apart to see how they worked will have retained our innate sense of curiosity and will be ready to explore novel ways of solving problems. We may well go into occupations where creativity is seen as appropriate, such as inventing, advertising or entertainment.

However, by the time we are adults, many more of us will have decided long ago to push much of our original creativity underground. We will accept that our work places more demands on our knowledge and experience than it does on our ability to produce innovative ideas. We will, therefore, display to the world our Adapted Child more often than we show our Natural Child. Indeed, over the years we are likely to forget that we ever had much creative ability and come to believe that our adaptation is really us. Hence the common myth that only some of us are gifted with creativity.

Reinforcing the learning and adaptation process of our Child ego state is our Parent ego state. This is the repository of all the things that people tell us and demonstrate to us. We store away copies of their behaviour and replay these in the future, both internally as memories and externally as ways to act towards others. If we were encouraged to be creative, we will have filed away copies of that behaviour which we will now use to encourage others in turn. We will also be comfortable about our own creativity.

However, many of us have different recollections. For example, if we were laughed at when we wore a pan as a hat, we are likely to laugh in the same way when we see a child doing as we used to. If we were told our ideas were impractical, we will tell others why their ideas are impractical. Thus, the implicit messages about creativity being stupid or a waste of time are passed on through generations. Check this for yourself by recalling what happens when you offer an idea. The more truly different the idea is, the more you are likely to receive a sceptical or outrightly adverse response.

Internally, we may react negatively to ourselves at the first sign of any creativity. Inside our heads we may replicate a scene from childhood; this time we have our copy of the grown-up stored in memory and we use it in as internal dialogue with our Child ego state. We then feel uncomfortable and decide our idea is not worth pursuing.

When we replay Parent in this way, we may also stimulate a corresponding replay of a recording in Child so that we feel discomfort that is related to the past. This feeling can be re-experienced powerfully enough in the present to stop us being creative even though other people are encouraging us to put forward ideas.

Our mediator between our own Parent and Child ego states is our Adult ego state. With luck, this ego state also filters the effects of other people so that we have some protection from their conditioning. When in Adult ego state, we think. We identify problems, recognise the need to find a solution, consider the advantages and disadvantages of various options, review the implications, weigh the probabilities of success, and make decisions. We may do this in fractions of a second or it may be a process that extends over days as we keep coming back to the problem.

Our input includes data from our Parent, which has stored away our experiences of how such matters were tackled in the past. This ego state will provide us with options that we recall being used successfully on previous occasions. It will be up to our Adult to analyse whether the current situation is similar enough to the past to make an option relevant, or to come up with combinations or adjustments of actions taken in the past.

The contribution to the problem solving process from Child is two-fold: it consists of our emotional response to the situation and, hopefully, our creativity. Our Adult may have to deal with feelings of discomfort if being creative led to unpleasant experiences in the past. It will also have to sift through any ideas we do have to check which ones could be implemented without too many problems. It is as if Adult takes the raw material from Child ego state, imagines what would happen if the various ideas were pursued, and then develops practicable options.

In practice, Adult is likely to arrive at solutions that are a mix of Child creativity and Parent experience. Provided we are not too cluttered with negative messages, our Child can see totally new ways of doing things. Provided we are not too set in our ways, our Parent sees the implications of the new idea based on what happened in similar situations in the past. Adult synthesises the two sets of inputs and adds any relevant external data, such as information and opinions from other people, before making the final selection of a course of action.

Brainstorming

Mention creativity and most people think of brainstorming. Like TA, brainstorming is an approach that is deceptively simple on the surface yet disappointingly ineffective if used without an understanding of the underlying dynamics. What many people experience as brainstorming will have significant omissions. Often, there is not enough attention placed on creating an atmosphere in which people feel free to be truly creative.

Brainstorming is a technique that should release us from the inhibitions that get in the way of our innate creativity. When used correctly, people are asked to put forward anything that occurs to them, without any consideration or censorship. A problem, a word, a picture – anything can be used as the initial stimulus – and the process should then be rather like a word-association method. Brainstorming can be done by one person but the advantage of a group is that each is stimulated by the others.

The major ground rule for brainstorming is that there be no evaluation. No comments are to be made on the ideas put forward. In ego state terms, this means that Parent and Adult ego states are banished from the room. This allows our Child ego state a high degree of freedom of expression, without fear of ridicule or contradiction.

Without this rule, Parent is likely to reject ideas that have not already been proved useful in practice. Adult will consider the potential difficulties in implementing the idea and may dismiss it before it is fully developed. More importantly, we will be reluctant to offer an idea if we believe that it will be renounced by our colleagues.

We need to be reminded that the ban on evaluation applies totally. Even apparently neutral comments, such as pointing out that an idea has been duplicated, indicates that the person is still thinking logically and is therefore using Adult instead of Child. Most importantly, we must eliminate any self-censorship. Worrying about how people might react to our idea is just as counterproductive as criticising their suggestions.

Understanding that we are aiming to release Child ego state during brainstorming gives us scope to increase the effect. Real children need the security of parents at hand in case of trouble. We provide this by having a facilitator who acts as Parent on behalf of the group, by challenging anyone who starts to evaluate or criticise. In other words, the facilitator's Parent makes sure the children play the game by the rules. They also decide when the game has gone on for long enough, or when the time limit has been reached for the end of the brainstorming session.

Creativity will be increased if several people are involved. It is not only because we stimulate ideas in each other that group brainstorming works better than individual efforts. It is also due to the effect of having several Child ego states active together. Being in the same position makes it easier for each of us to relax. It is as if we really are a group of children playing together. The quality of the 'protection' offered by the Parent ego state will also be significant here.

The more Child ego state there is in the room, the deeper each of us feels able to enter that mode. We become young once again in terms of our thinking, getting in touch with the levels of creativity that existed for us when we were small. In this way, our ideas will be even more original, with reduced contamination from previous experiences. This is also why some exponents of brainstorming suggest that creativity increases when 'naughty' topics such as sex and swearing are introduced; these tend to recall for us the times when we were young and talked about topics that were supposed to be the province of the grown-ups.

Once we have finished our brainstorming session, we need to move on to the original purpose of problem solving. For this, we fetch back our Parent and Adult ego states and then examine the ideas we have generated. We check to see which are feasible, and which offer most scope for further development. Omitting this stage is another common failing when brainstorming is done; this has led people to assume that the technique produces only impractical ideas. This final step is just as important as the ideas generation, although it may seem less fun.

INNOVATION

I think of innovation as applied creativity; organisations put the new ideas into practice. Again, there is a link with problem solving; innovation in organisations is about applying creativity to solve problems. And again, Chapter 6, Thinking Styles will provide useful information.

Stages of Innovation

There are six stages involved in going from initial stimulus through to implementation; as a memory aid I have given each step a name beginning with the letter I for innovation, as shown below:

Step 1	**Identification**	What is happening?
Step 2	**Information**	How is it a problem?
Step 3	**Ideas**	What could be done about it?
Step 3a	**Incubation**	An optional extra: forget about it
Step 3b	**Insight**	A flash of awareness from step 3a
Step 4	**Invention**	Develop an idea into a solution
Step 5	**Investigation**	Check solution for acceptability
Step 6	**Implementation**	Put solution into effect

Step 1 concerns identification. In this stage, we need to notice that something is happening. We may not yet recognise it as a problem but we need to be aware of what is going on. At the corporate level, this may involve us in monitoring levels of sales, of goods produced and rejects, of costs of supplies. Departmentally, it may be about noticing staff turnover or workload achieved. For an individual manager, it may also encompass knowing your staff, knowing their work and personal profiles, knowing equipment capabilities – and all the things that observant managers pick up when they get away from their desks and 'walk the floor.'

The second step is one of information gathering and analysis. Having noticed the raw facts, we now need to collect more data so we can determine whether a problem exists. We have to understand the significance of what we are observing. A decrease in sales figures could be a serious problem or could mask the fact that we are actually selling less at higher prices and making more profit. An increase in sales figures could hide a problem if we have put prices too low. I once belonged to an association which had run a membership recruitment campaign, with specially reduced fees, only to discover too late that they were failing to cover costs. Each new member meant more losses on the publications that had to be sent to them.

Third comes ideas. At this stage, we need to be able to recognise that the situation could be different. We then need to generate ideas for how things could change. Even impractical ideas are important; the truly creative solutions will start from the strangest beginnings. There may be two optional extras within this stage – incubation and insight. Incubation occurs when we stop working directly on the problem. Perhaps we sleep on it, or do something else for a while in the hope that we will have a sudden flash of inspiration. Insight is when we have that sudden flash of inspiration; when we realise that we know how to solve the problem or at least have the germ of an idea.

We then move onto a phase of invention. We must now work out how to develop our idea into something workable. This is typical of what inventors do; they have an idea and then they work out the practicalities of putting it into effect. This may be purely a mental process as we think through the steps to take to implement our idea. Alternatively, this step may involve designing tools and equipment, drawing up plans, or even building something tangible.

Next comes further investigation as we check out the acceptability of our new solution. We need to consider our own views of the idea; if we have doubts we are unlikely to implement it effectively. The views of others will also be important, especially if they are affected by the problem or the solution, and even more so if we will be requiring their involvement in the implementation. At this stage, we are, in effect, evaluating the chances of success for our solution. Will it work, will people apply it, will it really solve the problem, will it change the situation for the better?

Finally, we move on to implementation. We are now ready to put our solution into practice. This last step needs a level of energy and commitment as we will be changing the status quo. Any stages that we may have omitted may well impact negatively now, so that unforeseen objections are raised by people who were not consulted, or defects in the idea become apparent as we put it into effect. If we have moved through the steps, we will be ready to apply the results of our creativity and problem solving.

Innovation and Discounting

We can also contrast these steps with the patterns of discounting described in Chapter 6, Thinking Styles. In this way, we can better identify where creativity and problem solving are being lost within an organisation. This can make a major difference to the level of innovation being achieved by the organisation, and hence to long term viability.

Discounting Pattern 1 means we discount the stimulus; in other words we do not notice what is happening so the identification stage is missed. Pattern 2 concerns our failure to recognise the significance of the initial evidence; having done this we are unlikely to call for any more information about the situation. Pattern 3 occurs when we have the information but still believe that nothing can be changed, so we simply do not bother to look for any ideas.

Patterns 4 to 6 involve our thinking about people and their capabilities. Pattern 4 clicks in when we have ideas but do nothing with them because we doubt that anyone will bother to change what they do now; we decide that the idea is unworkable instead of recognising that our real difficulty is our opinion of human capability. Pattern 5 trips us up when we assume that we and others are incapable of solving the problem; we therefore neglect to investigate and gather sensible feedback because we assume that people will react negatively to our solutions anyway. Finally, with pattern 6 we tend to sabotages ourselves by acting with low energy and commitment; our implementation is unsuccessful because we seem to believe that someone like us will not succeed or that other people will not support the plans.

The Innovative Organisation

The amount of creativity and innovation within an organisation depends on the level of support for the range of ego states. Ego states are encouraged through stroking. Therefore, to measure an organisational climate we can look at the stroking patterns that exist.

In addition to the analysis suggested in Chapter 7, Working with Others, we can consider specifically:

- How much stroking related to creativity and innovation takes place? Do senior managers respond positively when suggestions are made to them? What happens when colleagues attempt to help each other?
- What recognition is forthcoming for Child ego state? Are the more creative people regarded as valuable or childish?
- What appreciation is there for the Adult ego state? How much attention is paid to assessing current and future circumstances? Is the respect paid to the past experiences of Parent ego states with long service kept in proportion?
- How much fun is involved in the rewards for people making suggestion scheme submissions? Serious awards are fine for Parent and Adult type suggestions for improvements but will not stimulate new ideas from Child ego state.

Problem solving

Another neglected area is the transformation of the initial ideas into workable options. Too often, participants are left feeling that the ideas they have dutifully contributed are impractical. To overcome this, I recommend a non-TA approach from Synectics. 'Synectics' is an invented word that is used to apply to a whole range of techniques related to creativity. One method in particular furnishes us with an excellent procedure to use in association with brainstorming for ensuring that creativity is followed by practical problem solving.

Practical Problem Solving

Synectics' practical problem solving technique fits around brainstorming to provide a very effective method for combining creativity with practicability. It also ensures that the problem-owner is in control of the process, so that solutions are not thrust upon them in an authoritative way. Another benefit is that the method avoids any tendency to 'Yes, but..', a conversation in which the problem-owner seems to find a reason why every solution proposed cannot be implemented.

Step 1 of Practical Problem Solving

The problem-owner sets the scene by:

- providing a headline that encapsulates the problem. This should preferably be a statement that starts with the words 'How to ...' and states what they want to achieve e.g. How to produce better quality goods, find a supplier, improve a relationship.
- giving the background to the problem. A short description of the situation and events leading up to it is given.

- saying what solutions have already been tried, and what happened, or what solutions have been thought of, and why not actioned.
- outlining their own ability to take action. What are their limits of authority, when do they have to get approval, what are their boundaries of responsibility?
- Describing their ideal solution. This can be a fantasy option, as outlandish as they like. It should be what they would like to do if there were no limits.

During this process, the rest of the group listen but do not ask questions unless there is jargon or technical language that they literally do not understand. They are recommended to use in-out listening – a Synectics technique whereby we listen (in); stop listening (out) while we make a note of an idea or thought; listen again (in); and continue alternating like this. This note taking ensures that valuable ideas do not get forgotten.

It may seem strange that no questions are allowed. However, in ego state terms this is very sensible. We are far too likely to shift into Adult or Parent ego state once we start questioning. That is how we normally solve problems. Parent wants to get more description to make it easier to select from memory a previous occasion on which the same problem occurred – so we can identify a previous solution that worked then. Adult wants more information so as to be able to take into account the implications of any suggestion – this will lead to ideas being killed off before we have been able to develop them.

Step 2 of Practical Problem Solving

The group, including the problem-owner and the facilitator, brainstorm. The facilitator writes up on large sheets everything that is said. Participants are encouraged to generate ideas as quickly as possible, with no pauses for evaluating or self-censoring. It can sometimes help to have more than one person writing up the ideas as they are called out, so as not to slow the process.

Step 3 or Practical Problem Solving

This is the step that really distinguishes this approach from simple brainstorming. The problem-owner selects from the lists one or more items which they would like to take further. In the Synectics version, they also give information about why they are making this selection. I have found this also works well if no explanation is given. Explaining helps to focus the participants in a particular direction; not explaining leaves them freer to continue to be intuitively creative for longer.

Having selected the item(s), the rest of the group are then invited to offer practical suggestions. They take the item further by proposing what action the problem-owner should now take. During this part of the process, only one participant contributes at a time. They are then responded to in a structured fashion by the problem-owner. Only after that can another participant offer a suggestion. This discipline prevents the session deteriorating into a normal meeting in which people interrupt, argue, insist that they understand the problem even though it is not theirs, and generally act as if they know the situation better than the problem-owner.

The problem-owner responds to each suggestion by:

- paraphrasing what has been suggested until the proposer is satisfied that they have been understood. At this stage, the problem-solver often finds that their first attempt to paraphrase indicates that they were about to disagree (or, rarely, agree) with an idea which they had not correctly grasped.
- giving three or more reasons why they like the idea. They may have to work hard here, mentally, to identify what they like about the idea. Their natural reaction may well be to talk instead about the impracticability of the idea. The facilitator needs to push them to see the benefits of the suggestion. This is rather like going for the burn in an aerobics session – painful at the time but you feel great afterwards.
- indicating what difficulty they see with the idea. When they do so, they are expected to state their rejection in the form of 'pointing a direction' – Synectics-speak for saying what drawbacks to the idea must still be overcome. As with the headline, they state the direction with a 'How to...' statement. e.g. How to raise the necessary finance; convince senior management; find time to implement.

The paraphrasing, giving of three plus points and direction pointing complete the interaction with the person who has made the suggestion. Once completed, anyone in the group may put forward the next idea. With luck, they will have been paying close attention to the conversation so far and can therefore offer a suggestion that relates directly to the direction headline just heard.

This procedure continues as the solution is gradually developed. The problem-owner remains in charge of the path of the discussion at all times. No time is wasted on suggestions that would be rejected anyway. Participants require considerable patience to stay quiet while others have the floor but can ultimately see how useful this has been.

Step 4 of Practical Problem Solving

The Step 4 Action Statement is really the culmination of Step 3. There will come a point when the problem-owner realises that they have a workable solution. At this stage, they outline for the group their action plan in terms of:

- what their solution is
- how it is different to ideas they had before
- how they will implement it
- what they intend to do now.

Why it Works

Why Does Practical Problem Solving Work? Obviously, one reason is because we have several brains working on the same problem. However, that rationale applies in ordinary meetings too yet these are not always distinguished by their problem solving capacity. There are several other causes of the success of the Synectics technique. TA concepts allow us to understand why this non-TA technique is so useful, by considering it in terms of the balancing of ego state contributions, the enhanced levels of stroking, and the avoidance of discounting.

One obvious facet of this technique is the way it creates an ego state balance. It brings back into action the Parent and Adult ego states after the creativity of the Child has been expressed during the brainstorming. It also balances the power between problem-owner and group member in a way that is often lacking in meetings, when whoever speaks most forcefully or loudest has an inordinate level of control.

In addition it also reinforces the impact of Adult over Parent. Parent provides opinions based on previous experience; these may be out-of-date or irrelevant now. Adult concentrates on the current situation. Being required to state the benefits of an idea forces us to relate it to the current situation. We could make one of our plus points the fact that it worked in the past but we will still need to identify two other advantages. We have little choice but to consider the idea in a truly open-minded fashion.

An equally significant aspect of the technique is its high level of stroking behaviour. Strokes were explained in Chapter 7, Working with Others; they are the units of recognition that we give to others. They may be positive or negative, reinforcing or undermining. Most of us prefer to receive positive strokes, which include constructive criticism that allows us to develop our skills, ideas and personalities.

The Practical Problem Solving process strokes in several ways:

- Listening. Insisting that only one person speak at a time gives us the pleasant experience of being attended to rather than interrupted.
- Paraphrasing. We have to really listen if we are to be able to paraphrase accurately. True listening is a powerful affirmation of the value we place on the other person. If we get the paraphrase wrong, more stroking occurs as we interact to correct our misunderstanding.
- Three Plus Points. Each favourable comment we make about their idea is a positive stroke. In order to identify at least three, we are required to think in depth about their suggestion, so our comments are anything but superficial.
- Action Statement. It is extremely reinforcing to hear someone turn our collection of thoughts into a practical plan that they intend to carry out. At this stage also, the genuine relief and excitement of the problem-owner is usually apparent.

Indeed, this solution stroking process is so powerful that it can be adapted for use on its own, as a way of encouraging ideas on a day to day basis. It then becomes a response pattern for use when an individual offers a suggestion, particularly an unsolicited one. Quite simply, it consists of listening, paraphrasing, identifying one benefit of the solution put forward and promising to think about it. We can do this without committing ourselves to accepting the idea.

We will, however, have a more positive impact on the other person than if we had told them what was wrong with the idea. Instead, we have reacted positively and can now take our time to give the idea further consideration. Used throughout an organisation, this style of responding will foster a climate of creativity.

Another explanation for the success of Practical Problem Solving is the way in which it challenges discounting. When we discount, we overlook problems or solutions without being aware of doing so. Each of us has blind spots – things we just don't notice. The Practical Problem Solving process helps us to see beyond our own blocks and grasp ideas put forward by others.

Often, when someone suggests a solution to us we are unable to see the relevance. We may already have struggled with our own range of options and cannot see how they can identify anything usable that we have not already thought of. So, we dismiss their idea before we have truly considered it. Paraphrasing forces us to pay more attention to the idea; identifying plus points causes us to change our perception of the idea itself.

At other times, we may have identified some options but do not believe that it will be possible to overcome the barriers to implementation. Stating these barriers in terms of how to resolve them forces us to acknowledge that it might be possible to do so. Being expected to consider carefully each new suggestion ensures that we give proper attention to the ways in which such obstacles can be surmounted.

The final level of discount occurs when we can see a solution but do not believe that we are personally capable of implementing it. It would work for others but we lack the skill, determination, confidence, knowledge, or whatever else is required. It is hard to maintain this distorted self-perception of our ability when our colleagues make it clear they think otherwise. Providing comments on the snags we see with their proposals compels us to bring our doubts into the open. They can then make further suggestions on how we can conquer our imagined limitations.

TRAINER EFFECTIVENESS
The Innovative Trainer
We all have the potential to be a creative trainer, and to be innovative in the ways we design and run our programmes. Check how much you have been influenced by your knowledge of other trainers. Are you modelling your approach to training on what you have seen in the past? This is fine if you have been lucky enough to be student or co-tutor with trainers who were creative themselves. It is not so good if you have experienced mainly trainers who preferred to play safe and use only tried and tested methods. There is a place for these but we need also to introduce new ideas and new techniques to keep our training fresh and alive.

Review your training repertoire. Make a list of every input, technique and activity that you use (or have used over the last 3 months). Now answer the following questions about each of them:
- How often and for how long do you apply it? What proportion of your total training time does it occupy?
- Where did you 'learn' it? Is it copied from training done by someone else? How much of your work is copied as opposed to devised by you?

- How much have you invented for yourself? How often do you repeat sessions that are your own creation? Are you in danger of overusing ideas that were once original but are now being applied more generally?
- What ego states do you exhibit when you are providing the training? Are you equally comfortable in any ego state? Which of your inputs, techniques and activities seem to work only if you adopt a specific ego state? Is it likely that you slip into the Parent style rather than using your own Child ego state to invite your students to have fun and be creative?

When you have answered the questions, review your responses and plan how you will introduce more creativity into appropriate areas of your work. The stages of innovation provide a useful checklist:

Identify – what happens in your sessions?

Review the information – look for possible problems; do they learn, what can they do better after the training, how do they evaluate your programmes; how do their managers evaluate your programmes?

Generate ideas – what might you change?

Incubate – sleep on it or do something else while your subconscious works on the problem.

Insight – keep notes of any ideas, however bizarre.

Invention – take your ideas and work them into practical options. Aim for alternative strategies so you can choose the ones that work out best.

Investigate – check out your ideas by talking to colleagues. Test feasibility by trying out one new approach at a time.

Implement – retain the best options and add them into your repertoire. Produce whatever course notes and handouts you need.

Then go back to the beginning of this process and start again, so that you are constantly expanding your range of options. The more you have, the easier it is to vary your sessions and the less likely you are to get bored with your own work.

ACTIVITIES
Activity 11.1 Kirton Adaptation-Innovation Inventory
The Kirton Adaptation-Innovation Inventory (KAI) is a short non-TA questionnaire that identifies cognitive style. It places people on a scale in terms of adaptation versus innovation. Adaptors prefer to operate within the current structure, so will be creative in

finding ways to do current tasks better. Innovators prefer to 'break the mould' so will look for new things to do.

The inventory takes only a short time to administer and score, and helps people see how their styles may lead them to interpret creativity and innovation in very different ways. Knowledge of their own preferences will help them to understand how they might be limiting themselves.

See the end of this chapter for details on obtaining certification in the use of KAI.

Activity 11.2 Creativity Puzzles
Any book of puzzles and creativity exercises from a high street bookstore will provide plenty of ideas for activities to use as warm-ups during training courses on creativity. Look near the books of crossword puzzles and on 'pop' psychology shelves.

Sunday newspaper supplements are also a good source of ideas, when they provide suggestions for family activities during national holidays, festive occasions and long journeys with children!

Activity 11.3 Brainstorming
This is an obvious activity to use to develop creativity. Put up plenty of large sheets to record ideas on, explain the process to participants, select a topic, and start writing.

It helps if you:
- laugh a lot and have fun
- reassure them that anything goes, and prove it by adding in items yourself
- write up exactly what they call out – any tidying up will be seen as censorship
- get them sitting in a circle without desks – these are too reminiscent of being at work or back at school. Sitting on a carpeted floor is even better for inviting them into Child ego state.
- don't have more than two people to write the ideas up – otherwise too many will call out at once and not all ideas will be heard. Being heard is important as recognition and for stimulating more ideas from others.

Note: there are variations of brainstorming in which participants write their ideas onto cards and pass them round or pin them up. These approaches are not as effective in developing creativity because they lack the group reinforcement of Child ego state and the facilitator challenges to Adult and Parent.

Activity 11.4 Practical Problem Solving
This combines creativity with problem solving so that participants can see how their creativity can be developed into something useful. When following the process outlined in this chapter, keep in mind the requirements below.

The problem-owner must have a real problem. It need not be a large problem but it must be current. Do not try this activity with a problem that is not really a concern for them, or one they have already solved. Check this carefully; beware the participant who invents a problem to help you out with the exercise. The dynamics will not work unless they want to find a solution.

When presented with suggestions during Step 3, some people will offer only superficial benefits or identify advantages with particular ease. In that case, make them think of more. The strokes have less value to the other person if they do not appear to be the result of serious consideration.

Occasionally people claim that they cannot think of anything positive to say about the idea presented to them. Let the rest of the group prompt them, but only for a few moments. If they persist in reacting negatively to the proposal, stop the exercise. Explain that you are unwilling to expose others to a similar experience. Describe, using TA stroke theory, how this discourages people from putting forward their ideas. If appropriate, restart the activity with a different problem-owner.

Activity 11.5 Listening and Paraphrasing: One to One
Any exercise in which participants are required to listen and paraphrase will be useful.

In threes or fours, ask them to talk to each other about their jobs, their hobbies, their ideas for improvements within the organisation, etc. Person A talks for 5 minutes, with appropriate pauses. Person B listens and paraphrases. Person C (and D) acts as observer.

Person B may not ask questions. If their paraphrase is incorrect, Person A must make the point again using different words.

After 5 minutes, Person A gives feedback on the accuracy of the paraphrasing. Person B gives feedback on how easy it was to listen to Person A. Person C (and D) comment on what they observed.

Activity 11.6 Listening and Paraphrasing: Group
With a group of 6-8 people, ask them to have a meeting on a topic of general interest which is likely to stimulate suggestions (e.g. bringing more tourists to the country, making the organisation more attractive as an employer). Set a time limit of 30 minutes to produce group proposals.

After the discussion has run normally for 5 minutes, they will be required to paraphrase what the previous speaker has just said before making any of their own points. Each person is to make a note of how accurate the paraphrase of them was; they should not interrupt to correct it but will give feedback later. (Make sure they understand it is only the previous speaker's own comments to be paraphrased – they don't need to paraphrase the previous paraphrasing!)

Review afterwards. Participants will generally find it very difficult to listen and paraphrase in this way. They will realise with a shock just how little attention we really pay at times to other peoples' ideas.

NOTES & SOURCES

Ego states is a concept originally introduced by Eric Berne. See Chapter 4 Interpersonal Styles, and Chapter 6 Thinking Styles. There are nowadays a range of models of ego states.

If you have read TA books, you are likely to have come across the term Little Professor. This has generally been presented in the popular literature as being the ego state that is creative. It is a fun sounding name for an ego state and you may well find that participants like it. If you do use this label, you may find you get questions on the difference between Little Professor and Adult.

'Little Professor' is the label Berne gave to part of Child ego state. When considering the developmental aspects of ego states, he showed a more detailed analysis (called second order) that divided Child into three components: Parent in the Child, Adult in the Child, and Child in the Child. Adult in the Child was the 'thinking' part of the little person, who did not yet think in the same logical fashion as a grown-up. Berne named this part 'Little Professor', to capture the essence of a mode of thinking that has magical, intuitive elements.

Little Professor refers therefore to an internal ego state, which may be displayed directly via Natural Child but which may also be hidden if we choose to suppress our intuition and creativity. It may also be displayed through any other behavioural ego state if that is what our Little Professor thinks will give us the best option for getting our own way! e.g. cool, calm and collected Functional Adult to impress a senior colleague; Nurturing Parent to convince someone we care about them even if we don't really.

Brainstorming is a non-TA term that has been misapplied so often that many people are unaware of its true format, and hence its real usefulness. As facilitators, we can increase the chances of 'real' brainstorming occurring if we are scrupulous about writing on the flipchart exactly what the participant calls out – with no censoring. We can also help by calling out items ourselves in a way that models the permission to say anything that comes to mind. Rude words and the names of parts of the human anatomy can be surprisingly effective in reassuring the Child ego states in the room that the Parent ego states really have been banished for the time being.

Practical Problem Solving and Synectics - non-TA - are described by Vincent Nolan in *Open to Change* MCB Publications, 1981. See www.synecticsworld.com and www.vincentnolan.co.uk

Stroking – see Chapter 7, Working with Others.

Discounting – see Chapter 6, Thinking Styles.

KAI – non-TA - for details see www.kaicentre.com.

CHAPTER 12: PROFESSIONAL SUPER-VISION

You may be wondering why this chapter is here, and why the hyphen.

The chapter is here because super-vision is essential for helping professionals. We use ourselves as the tools of our trade and hence need to maintain them. Super-vision is the process that equates to taking care of our tools, oiling them, adding new attachments as these become available. Just as we need to upload new software packages to our computer, check our virus protection and routinely clean up our hard drives, so we need similar processes for our psychological apparatus.

The hyphen is here to distinguish supervision as practiced by first-line managers from the sort of supervision that applies when helping professionals to develop themselves.

This chapter offers some ideas for how best to achieve good super-vision, and is especially targeted to you as a supervisee.

Within the chapter, I start by describing the key elements of super-vision, and how self-reflection is an important adjunct. I go on to explain transference and why this phenomenon represents a significant rationale for getting super-vision.

The next part of the chapter is about various techniques for reflection coupled with getting the most out of super-vision. The whole chapter is about the activity of super-vision but I do include some checklists at the end. These are for you to work through as you reflect rather than for you to use with participants attending your training. Some may also be applied to super-vision sessions.

WHAT IS SUPER-VISION?

As I mentioned above, the super-vision described in this chapter is very different to the way it is customarily used within industry to mean the activities of supervisors or first-line managers when they watch to see that work is undertaken in the way that their organisations (or said supervisors) expect. There may be elements of this managerial function within super-vision but the emphasis will be quite different, as will the way it is implemented. People are unlikely to review their development needs openly with supervisors who may later incorporate such information into an annual appraisal and use it to justify a lower salary.

A helpful way to consider the nature of super-vision is through three elements described around 20 years ago by Brigid Proctor (1986): normative, formative and restorative. I have renamed restorative as supportive as I think this better captures what is needed for developmental practitioners, who tend to encounter less 'distressing' client issues than the counsellors that Proctor was writing for.

For the normative aspects, the supervisor has a responsibility for ensuring that the practitioner is practicing in ways that are competent and ethical. This includes checking that the practitioner is working within whatever professional, organisational and national rules and laws apply. In other words, it is about ensuring that the practitioner is behaving as a good practitioner should and meeting the norms of the profession.

When it comes to formative, the supervisor has a role in the development and growth of the practitioner and may do this via feedback, direct guidance, role modelling or a variety of other options. The aim is to develop the skills, theoretical knowledge, personal attributes, self-awareness, etc. of the practitioner so that the practitioner becomes increasingly competent.

For the supportive element, the supervisor is there to support the practitioner when the inevitable doubts and insecurities arise, and to challenge and confront (supportively) when the practitioner's personal issues become evident. This includes providing a safety-valve for those times when a practitioner unwittingly seems to pick up the issues that the client has and starts behaving as if these are the practitioner's own issues. It also includes prompting the practitioner to see a therapist whenever the practitioner's own issues are getting in the way.

You can, of course, engage in a process of taking a meta-perspective with a colleague instead of with a formal supervisor. This is often referred to as peer supervision, and sometimes called intervision. You can still use the three elements as a framework, with some limitations.

When it comes to normative, it is not appropriate for someone to accept responsibility for checking that a colleague is doing their job properly. However, with a strong enough relationship, you can certainly draw a colleague's attention to any potential shortcomings in their professional activity.

On formative, there may be a significant contribution to the supervisee's learning because people often pay far more attention to a colleague's opinions than they do when an authority figure is involved. Comments from those in authority may well be dismissed on the grounds they have no idea what the job is really like. The same comment cannot be dismissed so easily when it comes from a colleague who is actually doing the same job as the supervisee.

Colleagues can be highly supportive and challenging. They become involved in similar situations so can empathise from the basis of their own experiences, which also makes it easier for them to spot and challenge inappropriate or inauthentic responses. However, if you engage in peer super-vision, you will need to guard against relating too strongly and losing your objectivity.

What is reflective practice?

Reflective practice refers to the same concept as super-vision but without the involvement of a supervisor or colleague. You can reflect as you review your practice across three timeframes – past, present and future. When you reflect on the past, you consider what you have done; how did you and the participant behave; what were the outcomes; how might you have acted differently and what might that have led to? Reflecting on the past can be done from memory but may be enhanced considerably through the use of recordings.

As you become accustomed to reflecting, it becomes easier to continue the process whilst with a participant and therefore to reflect on the present. Practice builds an ability to run a 'stream of consciousness' reflection in the background of the mind, whilst still paying attention to the participant. You may find it easier to reflect in the present if you choose a simple framework that you can bring to mind without needing to refer to notes.

The point of reflection is to enhance capability so time spent reflecting on how to behave in future situations allows you to identify more options and to plan for increased flexibility, with specific participants and more generally. NLP has a technique called future pacing, in which we are invited to go into the future in our imagination. The more vividly we imagine the future scene, the more real it feels. Our brain then records the future scene as if it has already happened. That way, when we reach that specific point in the future, it feels familiar to us and we are therefore more likely to behave in the way we previously chose. This can increase considerably the benefit we get from reflecting.

In addition to the significant learning that comes from reflecting and reviewing, the super-vision you receive will be far more effective when you have prepared for it via a process of self-reflection. Prior analysis of your own practice saves super-vision time and enables supervisors to operate at a higher level of intensity when they support and challenge you.

Why Bother?

It was not until I experienced super-vision as a trainee transactional analyst that I realised how valuable it is. Audio taping my work and listening to the tapes resulted in me noticing so many aspects that I had been unaware of. Presenting and discussing selected segments then led to even more insights. I often say, not completely as a joke, that I was able to increase my fees considerably over time as super-vision continued to contribute to my increased levels of professional competence.

One model for understanding the theoretical case for super-vision is that of discounting, as described in Chapter 6. This process, engaged in by all humans, means that we consistently fail to notice certain aspects of reality such as what we or others are saying or the real meaning behind the words.

We discount to maintain our existing frame of reference. Hence, if we have limiting beliefs about our own competence, we may accept a mediocre level of performance instead of realising that we could change our behaviours and learn new skills. We also discount about other people, so may need prompting to notice our limiting beliefs about what our clients or participants may be capable of.

I leave you to read the relevant section of Chapter 6 to learn more about discounting. With practice, you will become more skilled at noticing what is being missed in your interactions and also those between participants.

Another framework for recognising what we overlook, and hence why super-vision is so useful, is transference.

What is Transference?

An everyday use of English tells us that 'transfer' means something gets shifted across – as in footballers joining new teams. Transference occurs when clients shift across the characteristics of someone else onto the practitioner.

So participants may project their own good or bad points onto you, which will mean that some participants like you a lot because you seem to be just like them and some participants dislike you a lot because they have invested you with their own failings – in this case the participants probably also manage to repress any awareness of having the faults themselves. This is why it is easier to get on with people once we accept that we are not perfect ourselves. Once we recognise that we are still OK even with faults, we no longer have to project those faults onto others and can relate to people as who they really are.

Or it may be the characteristics of someone else that the participants transfer, as when they relate to trainers as if they are teachers from the past. In these cases, sometimes the trainer may compound the problem by acting like a school teacher. This reaction from the practitioner is termed countertransference. However, what is sometimes thought of as countertransference may be simply the person's own transference.

Professional helpers monitor their reactions for countertransference because this gives them valuable information about how to help their participants. If you recognise feelings of wanting to take care of a participant, you can check whether this is a realistic, here-and-now reaction that is also an appropriate thing to do – or whether it is a reaction to helplessness being exhibited by the participant. For instance, if a participant is clearly unable to deal with being bullied by a local manager, it may be appropriate (and an organisational requirement) for you to report this to senior management. However, a strong urge on your part to intervene with the participant's manager over something like management interference in a project may be outside the contract, part of a psychological game of 'Let's you and them fight'; and triggered by a combination of the participant's avoidance tactics and your tendencies to act as a Rescuer.

I categorise transference on two dimensions as shown in Figure 12.1: whether we are projecting elements of our self or of someone else (a third party) onto the person we are transacting with and whether we are projecting so that we appear to get on well with the other person or so that we have a problem relating to each other.

Note that it is possible to have a healthy dependency as a real child with a real parent. This is because such a relationship reflects reality and does not involve transference – children really do need parenting until they reach a certain age. Couples may also set up functional arrangements that look like transference but are not. For example, one does the gardening and the other cares for the house. No transference is involved as long as both recognise these as choices – and know that they are capable of swapping tasks if necessary.

We may also want to use the transference. It may seem strange to suggest this but therapists do so routinely to enhance their work with participants. A participant who thinks the trainer is a good parent will be more likely to act on the trainer's advice; a participant who thinks

Figure 12.1: Transference Formats

	Project self	
	Competitive	**Concordant**
	We project elements of our own Child or Parent ego state onto the other person and then get into a competitive symbiosis about whose Child or Parent will take precedence	We project elements of our own Child or Parent ego state onto the other person and then believe they are just like us and we are empathising with each other
	Conflictual	**Co-dependent**
	We project elements of 'a third party' onto the other person and then feel we must 'fight' in a Parent-Child or Child-Parent interaction	We project elements of 'a third party' onto the other person and then seek a Parent-Child or Child-Parent symbiosis
	Project someone else	

Have problem in relating (left side) — Appear to get on well together (right side)

the trainer is 'bad' can be allowed to work through their issues without being punished by the trainer. The same applies to supervisee and supervisor.

Awareness is the key – once transference and/or countertransference are recognised, the professional uses this knowledge to plan more effective ways of interacting.

Generally, the circumstances for a training programme or a super-vision session will mean that avoidance of transference is the better option.

See the details below within Figure 12.2 for ways to achieve this.

Figure 12.2: Avoiding Transference

	Project self	
	Competitive	**Concordant**
	Parent - Parent Check out the other person's views and paraphrase these; avoid direct disagreement	*Parent - Parent* Look for aspects where you have different opinions; emphasise these if necessary
	Child - Child Acknowledge the other person's stated needs; avoid sympathising and avoid playing 'My problems are bigger than yours'	*Child - Child* Look for areas where you experience different feelings; emphasise these if necessary
Have problem in relating	**Conflictual**	**Co-dependent**
	Parent - Child Clarify what they want you to do and explore their rationale for this; avoid making excuses or arguing	*Parent - Child* Look out for this when someone seems intent on taking care of you; thank them politely (and profusely) and explain you're fine without assistance
	Child - Parent Have a clear rationale when you ask for help; check you do not expect someone else to make your decisions for you	*Child - Parent* Watch out for times when you wish someone would take care of you; check whether this is appropriate and, if not, do it yourself

Appear to get on well together (right side label)

Project someone else

DOING YOUR REFLECTION

Having explained why super-vision is so important, below I will give some practical tips on how to prepare and do the reflection beforehand – super-vision may be useful at any of the stages, including why you might be avoiding getting started at Stage 1!

The underlying process is – set aside time to think about what you've done in the past and what you might do in the future – and take time during professional sessions to think about the process in the present moment.

We can consider this process in a series of stages that continually recycle:
1. Capturing events as they occur
2. Reviewing specific events
3. Reviewing a series of events to look for patterns
4. Planning ahead to incorporate learning points generally
5. Planning ahead for specific events
6. Implementing your learning

Stage 1: Capturing events as they occur

Note-taking

Some practitioners make notes during sessions but others prefer not to. The decision on note-taking is yours and will be influenced by personal styles and preferences, as well as by the type of practice being undertaken. For example, it will be highly relevant during any forms of coaching where you may provide advice, and contra-indicated whilst a participant is working through sensitive personal issues. It is more obtrusive in one-to-one sessions but there may be too much to note easily if you are working with a group.

Taking notes will give you a better basis than relying on memory but may mean that you miss something significant whilst writing down the previous point. Not taking notes will leave you free to focus your full attention on the participant(s), you will be more likely to pick up on the feelings behind the words, and that will contribute to a relationship that seems more intimate and less businesslike. However, not taking notes may mean that you fail to recall participant comments accurately, participants may feel uncomfortable with the intensity of your attention, or worry that you will not remember what they are telling you.

Stream of consciousness

Whether or not you take notes during sessions, it is also useful to get into the habit of writing a 'stream of consciousness' set of notes immediately the session ends. As well as capturing as much as possible, it serves as a sort of clearing process – once written down you can put that session out of your mind and concentrate on the next.

To use stream of consciousness effectively, it is important that you make no attempt to analyse or evaluate at this stage. Instead, write as much as you can without stopping to edit or think about what any of it means. Include any questions or insights that occur to you as you write, or that you were aware of during the session with the participant.

One way to do this is to divide a sheet into three columns. In one you note down whatever you recall of what was said by the participant. In the next, you note your own responses, alongside or below each participant interaction. Use the third column to note the questions and insights. Work right through the session doing this before you stop to think about what it might mean. Then go back over it, taking your time to reflect on what you've noted. Maybe use a different colour pen to add comments, extra insights, and more questions for you to think about. Finally, go through again and consider what actions you will take, either with a particular participant or in general in order to increase your professional competence.

Recording

An even better way of generating evidence for subsequent reflections is to record sessions. Audio recording is enough. Video is possible, of course, but a camera tends to be harder to ignore during the session, raises the issue of whether you point it at yourself or the participants, and is little use for later visual analysis unless you use state-of-the-art equipment. Audio taping also reassures participants because colleagues and supervisors are less likely to recognise them from voice alone. Video may of course still be useful for training sessions with peers as participants in one-to-one work.

I admit to being biased in favour of tapes over notes. This is because "we don't know what we don't know". What we write down during and after sessions consists of what we allow ourselves to be aware of. I referred to it earlier as stream of consciousness – and it lacks the unconscious or psychological level, of our interactions. We can't make notes about those aspects that are outside our awareness but if you listen to a tape of yourself you will begin to spot these. You suddenly hear yourself saying something in a particular way, or you notice how you overlooked a comment, or you recognise a new significance in what was going on. And, once you get beyond the natural tendency to punish yourself for being so unaware at the time, you begin to learn a great deal more about how you function.

Stage 2: Reviewing Specific Events

Having captured as much information as possible, whether through notes or recordings, the next stage is to initiate a review process. You might do this alone or in a group, with one or more peers, or within a supervisory relationship. You might also use a mix of these formats.

This is of course where you can use the range of TA concepts!

Stage 3: Reviewing to Look for Patterns

As well as reflecting on specific sessions, it makes sense to review across a series of sessions with the same participant, across sessions with a range of participants, and across sessions that cover the same topics. In this way, you will be able to identify any repeating themes, or patterns, in how you function.

For example, you might check the same stage for each of several sessions. Do you have any repeating patterns that occur when you are working to create the relationship with a new group, or any typical stumbling blocks around ending relationships, or do you fall into the trap of advice-giving when a participant needs to action plan?

Maybe you think about the ongoing process, such as whether you typically experience concerns about working with participants who have very different backgrounds to you, or you sense that participants are attempting to communicate more than they are saying, or you feel uneasy about participants who seem to want to be dependent on you.

Or review whether there are patterns that indicate you are more or less comfortable when the focus is on you or the participant or the participant's contacts, or whether your effectiveness changes according to the type of situation.

Keeping a Journal

Your session notes and subsequent reviews may well form the basis for a journal or learning log but the reflections across cases will be even more valuable. Unlike a diary, a development journal will contain far more than your instant reflections on events as they occur. You will use it to capture the themes and patterns you identify across your work.

There are many ways to operate such a journal, which can incorporate colours and symbols to highlight key points, spider maps to show relationships, drawings and even forms of collage for those who are stimulated by more than the written word – plus words are fine too.

At a practical level, you may want sections so you can file sessions by group topic, with a separate section for your reviews of these sessions (as these are about you rather than the participants). Then add a section for your cross-sessional reflections, with perhaps another for your action plans on how you will implement what you are learning. Plus perhaps the final step will be to plan for specific sessions with specific participants, thus closing the loop.

Stages 4 – 6: Planning ahead to incorporate and implement learning

If you've worked through stages 1 to 3, the fourth stage will be fairly straightforward – you select your learning points and think about how you will use them to develop your professional competence. You are then ready to move on to Stage 5, which consists of identifying future situations when you could apply your general learning in specific ways. Stage 6 then becomes a series of implementations as you put the learning from super-vision into effect across a range of situations, monitoring the results and adjusting as necessary as you go along.

SUPER-VISION FORMATS

There are options for how you organise your super-vision and some frameworks that will be particularly relevant.

One-to-one or Group

The most common format for super-vision is one-to-one working between supervisor and supervisee. This may be done privately but can just as easily be conducted in a group setting, with supervisees taking turns. Working privately may mean that a supervisee shares concerns more readily but working in a group has significant advantages. Supervisees can learn much from observing the super-vision of others. There are only so many variations of the issues that occur in professional sessions so chances are high that supervisees will realise that they share the issue currently under super-vision, and can work out for themselves what to do next. This leaves them free to bring a different issue when their turn comes with the supervisor – and this may in turn be enlightening for another supervisee.

Another advantage of having super-vision in a group is the way that it prompts supervisees to get beyond shame and to realise that mistakes are learning opportunities. It may take a while to pluck up the courage to present aspects of our work where we feel we make mistakes but when we do, we realise that our supervisor and the other supervisees are not judging us. Instead, we are more likely to feel validated by the reactions of others. This is potent learning that enables us to update our frame of reference, and hence empowers us to react to others in a similar manner.

Yet another benefit of super-vision in a group setting is that the 'audience' have the opportunity to monitor their own reactions as the super-vision progresses. They can check out whether their own issues are being triggered by what they are observing. If the supervisor runs a short process review after each super-vision, there is also the chance to share such reactions and explore how they might be resonating with the supervisee or their participant. This can provide valuable additional insights.

The above assumes that the group are an audience of silent observers whilst one supervisee works directly with the supervisor. This is itself is often a learning experience as some practitioners realise that they struggle to stay neutral and silent. If they are giving away their reactions in the super-vision group, what impact do they suppose those uncontrolled reactions may be having on their participants? Group super-vision can help practitioners develop poker-playing skills so they can avoid looking shocked or amused even when participants tell them shocking or inappropriately amusing things.

When a process review is conducted after each super-vision slot, it is important that the discussion does not stray back into the piece of super-vision. What is to be reflected on is the process during the super-vision – how supervisor and supervisee interacted, what reactions others experienced, exploration of the supervisor's choices of interventions – but nothing that might re-work the super-vision, no direct questions to the supervisee, no attempts to slip in some extra analysis or advice relating to the participant or client.

An alternative way of working with a group is for the group itself to provide the super-vision, with the supervisor acting as the back-stop. For this, the supervisee in question contracts with the whole group for what she or he wants. This might, for example, be to explore reactions with particular participants, or to consider options for a forthcoming session. The individual members of the group accept responsibility for working within the requested contract, or agree to stay silent if they have nothing to contribute.

Group super-vision can be a great way for a supervisee to hear many different perspectives or ideas. It can also be hard work for the supervisor who has to act as a kind of chairperson to ensure that group members keep in mind that the aim is to help the supervisee attain increased awareness and not to push their own opinions. It requires considerable self-discipline for the supervisee to be allowed time to think and respond before the next group member jumps in with their contribution. There is also the risk that the multiple perspectives mean that no one theme is progressed and underlying issues are missed. Plus there is the additional risk of a skilled supervisor stepping in just before the end to do the 'real work', leaving the group to feel inadequate. Group super-vision is, therefore, best suited to experienced supervisees who are confident enough to take charge of the process for themselves, and for matters that are relatively straightforward and not linked to deeper personal issues.

Another variant is cascade super-vision. For this, one person supervises the supervisee, and that person in turn is supervised on that super-vision by someone else, who may in turn be supervised on that super-vision by another person, and so on. Again, the 'official' supervisor may be the back stop. This can be an extremely effective way of identifying any parallel process that may be in effect.

Parallel process refers to the phenomenon whereby dynamics between people are repeated between others. It often happens that helping professionals react to participants in just the way that said participant is reacting to their own contact. For example, "this subordinate is so obstinate" may have the professional thinking "this client is so obstinate". The parallel process may extend to the supervisor, who starts thinking "this supervisee is so obstinate" Running a cascade increases the likelihood that someone in the sequence will avoid being drawn into the parallel process.

Group and cascade super-vision arrangements are useful for giving supervisees a different, broader perspective on super-vision processes. Doing it themselves adds another dimension to their experiences of receiving it.

Working with Colleagues

The formats described above for working with a supervisor can of course by utilised without a supervisor. Each group member in turn can contract for what she or he wants, there can be process reviews after each slot, there can be a cascade, and there can be one-to-one slots, privately or within the group setting.

To ensure that peer super-vision works well, it is important to take into account normal human difficulties about role switching – it is not easy to be supervisor one minute and supervisee the next. Instead, for one-to-one work, aim to have at least three of you in the group so that person A can supervise person B, person B supervises person C, and person C supervises person A.

Pay particular attention to contracting, so that each super-vision slot is set up clearly, and to staying within the boundaries of the contract. Keep in mind that you are supervising and not coaching, so your role is to help the supervisee to take a super-vision of the supervisee's own practice and what the supervisee is doing to help the participant rather than how you think the supervisee should have done it. Establish some clear ground rules and agree in advance how you will confront in respectful ways any potential or actual breaches (see below for some suggested ground rules). Share out the available time and monitor it – don't let people behave as martyrs who give up their time because others have over-run.

Finally, watch out for competitiveness and attempts to fill the vacant leadership slot – groups have a natural tendency to take on the characteristics of their members' families of origin and we need to guard against that. Watch out also for the opposite tendency – and of being too nice to each other, getting too cosy, unwittingly overlooking issues and failing to match support with challenge.

R4C4P4 – Ground Rules for Groups

If you decide to work in a group for super-vision, you might consider the following. The aim is that the group members choose those elements they want included and then discuss them to reach a shared set of meanings.

Respect – all opinions are respected and valued, all have equal rights, all will be treated respectfully, we will assume positive intentions for others' behaviours.

Responsibility – ground rules can only exist if all involved agree and take personal responsibility. Each person needs to indicate clearly to the rest of the group whether they accept shared responsibility for the ground rules – and for asking for re-negotiation if necessary.

Relationship – much development comes from being supported by others, we need to consider how we will support each other, how to establish close and trusting relationships.

Results – we need to remember purpose, such as to increase self-awareness, develop professional skills, etc. Ground rules need to reflect this emphasis on outcomes and not being simply somewhere to talk about problems.

Confidentiality – no-one gossips – what is said in the group room stays in the room - unless the person(s) who said it agrees otherwise.

Commitment – to the group and to ourselves – what we say we will do, we do – or we will explain why we changed our mind.

Communication – active listening, one person speaks at a time, plenty of paraphrasing and summarising to minimise misunderstandings.

Challenge – valuable learning comes from feedback – we need to give each other honest, constructive criticism and to balance challenge and support.

Participation – everyone participates – in addition to our own learning, we can help others learn by joining in.

Privacy – everyone has the right to pass – to decide not to reveal personal information about themselves, not to give specific feedback to another person.

Preparation – all will come prepared to each session, having prepared cases they wish to bring for reflection or super-vision in the group.

Practicalities – in the real world, things happen that make us late. Time, on the other hand, does not wait. We need to agree how long the group will wait for latecomers or whether to start exactly on time anyway. What is the routine for people to advise the group contact person (and who will do this role?) if they will be late or missing? What will be done about people who miss a session, how many missed sessions before we eject them from the group?

Analysing your Interventions using C5P5A5

C5P5A5 is called that as a memory aid, which prompts you to recall that there are five aspects starting with the letter C to pay attention to, then another five starting with P, and finally another five beginning with A. It can be applied to your processes of interaction with participants and those who commission your work, and also to analyse your super-vision processes.

C5P5A5
- What is the *context*?
- How well are we in *contact*?
- How clear is our *contract*?
- Is the *content* appropriate?
- How are we using our *contrasts*?

- Whose *paradigms* are in effect?
- How are we at the *personal* level?

- How are we at the *professional* level?
- What is happening at the *psychological* level?
- Are there any *parallel* processes?

- Are we being *autonomous*?
- Are we being *authentic*?
- Are *alternatives* being generated?
- Whose *aims* are being worked on?
- Are *actions* being committed to?

Note that although this model suggests aspects of process in an approximately chronological order, I am not proposing that these are stages to be worked through dutifully in sequence. Rather, they are elements to be paid attention to, in three clusters – five aspects to pay attention to as you start a session and a relationship, five that are significant during the middle and five more that generally come at the end.

The first cluster consists of context, contact, contract, content and contrasts. It prompts you to reflect on the context within which you and the participant (or you and your supervisor) are working, to consider how good the contact is between the two of you, to ensure you have a clearly defined and agreed contract for your work together and that are working within it, to check that the content of your interactions is within the boundaries of your contract and the context, and that you are extracting maximum benefit from any contrasts or differences between you, whether at the macro level such as race or the micro level such as how you dress (or anywhere in between).

The second cluster prompts you to think about whether you are working to your own paradigm, or model of the world, or the participant's – or is your super-visor imposing a paradigm instead of working within yours? In addition, how are you now relating to the participant (or supervisor) at the personal, professional and psychological levels? Are there any parallel processes, where you might be playing out the same dynamics as any of your participants?

The third cluster, which becomes more significant as the session progresses, contains prompts to check that you and the participant or supervisor are being autonomous and not letting someone else decide, and that you are both being authentic and not simply pretending to be polite. Is the participant (or you as supervisee) considering alternative options before making any decisions? And finally, is the participant or the supervisee committing to clear actions arising out of the session, and do these meet their own aims rather than yours?

C5P5A5 can be applied in several ways. You might use it to reflect after any session with a participant, to reflect after each stage with a participant, or to monitor the process whilst you work with a participant. In the latter case it would of course be used within your own head but not necessarily shared with the participant unless perhaps with a participant who is very advanced and genuinely shares responsibility for the relationship.

I include it here because it can also be applied as a framework for super-vision, this time with the supervisor and supervisee using it together, or inside the head of the supervisor or supervisee who can be running an ongoing reflection or analysis of the process as it occurs. Note that you can use it as the supervisee even if your supervisor is not familiar with it.

Finally, it serves as a prompt for reflection after super-vision as well as before it, and as a way to monitor the process during super-vision (in the head of the supervisor or the supervisee).

ACTIVITIES
Activity 12.1 Identifying Discounting
Use the following prompts to check out at which level you might be discounting. Repeat this activity frequently across a range of situations and with a variety of participants or groups.

Level 1: Situation
- What is actually happening?
- Have you missed any details?
- What might an impartial observer notice?
- Are there contextual elements that might affect your work?

Level 2: Significance
- What is significant about what is happening?
- Are there different significances for different parties?
- Have you identified the real problem(s)?
- Who owns the problem(s)? – is it you?

Level 3: Solutions
- What solutions or options have you already considered? what happened?
- What new solutions can you now consider?
- Who might help you to generate more options?
- What criteria apply as you decide which solution(s) to progress?

Level 4: Skills
- Do you have the skills required for your chosen solutions?
- If not, how will you acquire additional skills?
- When have you applied skills in different situations that will be useful now?
- Who might coach you in the necessary skills?

Level 5: Strategies
- What strategies do you need in order to implement your chosen solution(s)?
- What needs to be in your plan of implementation?

- What contingencies do you need in your plan for overcoming potential blocks to implementation?
- Who else needs to be briefed or involved so they will support your strategic implementation?

Level 6: Success
- How might you prevent yourself from unwittingly sabotaging yourself as you implement whatever you have decided to do?
- How will you deal with others who might prefer you not to change?
- How will what you do now contribute to your increased professional competence?
- How will you celebrate as you achieve increased self-awareness and greater autonomy that comes when we can recognise our own discounting?

Activity 12.2: Reflecting on Transference
Use the following prompts to check for transference with any of your participants (or indeed, with those who commission your services, such as human resource professionals, personnel directors, senior managers).
- Who does this person remind me of?
- How does interacting with them leave me feeling?
- Are there things I want to say to them that I'm keeping to myself?
- Do I feel drawn to reacting to them in a particular way?
- Do I wish I could behave differently towards them?
- Does the way I'm reacting to them have any similarity to ways I've behaved in the past with other people? Is that significant?
- Do I keep repeating unsatisfactory interactions with this person? Why might that be?
- Do I think this person is being childish? Or bossy? Or helpless? Or argumentative? Or any other annoying way of being? What is the evidence for that?
- Do I get an urge to tell them what to do? Or take care of them? Or argue with them? Or let them take care of me? Or any other inappropriate way of behaving towards them? Why might that be?

When you have responded to the questions, review your replies with a professional colleague. Identify any doubtful areas for further investigation with a supervisor.

Activity 12.3 R4C4P4
Use the R4C4P4 checklist within an intervision or peer super-vision/reflection group to set up ground rules for working with each other.

Activity 12.4 C5P5A5
Use the C5P5A5 checklist to review examples of your work. Look out for themes where you seem to focus on or overlook similar aspects in different situations.

Afterwards, review with colleagues or select specific segments to take to super-vision.

Activity 12.5 C5P5A5 applied to Super-vision

Use the C5P5A5 checklist to review a range of super-vision sessions that you have experienced. Consider what changes you can make in order to enhance the supervision you receive.

Activity 12.6 C5P5A5 with a Supervisor

Invite your supervisor (or peers) to join you in applying the C5P5A5 checklist to some of your super-vision sessions.

NOTES & SOURCES

NLP – Future Pacing – non-TA – you can find future pacing described in many NLP books, including my own Workbook and Tapeset - *Neurolinguistic Programming Practitioner Course* –Sherwood Publishing, 2001.

Many of the ideas in this chapter are covered in more detail in my book *Reflective Practice and Supervision for Coaches* – Open University Press 2007.

My ideas on transference have been influenced by previous TA works, including: Michele Novellino & Carlo Moiso, in *The Psychodynamic Approach to Transactional Analysis* in <u>Transactional Analysis Journal</u> 1990 20(3) pp 187-92 and Petruska Clarkson in *Transactional Analysis Psychotherapy*, Routledge 1991.

Parallel process - non-TA - is based on Searles, H. F. (1955) *The informational value of the supervisor's emotional experiences,* <u>Psychiatry</u>, 18: 135-46 (later reproduced in H. F. Searles, *Collected Papers on Schizophrenia and Related Subjects*. London: Karnac Books 1965).

APPENDIX 1: BOOKS BY ERIC BERNE

Beyond Games and Scripts Ed. C Steiner & C Kerr, Grove Press, 1977 Ballatine Books, 1978

Intuition and Ego-states Grove Press, Corgi Books, 1975

Games People Play Grove Press, Penguin, 1967/8

A Layman's Guide to Psychiatry & Psychoanalysis Penguin, 1971

Principles of Group Treatment Grove Press, 1966

Sex In Human Loving Penguin, 1973

Transactional Analysis in Psychotherapy Grove Press, 1961; Souvenir Press, 1975

Structure and Dynamics of Organisations & Groups Grove Press, 1966

What Do You Say After You Say Hello? Grove Press, 1972; Corgi, 1975

Many of these are re-published from time to time.

APPENDIX 2: ERIC BERNE MEMORIAL SCIENTIFIC AWARDS

1971   Claude Steiner SCRIPT MATRIX *Script and counterscript* <u>Transactional Analysis Bulletin</u>, 1966, 5(18), 133-135

1972   Stephen Karpman DRAMA TRIANGLE *Fairy tales and script drama analysis* <u>Transactional Analysis Bulletin</u> 1968, 7(26), 39-43

1973   John Dusay EGOGRAMS *Egograms and the 'constancy hypothesis'* <u>Transactional Analysis Journal</u>, 1972, 2(3), 37-42

1974   Aaron Schiff & Jacqui Schiff PASSIVITY & THE FOUR DISCOUNTS *Passivity* <u>Transactional Analysis Journal</u>, 1971, 1(1), 71-78

1975   Robert Goulding & Mary Goulding REDECISIONS AND TWELVE INJUNCTIONS *New directions in transactional analysis* In Sager & Kaplan (eds) *Progress in group and family therapy* New York: Bruner/Mazel, 1972, 105-134. See *Injunctions, decisions and redecisions* <u>Transactional Analysis Journal</u>, 1976, 6(1), 41-48

1976   Pat Crossman PROTECTION (award returned by Crossman 1979) *Permission and Protection* <u>Transactional Analysis Bulletin</u>, 1966, 5(19), 152-154

1977   Taibi Kahler MINISCRIPT AND FIVE DRIVERS *The miniscript* <u>Transactional Analysis Journal</u>, 1974, 4(1), 26-42

1978   Fanita English RACKETS & REAL FEELINGS: THE SUBSTITUTION FACTOR *The substitution factor; rackets and real feelings* <u>Transactional Analysis Journal</u>, 1971, 1(4), 225-230 and *Rackets and Real Feelings Part II* <u>Transactional Analysis Journal</u>, 1972, 2(1), 23-25

1979   Stephen B Karpman OPTIONS *Options* <u>Transactional Analysis Journal</u>, 1971, 1(1), 79-87

1980   Claude Steiner THE STROKE ECONOMY *The stroke economy* <u>Transactional Analysis Journal</u>, 1971, 1(3), 9-15

1980   Mellor & Eric Schiff DISCOUNTING & REDEFINING *Discounting* Transactional Analysis Journal, 1975, 5(3), 295-302 and *Redefining* Transactional Analysis Journal, 1975, 5(3), 303-311

1981   Franklin H Ernst THE OK CORRAL *The OK Corral; the grid for get-on-with* Transactional Analysis Journal, 1971, 1(4), 231-240

1982   Richard Erskine & Marilyn Zalcman RACKET SYSTEM & RACKET ANALYSIS *The racket system; a model for racket analysis* Transactional Analysis Journal, 1979, 9(1), 51-59

1983   Muriel James SELF REPARENTING *Self reparenting; theory and process* Transactional Analysis Journal, 1974, 4(3), 32-39

1984   Pam Levin DEVELOPMENTAL CYCLES *The cycle of development* Transactional Analysis Journal, 1982, 12(2), 129-139

1985   No award

1986   No award

1987   Carlo Moiso TRANSFERENCE *Ego states and transference* Transactional Analysis Journal, 1985, 15(3), 194-201

1988 - 1993   No awards. Awards broadened to encompass 4 areas: theory, research, practice applications and comparison and/or integration with theories and approaches

1994   Sharon Dashiell and John McNeel PSYCHOTHERAPY WITH THE PARENT EGO STATE *The Parent resolution process : reprogramming psychic incorporations in the Parent* Transactional Analysis Journal, 1978, 8(4), 289-294 (Dashiell) and *The Parent Interview* Transactional Analysis Journal, 1976, 6(1), 61-68 (McNeel).

1994   Vann Joines INTEGRATION OF PAUL WARE'S THEORY OF PERSONALITY ADAPTATIONS *Using redecision therapy with different personality adaptations* Transactional Analysis Journal, 1986, 16(3), 152 - 160. *Diagnosis and treatment planning using a transactional analysis framework* Transactional Analysis Journal 1988, 18(3), 185-190

1995   Peg Blackstone THE DYNAMIC CHILD *The Dynamic Child: Integration of second order structure, object relations, and self psychology* Transactional Analysis Journal, 1993, 23(4), 216-234

1995   Jean Illsley Clark PARENT EDUCATION *Self Esteem : A Family Affair* Harper Collins 1978, *Self Esteem : A Family Affair* Leader Guide Harper Collins 1981 Bredehoft, D. J. *An evaluation study of the self esteem : a family affair program with high risk abusive parents* Transactional Analysis Journal, 1990 20(2), 111-117

1996   Alan Jacobs SOCIAL APPLICATIONS *Autocratic Power* Transactional Analysis Journal, 1987, 17(3), 59-71, *Nationalism* Transactional Analysis Journal, 1990, 20(4), 221-228, *Aspects of Survival : Triumph over Death and Onliness* Transactional Analysis Journal, 1991, 21(1), 4-11 *Autocracy : Groups, Organizations, Nations, and Players* Transactional Analysis Journal, 1991, 21(4), 199-206

1997   Fanita English EPISCRIPT *Episcript and the 'Hot Potato' Game* Transactional Analysis Bulletin, 1969, 8(32), 77-82

1998   James and Barbara Allen THEORY *A new type of Transactional Analysis and One Version of Script Work with a Constructionist Sensibility* Transactional Analysis Journal, 1997, 27(2), 89-98. *Narrative Theory, Redecision Therapy and Postmodernism* Transactional Analysis Journal, 1995, 25(4), 327-334. *A Typology of Psychopathology and Treatment of Children and Adolescents* Transactional Analysis Journal 1997, 27 (4), 256-264.

1999   Richard Erskine, Rebecca Trautmann COMPARISON AND INTEGRATION OF TRANSACTIONAL ANALYSIS WITH OTHER THEORIES AND APPROACHES. *"The Process of Integrative Psychotherapy"* Transactional Analysis Journal 1996, 26 (4) 316-328; *Transference and Transactions: Critique from an Intrapsychic and Integrative Perspective* Transactional Analysis Journal, 1991, 21:(2) 63-76; *The Therapeutic Relationship: Integrating Motivation and Personality Theories from "Ego State Analysis: A Comparative View"* Transactional Analysis Journal 1981, 11(2) 178-185; *Ego Structure, Intrapsychic Function and Defense Mechanisms: A Commentary on Eric Berne's Original Theoretical Concepts* Transactional Analysis Journal 1988, 18(1) 15-19; *Methods of an Integrative Psychotherapy* Transactional Analysis Journal 1996, 26(4) 316-328; *Inquiry, Attunement, & Involvement in the Psychotherapy of Dissociation* Transactional Analysis Journal 1993, 23(4) 184-190; *Shame and Self-Righteousness: Transactional Analysis and Perspectives and Clinical Interventions* Transactional Analysis Journal 1994. 24(2) 86-102; *Theories and Methods of an Integrative Transactional Analysis*, A Volume of Selected Articles TA Pubs 1997.

2002   Leonard Schlegel *What is Transactional Analysis?* Transactional Analysis Journal 1998, 28(4) 269-287

2003   Michael Novellino *Unconscious Communication and Interpretation in Transactional Analysis* Transactional Analysis Journal 1990 20(3) 168-17

2004   Pearl Drego *Changing Systems through Correlations of Injunction Inventories* <u>The Maastricht Papers: Selections from the 20th EATA Conference</u> 1994 and *Building Family Unity through Permission Rituals: Permissions & Ego State Models* 1999 Bombay, Alfreruby Publishers

2005   Graham Barnes *Homosexuality in the First Three Decades of Transactional Analysis: A Study in the Theory and Practice of Transactional Analysis Psychotherapy.* <u>Transactional Analysis Journal</u> 2004 Volume 34 (2) 126-153

2006   Theodore B. Novey *Measuring the Effectiveness of Transactional Analysis: An International Study.* <u>Transactional Analysis Journal</u> 2002 32 (1) 8-24

2007   Helena Hargarden & Charlotte Sills RELATIONAL TA *Relational Transactional Analysis* 2002 Brunner/Routledge

2007   Bernd Schmid SYSTEMIC TA *Transactional Analysis and Social Roles in Growth and Change for Organisations* <u>Transactional Analysis New Developments 1195-2006</u> 2006, 32-61 eds Mohr & Steinert Kulturpolitische Gesellschaft

2008   Gloria Noriega Gayol MECHANISMS FOR TRANSMITTING TRANSGENERATIONAL SCRIPTS *Codependence: A Transgenerational Script,* <u>Transactional Analysis Journal</u> October 2004 and *"Construcción y Validación del Instrumento de Codependencia (ICOD) para Mujeres Mexicanas [Construction and Validation of the Codependency Instrument (ICOD) for Mexican Women]* Revista Salud Mental. April 2002

APPENDIX 3:   TA ASSOCIATIONS WORLDWIDE

International Transactional Analysis Association (ITAA) www.itaa-net.org

European Association for Transactional Analysis (EATA) www.eatanews.org

Western Pacific Association of Transactional Analysis (WPATA) www.wpata.co.au

ITAA and EATA webpages have lists of TA Associations around the world.

The following are intended to be communities and resources for those who share an interest in applications of TA in ways that develop others – and ourselves.

International Centre for Developmental Transactional Analysis www.icdta.net

International Centre for Developmental Super-Vision www.icdsv.net

APPENDIX 4: DEVELOPMENTAL TA QUALIFICATIONS

Note: this is a summary for guidance only and should not be relied upon when decisions are made – the original documents should be referred to before signing any contracts. Note also that requirements change from time to time so this document may not be up-to-date.

Terminology:

(P) TSTA – (Provisional) Teaching & Supervising Transactional Analyst – endorsed by EATA/ITAA/WPATA to provide advanced training and supervision. Advanced TA training and TA supervision can only be provided by PTSTA's and TSTA's. Such (P)TSTA's are not required to be qualified in the same field as the student. However, a sponsoring (P)TSTA is required to be in the same field unless this is impractical, in which case EATA may grant an exception.

Note: the only attendance certificate recognised by the TA community is for the TA 101. For all other levels, certificates are given after demonstration of competence. Attendance certificates may be signed by TA trainers/supervisors to meet cultural norms but have no status in terms of accreditation.

ICDTA International Centre for Developmental Transactional Analysis
EATA European Association for Transactional Analysis
ITAA International Transactional Analysis Association
WPATA Western Pacific Association for TA

EATA, ITAA and WPATA qualifications are equivalent under the Training & Certification Council of Transactional Analysis, which brings together those three bodies.

CTA – Certified Transactional Analyst

This is the internationally-recognised professional qualification.

EATA, ITAA, WPATA. Available in 4 fields – Organisational, Educational, Psychotherapy or Counselling – students opt for the field in which most of their work is done.

To become CTA, students must:
1. attend a TA 101 (or pass 101 exam)
2. sign a contract with a sponsor in the same field of application and have this contract endorsed by EATA. The contract need not be signed at the start of TA involvement but must be signed and endorsed at least 18 months before final examination

3. attend at least 600 hours of professional training of which at least 300 must be advanced TA training
4. receive at least 150 hours of supervision, of which 75 must be with a recognised TA supervisor and 40 of which must be with the sponsor
5. complete 500 hours of continuing professional development, which may include more TA training and supervision, non-TA training and supervision, peer group activities, reading, researching, etc. The type of CPD activities must be approved by the sponsor
6. complete at least 750 hours professional client contact, of which 500 must involve application of TA
7. items 3-6 must total at least 2000 hours in total
8. complete a written exam which comprises a professional self-portrayal, an account of learning during the training period, a description with analysis of a significant piece of professional work using TA, and a set of 6 theory essays chosen from a list of set questions
9. the written exam must be approved by their sponsor and then blind-marked as acceptable by another person qualified in TA
10. prepare a log showing how the various hours requirements have been met
11. produce 3 tape recordings of 5 minutes each, with transcripts, that are extracts from longer pieces of work and demonstrate the candidate's competence in the field of application chosen
12. sit an oral examination with a panel of 4 examiners, lasting about one hour, at which one or more tapes are played and the candidate's competence to practice is assessed

Note: on the basis of at least 16 days teaching and supervision per year, most candidates take 4-5 years to reach CTA status.

Note: CTA exams are run at most European and international TA conferences, and at some national TA conferences. Dates are published ahead of time in TA newsletters and websites.

ICDTA supports and also supplements the EATA/ITAA/WPATA qualifications as described below.

ICDTA Professional Qualifications

These operate at three levels - Master Practitioner which is the equivalent to CTA in a developmental field, Advanced Professional which relates to Diploma and Professional which relates to Certificate. Certificate and Diploma qualifications represent approximately 25% and 50% of the requirements for CTA respectively, although there is no requirement that students must continue to that level.

Because of the nature of transactional analysis, students are expected to spend a significant amount of time in self-study, application and/or research of TA in their professional context. They will also be expected to present their own work and obtain coaching and supervision within the training group. This will normally occur within specific supervision days.

In addition to the hours of self-directed practice/application indicated, students will be expected to have attained general experience in their chosen profession before any award is made.

The table below shows the requirements for the ICDTA certificate and diploma and how these relate to the CTA.

For each level, there are minimum requirements for:

- overall hours – the sum of training, supervision and professional development activities plus hours spent applying TA professionally.
- training hours – studying TA with an internationally accredited TA trainer (for CTA 300 hours may be on topics other than TA), these include sessions at conferences and other events.
- supervision hours – presenting own work to an internationally accredited TA supervisor; a set proportion of the total must be undertaken with the same supervisor so they get an overview
- application hours – using TA professionally to help others develop; this may be with clients or colleagues but may not be with subordinates as the dual relationship makes contracting impossible; may be coaching, team facilitation, mediating, consulting, teaching, training or similar activities.
- additional professional development hours – these may be additional training or supervision hours, time spent studying, researching, shadowing or co-working, or other activities approved by the sponsor.
- essays/case studies – these are defined for specific modules (and for CTA) and students have a choice of topics.
- portfolios/oral exam – these are collations of evidence including tape recordings, compiled to demonstrate competent application of TA together with ongoing development of the student's ability to analyse self and others.

Table 2 – Requirements Summary

	CERTIFICATE	DIPLOMA (ASSUMES CERTIFICATE COMPLETED)	CTA (TOTAL REQUIREMENTS)	GENERAL COMMENTS RE CERT & DIPLOMA
Overall hours	250	250	2000 (1025 hrs TA)	'hours' will be defined as per EATA custom and practice.
Training hours (with P/TSTA)	75 hours	75	600 (300 must be TA)	
Supervision hours (with P/TSTA)	10 of which 6 must be with sponsor	10 of which 6 must be with sponsor	150 of which 75 must be TA-based; 40 must be with sponsor	in group or one-to-one; includes tutorials no option to count hours when others get supervision

Table 2 – Requirements Summary(continued)

	CERTIFICATE	DIPLOMA (ASSUMES CERTIFICATE COMPLETED)	CTA (TOTAL REQUIREMENTS)	GENERAL COMMENTS RE CERT & DIPLOMA
Application hours	100	100	750 (500 TA)	mainly client contact time
Additional professional development hours	65 as agreed with sponsor	65 as agreed with sponsor	500 agreed with sponsor	can be whatever sponsor agrees is relevant – trainers will manage re consistency
Essays/ case study	1 essay 4,000 or 2 essays of 2,000 words (submitted at same time)	1 essay 4,000 or 2 essays of 2,000 words (submitted at same time)	24,000 words case study	marked by ICDTA trainers (not sponsor)
Portfolios/oral exam	3 portfolios with tapes (1 per mod) plus a reflective learning log	4 portfolios with tapes (1 per mod)	need tapes to play at oral exam	marked by ICDTA trainers (not sponsor)
101 Certificate	*Note that attendance at 101 Introductory Course is a requirement but that the hours for this are not credited towards any qualifications*			

ICDTA Supervisor Qualification

This option is currently available only to those who have attained either the ICDTA Master Professional Qualification or the CTA from ITAA, EATA or WPATA. Contact ICDTA for details - www.icdta.net

ICDTA Practitioner Award

For those who are already qualified in one of the 'helping professions' such as coaching, teaching, training, social work, etc but want to confirm their competence at incorporating DTA into their practice – but are not seeking full qualification as a DTA Professional. Contact ICDTA for details - www.icdta.net

ICDTA Vocational Award

For those not seeking professional qualification in TA, ICDTA offers an award that confirms their understanding and application of DTA within their own vocational context. This is suitable for anyone who has learnt some TA and is applying it in their work – such as managers, customer staff, social workers, teachers, teachers assistants, engineers, IT professionals, coaches, mentors – and any others where people contact is involved.

There are no prescribed lessons or activities; applicants are expected to demonstrate their understanding and application of at least six TA concepts. The following is not a complete list and is included here for guidance on the level at which TA theory may be regarded as a concept for DTAVA purposes.

Ego-states	Drama/Winners Triangles/Potency Pyramid	Affirmations	Discounting/Steps to Success
Transactions	Psychological Games	Scripts	Stamps
Strokes	Time Structuring	Working Styles/Drivers	BAR's/Racket System
Windows on the World/	Rackets/Substitute Feelings	Contracting	Life Positions

The emphasis in the award is on understanding and application. Applicants are also encouraged to provide a range of types of evidence. Possibilities might include: written accounts, correspondence, emails, meeting notes, diary notes, worksheet responses, drawings and diagrams, video footage, photographs, paintings, audiotapes, or web-based responses.

When participants have created an item of evidence – regardless of its format – they will include it in their portfolio and list it on a contents page at the front. This is to ensure the learner presents their understanding and application in a way that makes it easily seen by the moderator and others.

In addition to having evidence of individual assessment, participants are encouraged to build up evidence provided by their colleagues or fellow students. This evidence can again take different formats, for example through audio/video footage and/or written accounts.

APPENDIX 5: WINDOWS ON THE WORLD QUESTIONNAIRE

Please note that this questionnaire is included here for your personal use only. It is a copyrighted item and may not be reproduced. Copies are available for purchase in packs of 25 from Sherwood Publishing www.sherwoodpublishing.com

Circle the number next to the statement in each group that best describes you.

Be honest with yourself – don't just pick whatever you think is the 'best' answer.

A	1	I tend to interrupt others when they are speaking
	2	I prefer to take a back seat in groups and let others take the lead
	3	I do my best to avoid situations where you're expected to give an opinion
	4	I let other people finish what they are saying before I speak

B	1	I usually think that other people know best
	2	I stand up for myself when I feel that I'm right and expect others to do the same
	3	I insist that I'm right and expect others to go along with me
	4	I don't see any point in pushing my ideas as people rarely appreciate them

C	1	I resist making decisions or taking advice from others
	2	I let other people make decisions for me
	3	I make my own decisions based on what I feel is right and appropriate
	4	I often make decisions for other people

D	1	I tend to keep my voice low and avoid eye contact to prevent attention being drawn to me
	2	I sometimes speak loudly and expect to make quite an impact
	3	I can't be bothered to communicate much
	4	I generally match my level of communication to suit the circumstances

E	1	I tend to blame and find fault with others
	2	I sometimes hide my feelings and just go along with others
	3	I do my best to understand the feelings of others before letting them know how I feel
	4	I don't often feel that strongly about anything

F	1	I let others get what they want but I often feel resentful about it
	2	I talk through problems before they occur and find ways of coping with them when they do
	3	I make sure that things turn out the way I want them to
	4	I really don't mind if other people get their own way

G	1	I hold back on decisions so that others will make them for me
	2	I tend to avoid facing problems and keep putting decisions off until tomorrow
	3	I deal with my own problems and make my own decisions
	4	I provide solutions for people who seem unable to decide for themselves

H	1	I consider myself capable and equal to others
	2	I consider myself weaker and less capable than others
	3	I consider myself stronger and more capable than others
	4	I consider that most people are weak, including me

I	1	I avoid taking responsibility as it only gets you blamed when things don't work out
	2	I accept my responsibilities and am clear about what others are responsible for
	3	I take on responsibility for as much as possible, including the work of others
	4	I prefer it when someone else takes responsibility and I can follow their lead

To analyse your scores turn to the next page

Windows on the World - Scoring

Step 1. Using the chart below, circle the A, B, C or D that is alongside the number that you chose for each question. Then add each column to get a total score.

Q.A	4	A	2	B	1	C	3	D
Q.B	2	A	1	B	3	C	4	D
Q.C	3	A	2	B	4	C	1	D
Q.D	4	A	1	B	2	C	3	D
Q.E	3	A	2	B	1	C	4	D
Q.F	2	A	4	B	3	C	1	D
Q.G	3	A	1	B	4	C	2	D
Q.H	1	A	2	B	3	C	4	D
Q.I	2	A	4	B	3	C	1	D

Total A	Total B	Total C	Total D

Step 2. Now draw a bar chart of your scores by making horizontal lines at the score points.

Total score

8

7

6

5

4

3

2

1

0

A - win-win assertive	B – lose-win accommodating	C – win-lose aggressive	D – lose-lose
assertive	accommodating	aggressive	apathetic

APPENDIX 6: PERSONAL STYLES QUESTIONNAIRE

Please note that this questionnaire is included here for your personal use only. It is a copyrighted item and may not be reproduced. Copies are available for purchase in packs of 25 from Sherwood Publishing www.sherwoodpublishing.com

This questionnaire is also available in French and German.

INSTRUCTIONS

For each statement, allocate a score to show how much the behaviour is like the way you behave:

not true for me 0   partly true for me 1   moderately true for me 2   extremely true for me 3

ITEM	SCORE	
1.		I tell people firmly how they should behave.
2.		I tend to reason things out before acting.
3.		I do as I'm told.
4.		I behave sympathetically towards people with problems.
5.		I really enjoy being with other people.
6.		I enjoy taking care of people.
7.		I enjoy solving problems in a systematic and logical way.
8.		I tell people what to do.
9.		I let people know how I really feel without embarrassment.
10.		I am polite and courteous.
11.		I do the opposite to what people expect.
12.		When someone is new, I make an effort to show them where everything is.
13.		I can stay calm in a crisis.
14.		When I know I'm right, I insist that others listen to me.
15.		I ask a lot of questions when I'm curious.
16.		I am very enthusiastic about my work.
17.		People seem to expect me to know the answer.
18.		I'm asked to take care of new members of staff.
19.		I get on well with people who are polite to me.
20.		I keep on thinking logically even under pressure.

SCORE

21.	My working style is systematic and logical.
22.	I dress to match the sort of outfits that other people wear to work.
23.	I do things for people when I think they can't manage for themselves.
24.	I can quote my previous experience when problems occur.
25.	People tell me I'm creative and inventive.
26.	I prefer to take control rather than following someone else's lead.
27.	I fuss over people too much.
28.	I'm over-emotional compared to others.
29.	I expect my manager to set my terms of reference.
30.	I take all points of view into account when making decisions.
31.	I encourage people to test out their own capabilities.
32.	People complain that I'm bossy.
33.	I spend time enjoying myself.
34.	People tell me I'm especially courteous.
35.	I'm noted for my even temper and balanced comments.
36.	I show my feelings whether I am happy or sad, so that people can congratulate or sympathise with me.
37.	I've looked after someone even though they could have managed on their own.
38.	I'm tempted to analyse jokes, which spoils them for others.
39.	People do as I tell them.
40.	I go along too readily with what other people want.

Personal Styles Questionnaire - Scoring

Step 1. Transfer your scores to the summary below, against the question numbers, and add up each column.

	SCORE		SCORE		SCORE		SCORE		SCORE
1		4		2		3		5	
8		6		7		10		9	
14		12		13		11		15	
17		18		20		19		16	
24		23		21		22		25	
26		27		30		29		28	
32		31		35		34		33	
39		37		38		40		36	

Total

Controlling	Nurturing	Functional	Adapted	Natural
Parent	Parent	Adult	Child	Child

Step 2. Now draw a bar chart of your responses by marking horizontal lines at the score points.

Total score

24

21

18

15

12

9

6

3

0

Controlling	Nurturing	Functional	Adapted	Natural
Parent	Parent	Adult	Child	Child

APPENDIX 7: INTERNAL EGO STATE QUESTIONNAIRE

Please note that this questionnaire is included here for your personal use only. It is a copyrighted item and may not be reproduced. Copies are available for purchase in packs of 25 from Sherwood Publishing www.sherwoodpublishing.com

This questionnaire is also available in French.

INSTRUCTIONS

For each statement, allocate a score to indicate how much it matches your own thinking.

not true for me   0   partly true for me   1   moderately true for me   2   extremely true for me   3

ITEM	SCORE	
1.		I have strong opinions on some subjects.
2.		I like to balance the pros and cons before I make a decision.
3.		Children should be taught to respect their elders more.
4.		Most of my parent's views are totally out-of-date.
5.		I feel upset when people are angry.
6.		I take a moment to assess a difficult situation before I respond.
7.		I often go with a hunch when making a decision.
8.		I think about the implications before I do something.
9.		I rely on my experience a lot to make decisions.
10.		I can observe other peoples' reactions without necessarily feeling the same way.
11.		I often feel more mature than other people.
12.		I often feel as if I'm a lot younger than I really am.
13.		I am comfortable sharing decision making when relevant.
14.		I sometimes hide my true feelings from others.
15.		Sometimes I think other people behave childishly.
16.		I prefer it when someone else has to make the decisions.
17.		I have updated some of the views I learned from my parents.
18.		I expect to make my own decisions all the time.
19.		I resent it when people tell me what to do.
20.		I share many of the views of my parents.
21.		I can learn from younger people.

Internal Ego State Questionnaire - Scoring

Step 1. Transfer your scores to the summary below, against the question numbers, and add up each column.

	SCORE		SCORE		SCORE
1		2		4	
3		6		5	
9		8		7	
11		10		12	
15		13		14	
18		17		16	
20		21		19	

Total

Internal Parent   Internal Adult   Internal Child

Step 2. Draw a chart of your responses by marking horizontal lines at the score points for each ego state.

Total score

24

21

18

15

12

9

6

3

0

Internal Parent   Internal Adult   Internal Child

APPENDIX 8: WORKING STYLES PEN PICTURES

Please note that this set of pen pictures is included here for your personal use only. It is a copyrighted item and may not be reproduced. If you wish to use them as handouts, copies are available for purchase in packs of 25 from Sherwood Publishing www.sherwoodpublishing.com

LEE

Lee works steadily and produces work at a regular pace. Even when the pressure is on, Lee stays calm and continues to work at the same steady rate, never appearing to worry about the workload. Lee won't be hurried.

Lee seems to ignore how people feel and doesn't understand the need to be flexible to deal with those sudden emergency jobs - everything can just take its turn.

Lee prefers to work alone and never asks for help. Somehow, Lee appears aloof and almost unfriendly - it's as if there are no real feelings there. Occasionally, you wonder if the work is all being done or whether it is being hidden away in the desk and will be found one day when Lee is not at work.

ANDY

Andy is nearly always willing and helpful; nothing is too much trouble. Work gets accepted from just about anyone and sometimes Andy does things without even being asked. However, this means that Andy exercises little control over workload or priorities, so that jobs get left undone when someone else needs help.

Andy sometimes gets tired and emotional from being so helpful; at these times the normal behaviour changes to an irritable, sulky manner with Andy complaining about being misunderstood. Andy also gets very anxious and upset when people complain about missed deadlines or incorrect assumptions instead of appreciating the hard work and thoughtfulness.

PAT

Pat is meticulous, producing work that is virtually error free. Laid down procedures are followed absolutely correctly, even when this leads to bad feeling with those seeking an exception.

Pat often takes longer than expected to complete work: this is because everything is double checked and even minor errors are corrected carefully and painstakingly. Other staff sometimes complain that Pat is nit-picking, especially when their own mistakes are pointed out.

Meetings with Pat progress slowly as everything must be considered in great detail. Another thing people notice is that Pat often misses deadlines through taking too long to collect every single piece of information which could be relevant.

CHRIS

Chris gets through a lot of work, by doing everything very quickly.

Trouble is, every so often Chris makes a mistake through hurrying - and then it takes twice as long to put it right. One thing that people also notice is that although Chris does a lot of work, sometimes the less urgent items are given priority while important jobs are overlooked.

Chris is always rushing about, arriving late at meetings, leaving early to get to the next meeting and still not getting there on time. It is quite common for Chris to forget to bring the correct file to a meeting, yet manage to bring other work to do while the meeting is going on. Chris is impatient and interrupts a lot, so that people feel pressured and hurried.

ROBIN

Robin is enthusiastic and interested in all aspects of work, and is generally the first to volunteer when new tasks are being allocated. In fact, Robin is involved in some way in just about everything that is going on in the department and even outside it when opportunities arise. Indeed people sometimes ask for Robin's help in their section because they know the answer will probably be yes.

Robin likes to investigate all aspects of a task, but this often means that the work never quite gets finished - there always seems to be another important part of the job left to do.

It is not uncommon for projects to be handed over to someone else to be completed because Robin's time is taken up with other new work. This sometimes leads other people to complain that they have to pick up work which they feel is properly Robin's.

APPENDIX 9:   WORKING STYLES QUESTIONNAIRE

Please note that this questionnaire is included here for your personal use only. It is a copyrighted item and may not be reproduced. Copies are available for purchase in packs of 25 from Sherwood Publishing www.sherwoodpublishing.com

This questionnaire is also available in German and Romanian.

INSTRUCTIONS

For each item, give a score between 0 and 8, where 8 is totally like you, 4 is average and 0 is totally unlike you.

ITEM	SCORE	WHAT I TYPICALLY DO:
1.		I tend to wait until the deadline is near before I work on a task.
2.		I like to organise my work area efficiently.
3.		It is important to maintain harmony in working relationships.
4.		I enjoy starting new projects.
5.		I am very good at staying calm during a crisis.
6.		I work steadily and conscientiously at whatever is required.
7.		I am good at seeing the whole scope of a task and showing initiative.
8.		I enjoy encouraging people and doing things to help them.
9.		I plan ahead thoroughly so that I am ready for any problems that arise.
10.		I enjoy having lots to do (even if I complain about it sometimes).
11.		It is important to check so that there are no mistakes.
12.		I am usually more enthusiastic than other people.
13.		I am usually more balanced and even-tempered than other people.
14.		I am usually intuitive and sensitive to other people's feelings.
15.		I can usually finish tasks more quickly than other people.

Table continues on next page

16.	Sometimes people seem to think that I'm overly critical about standards of work.
17.	Sometimes I make mistakes because I am working so fast.
18.	Sometimes people act as if they resent it when I am only trying to help them.
19.	I sometimes miss deadlines because I find it hard to ask for help even when I have too much to do.
20.	I tend to start several projects but have trouble finishing any of them.
21.	People sometimes complain that I make tasks too big because I consider so many possible aspects.
22.	People sometimes seem to think I am aloof and unfriendly.
23.	I have problems saying no to people even when I already have too much to do.
24.	I feel impatient when people spend too much time discussing what to do.
25.	I sometimes miss deadlines because I need longer to check my work.

To analyse your scores, please turn to the next page.

Working Styles Questionnaire - Scoring

Step 1. Transfer your scores to the summary below, against the question numbers, and add up each column.

ITEM	SCORE		SCORE		SCORE		SCORE		SCORE
1		2		3		4		5	
10		9		8		7		6	
15		11		14		12		13	
17		16		18		20		19	
24		25		23		21		22	

Total

    Hurry Up   Be Perfect   Please People   Try Hard   Be Strong

Step 2. Now draw a bar chart of your responses by marking horizontal lines at the score points.

Total score

40

35

30

25

20

15

10

5

0

    Hurry Up   Be Perfect   Please People   Try Hard   Be Strong

APPENDIX 10: MANAGER WORKING STYLES QUESTIONNAIRE

Please note that this questionnaire is included here for your personal use only. It is a copyrighted item and may not be reproduced. Copies are available for purchase in packs of 25 from Sherwood Publishing www.sherwoodpublishing.com

For each item, give a score between 0 and 8, where 8 is totally like your manager, 4 is average and 0 is totally unlike your manager.

ITEM	SCORE	MY MANAGER:
1.		Sets very short deadlines for work to be done.
2.		Gives very thorough instructions on how things should be done.
3.		Can be very encouraging.
4.		Is enthusiastic and exciting to have around.
5.		Is calm and thoughtful whatever the circumstance.
6.		Has a strong sense of duty to the organisation.
7.		Has so many new ideas that it's hard to keep up.
8.		Shows an interest in me as a person.
9.		Can spot mistakes in most things.
10.		Talks fast and tends to interrupt.
11.		Takes a lot of care over quality of work.
12.		Goes off on tangents instead of finishing one thing at a time.
13.		Tells people what to do in a controlling manner.
14.		Avoids making decisions in case someone is upset.
15.		Gets a lot of work done very quickly.
16.		Complains about unimportant details.
17.		Comes late to meetings and is always in a hurry.
18.		Insists on helping me when I don't really need help.
19.		Is unemotional and even unfeeling at times.
20.		Turns small tasks into major projects - and then delegates the boring parts.
21.		Seems to judge my performance by how enthusiastic I am.
22.		Seems to judge my performance by how uncomplaining I am.
23.		Seems to judge my performance by how well I get on with other people.
24.		Seems to judge my performance by how fast I work.
25.		Seems to judge my performance by how accurate I am.

Manager Working Styles Questionnaire - Scoring

Step 1. Transfer your scores to the summary below, against the question numbers, and add up each column.

ITEM	SCORE	SCORE	SCORE	SCORE	SCORE
1	4	2	3	5
8	6	7	10	9
14	12	13	11	15
17	18	20	19	16
24	23	21	22	25
Total					
	Hurry Up	Be Perfect	Please People	Try Hard	Be Strong

Step 2. Now draw a bar chart of your responses by marking horizontal lines at the score points.

Total score

24

21

18

15

12

9

6

4

0

| Hurry Up | Be Perfect | Please People | Try Hard | Be Strong |

BIBLIOGRAPHY

Barnes, Graham. *Transactional Analysis after Eric Berne: Teachings and Practices of Three TA Schools*. Harper's College Press 1977.

Barnes, Graham. *On Saying Hello; The Script Drama Diamond and Character Role Analysis*. Transactional Analysis Journal Jan 1981, 11(1), pp 22-32.

Berne, Eric. See Appendix 1 for a list of books by Berne.

Cowls-Boyd, L and Boyd, H. *Play as a Time Structure*. Transactional Analysis Journal 1980, 10(1), pp 5-7.

Crossman, Pat: See Appendix 2: Eric Berne Memorial Scientific Awards for details of the relevant article in the Transactional Analysis Journal – 1976.

Dusay, John: See Appendix 2: Eric Berne Memorial Scientific Awards for details of the relevant article in the Transactional Analysis Journal – 1973.

English, Fanita. *The Three Cornered Contract*. Transactional Analysis Journal 1975 5(4), pp 383-4.

English, Fanita: See Appendix 2: Eric Berne Memorial Scientific Awards for details of the relevant article in the Transactional Analysis Journal – 1978.

Ernst, Franklin: See Appendix 2: Eric Berne Memorial Scientific Awards for details of the relevant article in the Transactional Analysis Journal – 1971.

Erskine, Richard and Zalcman, Marilyn: See Appendix 2: Eric Berne Memorial Scientific Awards for details of the relevant article in the Transactional Analysis Journal – 1982.

Goulding, Robert L. & Mary M. *The Power is in the Patient*. TA Press 1978.

Goulding, Robert L. & Mary M. *Changing Lives through Redecision Therapy*. Grove Press Inc, 1979.

Goulding, Robert L. & Mary M: See Appendix 2: Eric Berne Memorial Scientific Awards for details of the relevant article in the <u>Transactional Analysis Journal</u> – 1975.

Harris, Thomas. *I'm OK, You're OK,* Pan 1973.

Hargaden, Helena & Charlotte Sills *Transactional Analysis: A Relational Perspective,* Brummer-Routledge 2002

Kahler, Taibi: See Appendix 2: Eric Berne Memorial Scientific Awards for details of the relevant article in the <u>Transactional Analysis Journal</u> – 1977.

Kahler, Taibi: *Drivers: The Key to the Process of Scripts,* in <u>Transactional Analysis Journal</u> 5:3. July 1975

Karpman, Stephen: See Appendix 2: Eric Berne Memorial Scientific Awards for details of the relevant article in the <u>Transactional Analysis Journal</u> – 1972.

Kubler-Ross, Elizabeth. *On Death and Dying,* MacMillan, 1969.

Levin, Pamela. *Becoming the Way We Are,* Health Communications Inc., 1974, 1985, 1988 now incorporated into *The Cycle of Life,* The Nourishing Company, 2007

Levin, Pamela. *Cycles of Power: A User's Guide to the Seven Seasons of Life,* Health Communications Inc., 1988 and The Nourishing Company, 2007.

Levin, Pam: See Appendix 2: Eric Berne Memorial Scientific Awards for details of the relevant article in the <u>Transactional Analysis Journal</u> 1984.

Loria, Bruce *Integrative Family Therapy: A Constructivist Perspective in The Stamford Papers,* Selections from the 29th Annual ITAA Conference, Omnipress 1991

Mellor, Ken and Schiff, Eric: See Appendix 2: Eric Berne Memorial Scientific Awards for details of the relevant article in the <u>Transactional Analysis Journal</u> – 1980.

Micholt, Nelly. *The Concept of Psychological Distance,* <u>Transactional Analysis Journal</u> 1992 Vol 22(4) pp 228-233.

Nolan, Vincent. *Open to Change,* MCB Publications, 1981.

Peck, M Scott. *The Different Drum,* Rider & Co (Century Hutchinson imprint) 1987.

Rackham, Neil and Morgan, Terry. *Behaviour Analysis in Training,* McGraw-Hill, 1977.

Rogers, Carl. *Client Centered Therapy*. Constable & Co. Ltd. 1951, reprinted 1986.

Schiff, Jacqui Lee. *Cathexis Reader*. Harper & Row 1975.

Schiff, Jacqui Lee with Day, Beth. *All My Children*. Jove Publications Inc., 1979.

Schiff, Aaron and Schiff, Jacqui: See Appendix 2: Eric Berne Memorial Scientific Awards for details of the relevant article in the Transactional Analysis Journal – 1974.

Schutz, Will. *The Truth Option*. Ten Speed Press, 1984.

Searles, H. F. *The informational value of the supervisor's emotional experiences*, Psychiatry, 18: 135-46, 1955 (later reproduced in H. F. Searles, *Collected Papers on Schizophrenia and Related Subjects* Karnac Books 1965.)

Sheehey, Gail. *Passages*. Dutton, 1976.

Steiner, Claude M. *Scripts People Live*. Bantam Books, 1975.

Summers, Graeme & Keith Tudor. *Cocreative Transactional Analysis* in Transactional Analysis Journal Oct 2000 Vol 30 No.1 pp 23-40.

Tuckman, B. *Developmental sequence in small groups*. Psychological Bulletin 1965, 63 pp 384-399.

Tuckman, B. and M.A.C. Jensen. *Stages of small-group development revisited*. Group and Organisational Studies 1977, 2, pp 419-427.

INDEX

101, 7-8, 255, 258
202, 7-8

5 OK, 61

A

absenteeism, 113, 128-130
abuses (of TA), 1, 12-13, 160
acceleration (AP³) – see also
    acceleration/patience and active/people,
    passive/people, active/alone, passive/alone,
    190, 193, 194
acceleration/patience (AP³), 185, 190, 191, 192,
    193
acceptance – see competence curve
action learning, 2
action, action plan, planning, 20, 31-37, 39-40,
    109, 111, 132, 196, 211, 224, 225, 240
action statement, 225, 226
action(s) (BAR), 17, 121, 123-126
action(s) (C5P5A5), 245
action(s) (NOICISED), 121
active/alone, 186-187, 191, 192, 193, 194
active/people, 187-188, 190, 191, 192, 193, 194
activity, activities (time structuring), 167, 168,
    176, 183
Adapted Child, 65, 66, 67, 69, 70, 71, 72, 75, 77,
    78, 79-80, 82, 84-85, 86, 87, 88, 90, 91, 92,
    93, 119, 137, 191, 219
adapted group imago, 173-174, 175, 178, 179,
    181, 183
adjusted group imago, 172-173, 175, 177, 179,
    181, 183

administrative (contract) – see also procedural, 21
Adult – see also Functional Adult, Internal
    Adult, 10, 62-64, 94, 137, 184, 216-220,
    223, 224, 226, 228, 231
Adult in the Child, 231
adult(s), 3, 7, 54, 62, 68, 72, 131, 140, 198, 204,
    218
advantages (of games), 138, 152-153, 164
agitate, agitating, 131, 135
ALAT, 7
alienated group imago, 174, 175-176
alone (time structuring), 16, 143, 165, 166, 169,
    176, 180, 181, 182, 183, 185
alternatives (autonomy), 4
alternatives (C5P5A5), 245
anticipatory group imago, 170-172, 173, 174-175,
    177, 178-179
AP³, 2, 184-197
application – see competence curve
application (of TA), vii, 3, 18, 19, 147, 255, 256,
    257, 258, 259
Argentina (game), 164
assertive, assertiveness, 2, 6, 10, 12, 45, 58, 103,
    121, 125, 261-262
attached group imago, 174, 175, 178, 179, 182
attachment (autonomy), 4
attitude(s), viii, 2, 12, 23, 33, 41-61, 134, 148,
    152, 171, 172, 201
attributions, 54, 55-56, 58, 60
audio-taping (recording), 87, 234, 239, 259
autonomy, 4, 5, 15, 16, 17, 18, 44, 247
awareness (autonomy), 4, 18
awareness (out of – in games), 147, 162, 168